AMERICAN POLITICAL THOUGHT

The Philosophic Dimension of American Statesmanship

AMERICAN POLITICAL THOUGHT

The Philosophic Dimension
of American Statesmanship

EDITED BY

Morton J. Frisch
NORTHERN ILLINOIS UNIVERSITY

AND

Richard G. Stevens
THE UNIVERSITY OF WATERLOO

Charles Scribner's Sons
New York

Printed in the United States of America
SBN 684–41253–5 College
SBN 684–10190–4 Trade
Library of Congress Catalog Card Number: 73-135390

To The Memory Of
FRANKLIN DELANO ROOSEVELT
and
FELIX FRANKFURTER
and to the noble
employment of the
powers they once
wielded

PREFACE

This is a book on the political thought of American statesmen. Why statesmen? The very fact that there are no American political philosophers means that the only proper objects for study are sub-philosophic. But we differ from a great many students of American politics who hold the view that statesmen are altogether thoughtless, that they are moved solely by forces, impulses or interests or that they are merely clever "operators"—alternately the sheep and goats of the group theory of politics or the lions and foxes of Machiavelli. We believe that our statesmen have had more or less consistent and comprehensive views of the good of the country and that their actions have been constantly informed by these views (that is, that their views have been crucial moving forces in American life). We further believe that political life in America has been punctuated by three great crises, and that the statesmen having political responsibility at these critical moments in American history, in facing up to the problems those crises presented, have come nearer a philosophic treatment of the problems of liberal democracy than have any other Americans. While not political philosophers of the rank, say, of Aristotle, or Locke, their political thought is of a far higher rank than that of, say, Thoreau or Melville or John Dewey.

We do not propose to "cover" American political thought comprehensively, but rather to try to grasp its essential character by reference to the three crises and by examining with care a selected group of statesmen involved in those crises. The collection, as such, tries to provide "coverage" in the *best* sense, that is, only by reading the essays in company might one hope to grasp the whole of American political thought and be pointed toward a recovery of the most nearly philosophic parts of it. The precise nature of the contribution of this work, moreover, would be its restoration in commentary of the relationship, which in fact does exist, between theory and practice—between the political philosophy which is reflected in the thoughts of those selected statesmen and the political actions which they initiated.

There is general agreement among the contributors to this book that *statesmen* do things, and that their doings are moving forces as much as are the "events of history." Their doings proceed from and as a consequence of their views of the good and of the attainable good. What is more, America has been benefited with a substantial number of statesmen whose views are well worth study and, in fact, *almost* nobody in America has views of politics as worthy of study. What might be called the master idea of this book is that the highest political thought in America is that of its statesmen, that that thought is surely high enough to merit study in itself—quite aside from its interest because it is *ours* and because it is all we have—and that, finally, a proper understanding of it revolves around an appreciation of its relative connection with the three great crises of American history.

There is, of course, an emphatic appreciation on the part of the editors that what truly matters is the thought, and that a consideration of statesmen could lead one into the merely historical concern for contingencies and perhaps even personalities. We have always been agreed that that is the danger away from which we must steer, but that danger does not gainsay the fact that the highest and best political thought in America has been the thought of its statesmen and, as long as we steer close to the shore of their *thought* and stay away from the enticements of dealing directly with the historical episodes, except as it is necessary to do so in order to show the arena of their thought, we shall stay on the proper subject.

Present approaches to the study of American political theory tend to look upon the American political tradition as being made up of thoughts (i.e. "isms") which flow and ebb and grow and atrophy, but which are wholly independent of the thinkers themselves. Our approach, in contrast, emphasizes that thought can only be understood by thinking and that only thinkers think thoughts which can be understood as such. Instead of themes floating, as it were, on the stream of history, we will examine political thought as it is *thought*.

MORTON J. FRISCH
RICHARD G. STEVENS

August 1970

CONTENTS

AMERICAN POLITICAL THOUGHT

The Philosophic Dimension of American Statesmanship

★ INTRODUCTION

In every country which is ruled more or less as countries should be ruled, that is, in every country which does not lie under the boot of an absolute tyrant, statesmen cannot act without making public explanations of their actions from time to time. Every action which the statesman proposes to take must be defended and justified in the name of the common good and in the name of justice or right. Clearly the activities of the statesman and those of the political philosopher differ. Until recently, the peculiar virtue of the statesman was understood to be practical wisdom or prudence, and prudence was understood to be the special capacity to grasp the connection between theory and practice and to fashion one's practices accordingly. But only in the highest sense would theory and practice be linked directly. That would only happen in that country where philosophers proper actually rule. So far, such a rule has only occurred in that city of which Socrates speaks in Plato's *Republic*. That was a city which existed only in speech and, even at that, it did not last very long. Toward the end of the *Republic*, Socrates describes its eventual dissolution. In the ordinary sense, therefore, theory and practice are separated by an enormous gulf which must be bridged.

All political action is based on some implicit view of what is better and what is worse. At the crudest level, this amounts to no more than the desire to have more without regard to the cost or consequences for others. But that is precisely the crudest level. The difference between the statesman's views and those crude views is precisely that the statesman's views are more thoughtful. They involve, to begin with, reflection on whether the consequences to others of this or that gain for oneself might not elicit a reaction which involves a loss costlier than the gain achieved. And, by easy stages, thought can become more and more complex, comprehensive and reflective. One can immediately see that one of the hard questions for the student of politics is whether political thought, as it becomes more complex, comprehensive and reflective, ever becomes truly transformed or forever remains merely an intricate calculation from the desire for private gain. But if political thought can be crude or complex, narrow or comprehensive, reactive or reflective, and if the difference between statesmen and others is the intricacy, breadth and depth of their thought, then the difference between better and worse countries is chiefly made by the difference in the quality of their statesmen. Surely everyone who does not take a frivolous view must see that the well-being of a country turns on which men are in and which out of political office.

It is our contention that the United States has been benefited at various critical moments in its history with the presence of statesmen of great quality, and that the highest political thought in America, given the absence of American political philosophers, has been for the most part the thought of certain of its statesmen. We agree that just as an understanding of the Soviet Union involves understanding the political philosophy of Marx, an understanding of American democracy involves an understanding of the political philosophies of Locke and Montesquieu and others. But our argument here is that there is a political thought which belongs to America as such and within that body of thought the highest reaches are to be found in the political thought of America's statesmen. Therefore, to understand American political thought and so, American politics, is to identify those statesmen and to subject their thought to careful inquiry. To do so requires that we examine the nature of statesmanship itself and inquire into its particular character in democracies generally and in the United States specifically. This, in turn, requires that we identify the great political crises in American history.

We are reminded of an objection to our assertion that the highest political thought in America is the thought of its statesmen by recalling that famous aphorism of Speaker Joe Cannon of the House of Representatives at the beginning of the twentieth century that a statesman is a politician who has been dead a long time. But what did "Uncle Joe" mean by that? Did he mean that it is foolish to venerate as statesmen those who, upon a closer view, would be seen to have been "merely" politicians? Or did he, on the contrary, mean that one ought not to demean politicians because, upon reflection, one could see that they might well be acknowledged later to have been true statesmen?

What we *think* Cannon meant by that aphorism depends on what we have been taught to think about politics generally and all of us in the United States have been taught a particular view of politics for the past half-century. That view may compendiously be identified by the word "debunking." The dominant trend of scholarship for the past half-century has led to the study of the actions of statesmen informed by a conviction that those statesmen could not possibly have meant most of what they said. Since the actions of statesmen consist largely in *saying* things, to study those actions under the thrall of that view means to study an object without taking seriously the object of study.

Even the avid supporters of statesmen cannot truly give them support under this cloud, for to support a statesman means to approve of him as statesman and, if one believes that all statesmanship is merely a cover, there is no such thing as excellent statesmanship, or better or worse statesmanship. One cannot truly approve of this or that statesman because nothing, properly speaking, deserves approval. One sees only the surface manifestations of the character of the statesman and misinterprets those manifestations. Not knowing *why* the statesman did this or that thing, the scholar supposes that the statesman did not know why, or that he actually had no reason, or that he had some narrow, mean or devious reason. Therefore, support for a statesman, since it cannot be genuine support in the name of the public good, becomes a kind of chronicle of the intricacy and cleverness of his acts. The old histories full of kings and generals whom our ancestors foolishly mistook for heroes are, we suppose, to be replaced by a kind of hall of fame of clever operators.

Against the stream of this orthodoxy which dismisses all statesmanship as mere cleverness or which denies that there is such a thing as statesmanship at all and which argues that statesmen merely react or are merely moved by this or that invisible hand or force—this view that sees statesmen alternately as lions and foxes or as sheep and goats—we contend that there is such a thing as statesmanship and that there have been some excellent American statesmen. We further believe that their actions, sayings, thoughts and intentions are worthy of the most serious study. We also contend that the best of them have had thoughts of such a high order as to be the nearest approximation this country has had to political philosophy in the proper and full sense. These men are, we believe, worthy of study not only because they are *ours,* though they are worthy on that account, too, but because they are of a high enough order in themselves to merit inquiry. Finally, we contend that their highly formed and well formulated thought has been the mainspring of their political actions. Thus, to understand what the statesman's actions truly were, one must truly know what he was "up to" and to know that means to discover the nature of the good and of the attainable good which he had in mind.

But to get at that thought is a very difficult thing. All political thought of a high order is hard to grasp precisely because it is of a high order. The object of study, politics, is difficult, and attempts to come to an understanding of it must involve a great effort by serious minds. The work of understanding the products of those minds is perhaps not as great as the original work of those minds themselves, but it is great. The student of those minds cannot play the "consumer" and merely turn them on as one turns on a tap. Thought can only be understood by thinking.

Let it be granted that there is not a *single* American who is generally recognized as a political philosopher. Yet we would argue that, while America has not had a political thinker of the rank of Aristotle or Locke, it has had some thinkers who truly deserve study. The American political thought most worthy of study has been that of its statesmen. But what about the character of statesmanship in America? It is an old saying that "politics is the art of the possible," but like the aphorism of Speaker Joe Cannon, it takes a moment of thought to see what that saying might mean. In the mouth of a prudent statesman, that saying might be a counsel of moderation, a suggestion that one ought not to seek too much, for the cure accomplished might be worse than the disease purged. On the other hand, that saying might be taken as an excuse for not studying politics seriously because, as it is so used, it argues that statesmen are only interested in the moment and success. But the question needs to be asked, "success at *what?*" Of all the "possibles," why does the statesman under study prefer the *particular* "possible" to all the others? If the statesman is *not* a man buffeted from day to day by circumstances, who takes what he can from day to day without asking whether he *wants* what he can get, and without looking to tomorrow, must one not ask this question: If the statesman settles for some proximate good, what makes it even proximately good? Why is one thing better and another worse? Relative to *what* is a thing better? What is the good seen by the statesman which is merely reflected in the approximation he finds acceptable? If politics is *merely* the art of the possible, then the greatest politician is one who can keep all sorts of committees rambling, a kind of legislative and administrative game of keeping the pot boiling. Indeed, we know many individuals who believe that that is exactly what it is: that success is measured not by what is done but by the fact that one keeps doing and doing and doing. Politics becomes like a war in which the aim of the generals is simply to stay alive. Battles become stately minuets. Anyone who dies is a fool who spoils the game. Those triflers who pretend to study politics as though it were a game fail altogether in their attempt to understand what they study because in order for them to succeed it would, in fact, have to be played as a game. And it is not. The number of men who have died in battle throughout history shows that politics is not a game to the "players."

If politics is not a game, then the expression "politics is the art of the possible" must be understood to mean that the political practitioner fashions some practicable good with a view both to the conditions which limit him and that good which he would fashion were he not constrained by those limits. Perhaps the best way to explain the phrase "politics is the art of the possible" would be to say that the statesman does as much good as he can get away with. This has somewhere been described as removing the greatest amount of evil while disturbing the least amount of prejudice. Of course, not everyone who is in political office knows where he is taking his country and not everyone who knows where he is taking his country succeeds in arriving there and, finally, not everyone who succeeds in taking his country where he would take it takes it where it ought to go. But this does not preclude the possibility of excellent statesmanship. There are plenty of triflers, drifters, dreamers, fools and knaves in politics—plenty of the "pedlers, pickpockets, highwaymen and bullies" of the modern legislature conjured up for Gulliver in Glubbdubdrib.[1] This fact affords perhaps the strongest proof that the difference between better and worse countries is, not simply, but largely, the difference between better and worse statesmen.

To say that the statesman removes the greatest amount of evil while disturbing the least amount of prejudice is to say several things at once. It is to say initially that the doing of political good at any given moment is, for the most part, a negative thing. It is the destruction of evils, such as vice, poverty, oppression, weakness in war, civil discord and the like. These things can be stated positively, as witness the Preamble to the Constitution of the United States. But chiefly it is a business of cure. The excellent statesman will, if he can, play the nurse, but he can and he will, if he must, play the surgeon. But even Plato's *Republic*, while showing the necessity of reflecting on radical political surgery in order that one might envision a country in good health, soberly reminds us that cures are sometimes worse than diseases. It reminds us of this by effecting *its* cure, destined to last for only a short time, by banishing from the country everyone over 10 years of age.

Radical surgery may sometimes be necessary, but such surgery is a last, desperate, bloody business undertaken when, judgment shows, death will come anyhow from the disease or the disease makes life not worth living. Not going to surgery means staying with milder cures, which, in our figure, we call nursing, but whether one engages in quiet nursing or in radical surgery and harsh purgatives, the central problem is the same—to alleviate wrongs while saving the patient. In politics, to save the patient means to preserve the country. One can only save the country, however, if he has some sense of what the thing is that he hopes to save. What makes a country a country? The answer to that question comes by way of the assertion that the essential character of a country—the thing public, the common wealth, the public good —is a thing which belongs to all and yet which cannot be divided up and parcelled out to each citizen. That public thing, that thing which is held *truly* in common, is a common view of the political good. That is what a constitution is. That is what the constituent principle of a country is—a common view of the nature of justice. But such a common view, of course, could not be the correct view, simply, because whatever the correct view is about justice, like all hard questions, it is not the sort of thing which is capable of being grasped by great multitudes, some of which are bound to be less thoughtful. Therefore a *common* view of justice is at best right opinion, or an approximation to the correct view, some salutary near-correct view—that is, a prejudice. And if that is shattered, that bond of fellow-feeling which fellow-citizens feel for each

[1]Jonathan Swift, *Gulliver's Travels*, Book III, Chapter vii.

other is destroyed. They begin to wonder what they have in common that they should so live together. Only someone who thinks that all men may live from day to day on the basis of reason alone supposes that statesmanship consists in purging a country of all prejudice. On the contrary, as we are suggesting, the statesman will disturb only as much prejudice as he has to disturb in order to remove evils which can not be tolerated.

That the statesman does his work by way of removing as much wrong as he can while unsettling as little prejudice as possible shows that the job of the statesman is the job of forming and reforming the characters of the citizens by calling forth from them a readiness to behave in a way which is good both for them and for the country as a whole. This must be done in such a way that the citizens can see that they are in fact doing what their common view of the good calls upon them to do anyhow; that is, the statesman must call forth from the citizens an eager willingness to be their best selves and must make them see that this is what they wanted all along. That is a peculiarly difficult task in a democracy because the principles of a democracy are freedom and equality and these principles, in addition to existing in a state of tension with each other, exist in a state of perpetual tension with the idea of statesmanship as well. That is, the statesman in a democracy must legitimate the actions he seeks to elicit from the citizens by referring these actions to prejudices which hover constantly on the fringe of denying the legitimacy of the existence of statesmen. The democratic statesman must make the most and best of the democracy by appealing to principles which threaten to tear the democracy asunder.

To understand American political thought, and its approximation to political philosophy in the highest and fullest sense, is to put together these observations on the relation between political philosophy and statesmanship with the facts about statesmanship in America in particular. Since a statesman plays the nurse if he can and a surgeon if he must, it is probably true that the crises in the life of a country call forth to statesmanship those most suited to the steady but hard business of surgery. That's why Lincoln left his law practice to reenter politics in 1854. Indeed, if the country survives the crisis, it is proof that it has found within itself and called forth to duty such a man. What are the crises in the life of the United States? What could the word "crisis" mean when one is speaking of the life of a country? Who are the statesmen who have been her nurses?—and her surgeons? What were the principles of political right which guided them?

★ ★ ★

As we see in retrospect, there have been three great crises in the life of our country. They are the critical moments in the fulfillment of the words and phrases of the Declaration of Independence. The first crisis is the crisis of the

Founding itself, the founding of a true Union with a genuine government based on popular republican principles—the crisis, if you will, of *actualizing* the principles asserted in the Declaration. To appreciate the alternative prescriptions, one would have to examine the political thought of Thomas Jefferson, Richard Henry Lee, Roger Sherman and others. The second crisis is the crisis of the House Divided: whether, that is, any nation so conceived and so dedicated can long endure or, on the contrary, government of the people, by the people, and for the people must perish from the earth. One man stands out here as surgeon and nurse, prophet and sacrifice—Abraham Lincoln. But one also would have to know about John Marshall and John C. Calhoun and perhaps Henry Clay, Daniel Webster, Roger Taney, and others. The third crisis is the crisis of the confrontation of liberal democracy with its great twentieth century alternatives which shows itself dramatically in the Great Depression, and which continues to show itself in the struggles the country has experienced attempting to formulate and reconcile internal and external policy. Though first presented in the form of the Great Depression, on reflection we see that "Making the World Safe for Democracy," "Clear and Present Dangers of evils Congress has a right to prevent," and "Black Power" are all a part of this crisis. The towering figure of this struggle is Franklin D. Roosevelt who, as John Maynard Keynes said in December 1933, made himself "the Trustee for those in every country who seek to mend the evils of our condition by reasoned experiment within the framework of the existing social system."[2] But one would also want to examine the thought of such men as Oliver Wendell Holmes, Felix Frankfurter, Woodrow Wilson, and perhaps others.

We have described the first great crisis as the crisis of the Founding. There was, of course, an incipient Union before it was perfected in the Constitution. The Declaration of Independence is surely a great—and the first great—act of Founding, but the Declaration would have had a hollow ring if it had not been fulfilled by the Articles of Confederation, and the Articles were, as every schoolboy knows, imperfect and had to be transformed by the Constitution into "a more perfect Union."

But Union, as such, is not good in itself. It is only good if it is good *for* something. It is good not so much as an end as it is a means to a higher and better end. That higher end is truly republican, the perfected republican government. There had, of course, been republics in antiquity, but they all had been wretched and violent, and most had been short-lived. The task at hand was to found a republic as strong, as stable, and as consequential as the strongest monarchy, but characterized by the freedom, equality and self-mastery of

[2]See *Roosevelt and Frankfurter: Their Correspondence, 1928-1945,* annotated by Max Freedman (Boston, 1967), p. 178.

the simplest republic. That is, the task was to found a republic free of the characteristic vices of republics—violence, faction and instability—and yet clearly committed to the unmixed principle of republican government— majority rule. The Founders' answer was the first large republic in history and if one wanted to find the shortest possible description of the American polity, it would be just that—a large republic.

Of all the Founders, Alexander Hamilton is, we would assert, the most comprehensive, the most consistent, and the most single-minded political thinker. The opposition to his views was, of course, not simply mean-spirited or self-interested. It, too, was moved by some general view of the larger good. It is usually that way in politics: the contending views are not those of the "good guys" and the "bad guys," but two contending visions of the general good each of which has some merit and neither of which is simply and un-equivocally right, but one of which is more right than the other—more right in general, or more right in the particular circumstance, or both. It is not always the man guided by the better vision who wins, moreover, and, in politics, it seldom happens that the winner wins without making some conces-sions to the other side.

The two visions which dominated politics at the time of the Founding may fairly be called Hamiltonian and Jeffersonian. It is usually said that Hamil-ton wanted commerce and cities and that Jefferson was an agrarian, and that is certainly correct. But our characterization of the struggle is to say that Hamilton wanted national greatness and Jefferson wanted civic simplicity. Each believed that a fair portion of the other's goal could be achieved if his own goal were pursued as the chief goal. We can make some sense out of Hamilton by reflecting on his general purpose and on the character of his statesman-ship in the context of the views of the men who opposed him and his vision.

James Madison is rightly called the Father of the Constitution. It was he, along with his colleagues from Virginia, who presented the Virginia Plan to the Constitutional Convention. That plan would have established an unencum-bered national government with supreme legislative, executive and judicial powers—unencumbered by doubts as to its single and simple sovereignty and supreme over all of the governments of the states in all questions and in all contests. The Convention rather quickly accepted that plan, in principle, by a large vote, but then, when it went on to discuss the details, several members began to have second thoughts. They hesitated and questioned, and offered provisions and restrictions. It is *not* proper to refer to these hesitant men as "states' rights" advocates. To call them such would be to speak in anachro-nisms. At first, the resistance was based on the view that only a small country could be governed on republican principles. The doctrine of the "small republic" was, in the course of argument, transformed into a small-state versus large-state position, later in the Convention's proceedings. It was only later in the eighteenth century, that the intellectual descendants of the small republic and then the small state position began to form their arguments into the terms of state's rights. In other words, the "states' rights" position, as it is presently understood, was not present in the Convention which created the Constitution.

It surely would be proper to say that there was a hesitancy—call it a party of hesitancy, if you like—respecting the fulfillment of that intention which the Virginians had and which James Wilson and Gouverneur Morris of Pennsylvania and Hamilton of New York shared. The vision was that of a great republic—a republic characterized by greatness, meaning great men and great deeds. The hesitancy revolved around the question whether that greatness might not destroy the republicanism. This was based on the observation, to which Montesquieu attested, that in the past there had only been small republics and large monarchies. Out of that hesitancy arose the New Jersey Plan and, in response to that, Hamilton presented his plan. It was surely an enormously strong government which he proposed and one which was organized around a national center which owed no apologies to the parts for its strength and unity, and it was to be a stable government, made up by men many of whom held office during good behavior. Most of these were to have been merchants or professional men. But Hamilton did not seek a monarchy, as Jefferson charged privately to President Washington in 1792. We do not believe that he even sought a "mixed government"—mixed, that is, of republican and aristocratic principles.

The plan Hamilton presented to the Convention called for a truly stable, very strong, and fully central government—but a government exactingly republican in character. The crucial proof of this is its ultimate reliance on majority rule and the complete absence of hereditary rank—principles fully consistent with the fundamentals of the Declaration of Independence. It is true that the country would have been dominated by merchants, lawyers, and bankers—but they would have been *elected* and, in the final case, anyone could aspire to being a merchant, a lawyer, or a banker. It is true that Hamilton favored a government entrusted to such men, but he knew what he was doing and he did it without regard for his own interests out of a clear and consistent view of the right kind of government and the right life for man. But nothing came of Hamilton's plan of government. The Virginia Plan won out with only modest concessions to the party of hesitancy.

Hamilton and the Virginians shared the view that the defect of the New Jersey Plan was precisely its hesitancy, that is, that it really wanted more than it knew how to get. It really wanted strong national government, perfect union, national consequence, strength, an end to the petty bickering between and within the states, and an assurance against Balkanization in America. Hamilton's whole life was devoted—in his modest contributions to the Convention and his profound contribution to the *Federalist Papers*, and in his domination of the course of the government during Washington's first administration and his off-stage dominance during Washington's second administration—to a clear and consistent plan for a large, powerful and commercial but perfectly republican republic. Against all the forces of the party of hesitancy who would have strangled the infant nation, Hamilton succeeded. We are not merely suggesting that Hamilton and Madison were more clever *in* their day *for* their day. We are arguing that they had an understanding of fundamental, therefore permanent, questions of politics. They are not merely historical figures and this book is not a history. To study these men is to understand the American Constitution better *now*. To learn what Madison teaches is to understand American politics better *now*. If Hamilton were revived from the grave and were given a few months to catch up on his newspapers he would make a consummate Secretary of the Treasury *now*.

★ ★ ★

The second great crisis in the course of American history is the crisis of the House Divided. The Declaration of Independence declared the independence of a nation conceived in liberty and dedicated to the proposition that all men are created equal. The Constitution enacted the princples of the Declaration, but while the founders were opposed to slavery, they were, despite its radical inconsistency with the principles of the Declaration and the Constitution, unable to resolve it. They left the matter tolerably well satisfied that the blight would, in due course, be removed. But circumstances conspired to revive slavery and the institution which began as an exception to and imperfection of the system grew to a point where it contended for the principal direction of the system. Lincoln saw that a house divided against itself could not stand, that a nation half free and half slave would willy-nilly become all one or all the other and, lest it become all slave, he set himself to putting it back on the footing on which it had first stood—a free nation. For the sake of peace, and because he was a lawful man, he was willing to leave those vestiges of slavery which the Constitution itself had allowed. Left at that, it might have withered and died. But, wholly contrary to the manifest tenor of the Constitution, slavery had been increasing in strength rather than disappearing and Lincoln set himself against its gaining another inch even if it meant war to stop it. Then, as now and always, there are some things worse than war. With clarity of mind and charity of purpose, he set about to make the nation more perfectly

what the Declaration and the Constitution had all along intended, namely, a
nation of freedom and equality for all men.

✷ ✷ ✷

According to the *Oxford English Dictionary,* the word "crisis" means primarily
a vitally important or decisive stage in the progress of anything; a turning
point; also, a state of affairs in which a decisive change for better or worse is
imminent; now applied especially to times of difficulty, insecurity, and sus-
pense in politics and commerce. Any attempt to understand the crisis of the
Great Depression must begin with Franklin Roosevelt. Said in the greatest
generality, Roosevelt stands in the same relation to the American political
experience as Abraham Lincoln, for his intention was to demonstrate the
viability of liberal democratic institutions in a period of crisis. Still the circumstances of 1860 were very different from those of 1933. The crisis of the
depression was essentially unprecedented; there were massive dislocations in
the economy. As Justice Brandeis described it: "The people of the United
States are now confronted with an emergency more serious than war. Misery
is widespread, in a time, not of scarcity, but of overall abundance. The long-
continued depression has brought unprecedented unemployment, a cata-
strophic fall in commodity prices, and a volume of economic losses which
threatens our financial institutions. Some people believe that the existing
economic conditions threaten even the stability of the capitalistic system."[3]
Hence the central problem for Roosevelt was the restoration of a healthy
economy. The great series of economic measures of the New Deal, by which
the government assumed responsibility for the management of the economy,
including fair labor standards, the regulation of wages and hours, money and
banking, security exchanges, and so on, meant a significant alteration in the
capitalistic system. But these regulatory measures were never admitted by
Roosevelt to be anti-capitalistic. On the contrary, he presented them as essential to prevent the collapse of capitalism.

To understand the crisis of the depression, needless to say, one would
need to understand the economic circumstances of the times. Roosevelt, when
speaking of "horse and buggy" thinking in his famous press conference in
1935, vigorously and publicly argued that the Supreme Court under Chief
Justice Hughes had blithely ignored these circumstances. "The Nine Old
Men" were impervious to the political setting of economic activity and hence
abstracted the commerce clause from its context. It was the commerce clause
which comprised the direct source of some of the most important actions of

[3] *New State Ice Co.* v. *Liebmann,* 285 U.S. 262 (1932) at pp. 306–07.

the New Deal. The Hughes Court, in giving this and other constitutional clauses the narrowest of interpretation, resisted the whole trend of New Deal legislation. The more flexible interpretation of the commerce clause, which Roosevelt advocated, was based on principles originally stated by Chief Justice Marshall, the founder of our constitutional law, in the *McCulloch* v. *Maryland* and *Gibbons* v. *Ogden* decisions. But the Hughes Court construed the same commerce clause as Marshall and it drew virtually the opposite conclusion in the Railroad Retirement and Schechter Poultry cases. That Court believed that the legislation under consideration in these cases would push governmental centralization too far and hence detract from the democratic character of the system. It was with respect to these decisions especially that Roosevelt collided with the Hughes Court. The peculiar narrowness of the Hughes Court's views, its ill-conceived effort at blocking the regulatory legislation of the New Deal, served to convince him that he would have to make a political issue out of their rigid opposition to social change. The fundamental question, as he saw it, was whether the Constitution gives the national government a set of regulatory powers adequate to the task of managing the national economy.

In his later formulation of the argument, Roosevelt emphasized the different construction of the different clauses of the Constitution. Some clauses, he noted, canalize interpretation within narrow limits, whereas others are clearly general. Where a power is expressly granted in general terms, as the commerce power is, the exact limits of the powers of the general government may not always be capable of being defined or ascertained. The broad and general language here is intended to allow variations in detail which changing circumstances might require, that is, which flexible statesmanship of the future, within the Constitution, could adapt to time and circumstance.[4] He emphasized, moreover, that an adequate understanding of the clauses of the Constitution requires more than an understanding of the words of the Constitution, for, behind the words of the Constitution are the working principles of democratic government. The Constitution is a layman's document, not a lawyer's contract.[5] Thus the Constitution points beyond itself to the intents and purposes which it serves.

The problem posed by the controversy between Roosevelt and the Hughes Court can only be resolved by a fundamental reflection on the question of the relationship between the government and the economic system. Surely the crucial difference between progressivism and the welfare state, which characterizes the New Deal, has something to do with the terms of that relationship. In the "Progressive Movement" at the turn of this century,

---

[4]Franklin D. Roosevelt, *The Public Papers and Addresses of Franklin D. Roosevelt*, compiled by S. I. Rosenman (New York, 1938–1950), VI, 363.
[5]Roosevelt, *The Public Papers and Addresses of Franklin D. Roosevelt*, VI, 362.

governmental regulation found a place. Theodore Roosevelt, William Howard
Taft and Woodrow Wilson all presided over the country during the introduction of some regulatory measures. But that regulation was not based on solid
reflection on the relation between politics and the economy. The governmental regulation of progressivism did not re-examine the doctrines of nineteenth century economic liberalism according to which the end of
government was simply the fostering of life, liberty and the pursuit of happiness. Happiness itself was thought beyond the reach of governmental provision. Happiness as an end of man was not thought to be the government's
business because ends, as such, were not thought to be the government's
business. There was, as it were, a tendency in nineteenth century liberalism
to reduce politics to formalism. The New Deal, driven by its motive force—
the mind of Franklin D. Roosevelt—saw politics as aimed at some substantive
good for men. The subordination of the economy to the government which
the New Deal sought to accomplish through regulation integrates economic
well-being, or welfare, into the purposes of government and, in doing so,
points beyond the prior formalism. That change required the emergence of a
higher plane of thought which, at least within the limits of modern political
philosophy, constituted a new departure.

In what is apparently the generally accepted understanding, the New
Deal was constituted essentially by the multiplicity of *ad hoc* responses to
immediate problems, and that understanding is therefore incapable of taking
very seriously the statesmanship of FDR. But if statesmanship means meeting
the particular requirements of the circumstances, or doing what is deemed best
in the circumstances, then it means making some measured judgments about
those circumstances in which some improvement may be possible. What is
deemed best in the circumstances surely depends ultimately on principles of
preference whose political implications, if fully elaborated, would present a
complete picture of maximum political improvement. According to our understanding, any adequate explanation of the New Deal must take into account
the dimensions of the Roosevelt Revolution, for implicit in that revolution was
a conscious and deliberate attempt, on the part of FDR, to effect a fundamental
change in orientation of government in its relationship to economic life—the
coming-into-being of the welfare state, with its regulated or controlled
economy. Accordingly, that fundamental change in orientation accomplished
by the New Deal depended on the solution of a theoretical question: What is
the purpose of democratic government? Is it to provide merely for the conditions of happiness or must it not supply something of happiness itself, understood as well-being or welfare? It is in the context of these considerations that
one must reflect on the crisis of the depression if one is to grasp its essential
character.

When viewed from the perspective of the great crises in American history, the American experiment in self-government was faced in the 1930s with what was perhaps its greatest test for, while in the crises of the eighteenth and nineteenth centuries America was to be regarded as a test case for liberal democracy, in the crisis of the twentieth century America is not the mere example, but the very citadel of liberal democracy. In that difficult and most critical period, Roosevelt won the allegiance of a restive democratic nation and, at the same time, moderated its extremist tendencies toward state corporatism on the one hand and the class struggle on the other. For, in a very emphatic sense, the crisis of the depression was a crisis of the confrontation of modern liberal democracy with its great twentieth century alternatives—fascism and communism. One could almost say that FDR insinuated his version of liberalism into the American political mind which, as such, provided a viable alternative to the extremist ideologies of the right and left. Hence FDR's New Deal leads to the dominance of a certain version of liberalism in the American political system of the twentieth century.

Indeed, it would be no exaggeration to say that Roosevelt so completely set the tone for the politics of succeeding generations that we still think and act largely within the broad lines of the liberal doctrines which he articulated during the New Deal period. But in any attempt to secure that necessary balance between stability and social change in a political democracy, there is nothing more needed than the peaceful confrontation of liberal and conservative principles and, as a result of their action and reaction on one another, the producing of orderly change (that is, reform rather than revolution). Surely part of the reason for the complacent character of present-day liberalism (in spite of attacks from the extreme left) is the absence of a respectable alternative to that liberalism, for in the place of a healthy conservatism with sound and generous principles and with eloquent spokesmen, there exists only a shadow which can be easily dismissed as mere reaction or mere selfishness.

Prior to the philosopher Hobbes and even up until the philosopher Kant, who was an older contemporary of Alexander Hamilton, there was a view that understood despotic authority as the opposite of freedom. It is now the prevalent view that *all* authority is the enemy of freedom. But what is needed, now as always, is not less government. The way to avoid bad government is not to have as little government as possible. What is wanted is more good government. A vulgarization of Jefferson's view can be seen in the latter-day conservative view which regards big government as centralist, bureaucratic and socialistic. Therefore the alternative to the liberalism of the present-day is a most unattractive alternative from which that liberalism can learn nothing but self-complacency. This is very likely what stands in the way of our facing and resolving the crisis of our time, for the absence of a viable conservatism has led to the degeneration of the liberal viewpoint. But a conservatism whose discussion of political issues would again bear some relation to our national needs and consciousness would have to restore Hamilton's regard for strong government and for strong national government.

As we try to grasp and weigh liberalism and conservatism as viable political viewpoints, it would be important for us to restore their original dimensions. But in order to see what liberalism and conservatism originally meant as respectable partisanships, we must drop the 'ism' and think of the words in their sense as adjectives. Both "liberal" and "conservative" were once understood as terms of praise. Every gentleman was supposed to be both liberal and conservative. To be liberal meant to be endowed with liberality, and, in the modern sense, this meant to be open-minded, open-hearted and open-handed. The open-handed man is fair, plain-spoken and above-board in all his dealings. He does not wish to gain by force or fraud or by narrow shrewdness in the market. He respects the opinions and interests of others. To see the virtues of the liberal man more fully, they must be constrasted with the vices of the peasant. The peasant is shrewd, selfish and bigoted. He supposes that running the country is like ploughing an extra large field. Of course there are no peasants in America, but there are housewives, factory workers and small town merchants and not a few of these fall far short of what is here described as liberal. Imagine a small town merchant whose conception of politics is that the country is like an overgrown hardware store. Statesmanship consists in making a "good deal" when we can, sweeping out the stockroom on occasion, and preserving a good credit rating in the bank.

And what was it to be conservative? The conservative gentleman wishes to conserve all good things, both public and private. He has enough doubt about the perfection of his own judgment not to destroy lightly old ways and old things. He recognizes the debt the excellences of the present owe to the labors of the past. He is not a spendthrift, but neither does he practice false economy in public or in private matters. He is not the enemy of spending. In fact, he advocates spending for good value. He would never think of saving his money by building a house of cheap materials, or saving "his" tax money by refusing to build a dam for flood control. He knows the value of money. And he knows the value of tradition. But he is not against change. He simply insists that proposed change bear the burden of proof of its own value. Nor is he against government. He knows that things must be governed or they will run amuck, and he abhors violence and civil discord. He is not for "more" government or "less" government, but for just so much government as circumstances demand and he knows that circumstances vary with time and place. He is not for "local" government or "central" government, but for that government which in the circumstances, and with a view to long-range consequences, governs best. The best government is that which preserves health, peace, property and the good character of the citizens.

To what extent can present-day "conservatives" in America properly lay claim to that term? They profess to believe in order, but often that is a belief based on narrow self-interest. They claim to revere tradition, but that tradition often goes back no farther than the day-before-yesterday—back to a Supreme Court ruling which they liked and was just overthrown but which itself had run roughshod over earlier views. They profess to adhere to the Constitution, but their arguments often show their apparent adherence to be a camouflage for narrow interests. They profess to love their country, but it is a strange love of country that forbids the country, as country, ever to act except negatively as a policeman acts.

Reduced to their barest essentials, the older views of liberalism and conservatism as fundamental doctrines of political opposition can be stated this way: the liberal was optimistic about change and about the good which rational calculation can engender; the conservative, while equally committed to reason, had reservations about its ability to come at the right answer in the course of one, good, long argument and knew that a good deal of what goes on in life, public and private, is moved quite as much by other things as it is by reason. But what about now? The liberalism which exists today seldom rises above simple-minded libertarianism. The cracker-barrel conservatism, which is a reaction to that liberalism, is largely compounded of a merely older liberalism, on the one hand, and sheer mean-spiritedness on the other.

The contemporary opposition between liberalism and conservatism in America has shifted its emphasis from the economy to the sphere of civil rights. It is concerned with the extent of protection for civil rights, and their expansion, and with control over civil disorders. The radical libertarian viewpoint does not truly understand what civil rights are. That viewpoint does not recognize that there is such a thing as civil conduct and rights appropriate to that conduct. The right-wing defenders of law and order, on the other hand, often mean only to defend the material *status quo.* They would subordinate civil rights to property rights in the interest of selfish convenience. It is somewhat ironic to see that they are now placed in the position of relying more heavily on the support of government than they would have admitted necessary when economics was at the center of their controversy with the liberals. But neither viewpoint has sufficiently considered the proper relation between freedom and a democratic society.

The radical libertarian must recover his senses about what are and what are not "civil rights." Indeed, not all those who are clearly advocates of rights deserve to be called advocates of civil rights, for the word "civil" is an adjective that modifies the word "rights" and gives the term its distinctive meaning. If a man enters a contractual relationship, he has out of it certain contract rights. It would be utterly foolish for a man to enter into a marriage contract one day and a business contract the next and to confuse the rights connected with the two contracts. More specifically, one does not have a right to deep understanding and affectionate forbearance from one with whom one has contracted, say, to build something for a sum of money. Thus, one is not a proper civil rights advocate unless the rights he advocates are proper to civil society, civilization and civility. We do not suggest that the Constitution is to be read as though it were a mere contract, as the subsequent chapters on Marshall, Holmes and Frankfurter show. We do not mean that it is to be read with nitpicking particularity in this regard. Surely a free country is one in which the rights of individuals are provided and construed with liberality and generosity. One has a right to expect more than is spelled out with lawyer-like care. That is the meaning of the Ninth Amendment.

Surely the spirit of the civil relationship, the high ends of the polity, are the bounds of civil rights, not the narrow bounds of the letter of the law. But the ends of the polity *are* the bounds. "Civil rights" are not boundless. There is no civil right to be uncivil, to be uncivilized. There are exceptions. Circumstances may indeed make it wiser to tolerate a particular evil than to suppress it and that toleration may be written into the Constitution. Such a right is not a civil right by its *nature* but only by specific constitutional enactment. If such an evil *is* tolerated by specific constitutional right, then, surely, toleration of it cannot be ended but by the proper form of constitutional amendment. But if a thing is not specially preserved by the letter of the Constitution, then it can only be preserved by its spirit, or end, or general tenor, and so a right which is not granted in explicit terms must, to be a "civil right," be conducive to the end of civil society.

We say all the time that democratic government is necessarily responsible government, or government responsible to the governed, but it would seem more important to consider whether the responsibilities of governing and being governed were exercised with a view to the wants or needs of men. We believe that we cannot take our bearings by our wants, because we may want what is not good for us. It is therefore necessary to make a distinction between wants and needs, and it follows that making reasonable choices between various wants determines need or, what is the same thing, only reasoning, in contradistinction to wanting, can show us what are our needs. This view, however, would impose an overriding obligation on the citizen, for self-control would be a particular necessity in a reasonable society. The very possibility of democracy as a rational society, as a society in which there is a compatibility between choosing and choosing well, would require that its members have the requisite intellectual and moral virtues for ruling themselves and one another well. It is for a very good reason that self-government can only be understood as one part of the self ruling over another.

This need democracy has for men of reserve and self-mastery leads to a most serious difficulty. Insofar as liberal democracy is understood as *limited* government whose end is mere self-preservation, it is inhibited from performing that vital business of any government, the making of citizens of the right character. That is, democracy *needs* democratic citizens. If it does not *fashion* them, it is dependent on something or someone else to fashion its citizens for it. Yet it is, by its very nature, most reluctant to fashion men at all. It seems, at least to begin with, to rest its hope in the provision of those minimal conditions upon which democratic government *must* depend and out of which democratic government *might* arise—security of life, liberty and the pursuit of happiness. In fact, understood *quite* minimally, the provision for the "pursuit of happiness" can be seen as the provision for the preservation of property. The great virtue of Franklin D. Roosevelt is that he led the country to a level of understanding higher and grander than that which rested on the mere minima. But he knew that to transcend those minima was not to abandon them. The "welfare state" differs from Marxism precisely in that it does not abandon the principles of liberal democracy which call for the establishment of and respect for individual rights to life, liberty and the pursuit of happiness, including the ownership and enjoyment of property. If the crisis of the twentieth century is to be survived by America, it will be by virtue of the statesmanship of a man of the rank of Abraham Lincoln, or, at least of the rank of Franklin D. Roosevelt—a man who shows us in the realm of liberty, as Roosevelt did in the realm of welfare, or property, how to ward off those doctrines of abandon of the left and of the right which, in the name of liberty and philanthropy, promise only slavery and the reduction of man. But because of the inhibitions democracy feels respecting the formation of the characters of its citizens, such a statesman must be a transcendent teacher. He must "take the whole nation to school."

The simplistic criticism of American democracy always starts from the view that it is not democratic enough. But what that view does not take into account is that the best kind of democracy is one which makes allowance for politically relevant limitations on freedom, because what ultimately counts is how we use our freedom. It is therefore not sufficient to know that in a democracy there is danger of unfreedom for minorities. The limitations on the freedoms of majorities in their exercise of freedom cannot be articulated, or even properly understood, unless we realize that the commitment to freedom implies and requires a commitment to certain fundamentals beyond the reach of all majorities. Lincoln understood the problem very well. When he denounced the freedom of Kansans to have slaves if they wished, although that freedom had already been established by congressional legislation in 1854, he clearly indicated that there are limitations on the freedom of majorities. But once a democratic society convinces itself, or allows itself to become convinced, that the common interest is necessarily identical with the majority interest, then everything is permitted, including the freedom to make others unfree. The common interest may very well appear to be identical with the majority interest; it consists, however, not merely in the wants of many individuals, but in the preferences of reasonable individuals. It is indispensable to political freedom that the citizens who would be free are self-governed and self-disciplined and surely those who exercise the decisive influence in such a government must be so.

Not all the statesman examined in this book held views with which we can wholeheartedly agree. But they were all men earnestly devoted to the common good, they were all men of great understanding, and they all reflected penetratingly and intensively on the problems of democracy in America as those problems have shown themselves in the great crises of the eighteenth, nineteenth and twentieth centuries. We do not speak of their several "philosophies" or of the several dimensions of statesmanship because we do not share the presently dominant opinion that the word "philosophy" is equivalent to the word "ideology," and that there is an indefinite number of "ideologies" or "philosophies." Not all political thought is political ideology. Thought that rises toward philosophic rank is, in our view, emphatically not ideology. The penetrating and intensive thought which American statesmen have given to the problems they faced is our project of study. It is that aspect or dimension of their work which is most nearly philosophic. It is the philosophic dimension of American Statesmanship.

★ THOMAS JEFFERSON *Harvey C. Mansfield, Jr.*

All honor to Jefferson—to the man who, in the concrete pressure of a struggle for national independence by a single people, had the coolness, forecast and capacity to introduce into a merely revolutionary document, an abstract truth, applicable to all men and all times. . . .

Mr. Jefferson . . . was, is, and perhaps will continue to be, the most distinguished politician of our history.

These two judgments of Abraham Lincoln on Thomas Jefferson, the one praising him for giving a national struggle the dignity of a human struggle, and the other suggesting his partisan skill, may be considered to set the problem of Jefferson's political thought. As the author of the Declaration of Independence, Jefferson made himself one of his country's Founders as well as one of mankind's benefactors, though he was not present at the Constitutional Convention and hence was not one of the "Framers." Yet he was also a supreme partisan. He fought three remarkable adversaries, John Adams, Alexander Hamilton and John Marshall, in contests so stirring that historians today still cannot describe them dispassionately; he founded the oldest political party in the United States; and beyond this, he founded the very institution of partisanship, party government, which settled into the two-party system we maintain today. Why did Jefferson decide that the "abstract truth" must be sustained in a party or that the party must promote an abstract truth?

THE DECLARATION OF INDEPENDENCE

The "abstract truth" Lincoln meant was the "self-evident truth" of the Declaration of Independence that "all men are created equal." Jefferson was the author of the Declaration, but he wrote it at the behest of a committee and for the approval of an assembly. He said later that its authority rests on "the harmonizing sentiments of the day," not on any "originality of principle or sentiment."[1] The Declaration cannot be taken simply as an expression of Jefferson's own political thought because he was speaking in the name of a

---

[1]Letter to Henry Lee, May 8, 1825, Thomas Jefferson, *The Writings of Thomas Jefferson*, ed. P. L. Ford (New York, 1899), X, 343. Hereafter cited as *Writings*.

nation. Yet it was the very basis of his partisan career too. In the 1790s he formed his Republican party to recover the principles of the Declaration and to inspire the country with the revolutionary fire of its signers. It is an uncanny fact that Jefferson (and John Adams) died on the fiftieth anniversary of the signing of the Declaration.

If the Declaration harmonized the sentiments of the day (Jefferson specified that he meant the *Whig* sentiments, favorable to independence from Britain), it was not therefore merely in harmony with those times. Lincoln's praise was for something more, and the phrase "self-evident truth" did not mean a truth then thought obvious. A self-evident truth may be obvious or obscure, but it must contain its meaning within its own terms rather than look to something outside. To see that all crows are black one must look at the crows, but to understand what "all men are created equal" means one must know only the meaning of "man." This is said to be a "truth," be it noted. It is not a concept created by men, for men have themselves been created. Men must make their way in a world and be guided by a truth they have not made. Since their freedom is based on this truth, they are not free to deny it. Nor may they regard this truth as an ideal to be aimed at, for it states the real nature of man from which and by which men must build. What, then, can be found in the "self-evident truth" that all men are created equal?

The Declaration is not a proclamation from a superior or chosen people. Its object, Jefferson said later, was to present "an appeal to the tribunal of the world" and it implies, as the document itself says, a "decent respect to the opinions of mankind."[2] Although it also appeals to the "Supreme Judge" for the rectitude of its intentions, its addressee is chiefly the present generation of human beings, who are created equal. Since they are equal, they hold unalienable rights to life, liberty and the pursuit of happiness; for nobody can reasonably yield or alienate these fundamental rights to his equal, or justly ask his equal to alienate them to him. But the rights by themselves are not secure. Though they cannot be alienated to rulers who rule by the favor of nature or the grace of God, they can only with difficulty be limited and made consistent with each other. It appears that government is required as much when men are held to be equal as when they are held to be unequal, and government must get obedience by consent in the first case when it could ask for deference in the second.

To secure these rights, governments derive their just powers from the consent of the governed, and when "any form of government becomes destructive of these ends, it is the Right of the people to alter or abolish it, and to institute new Government. . . ." Americans, however, could not institute

<hr />

[2] *Writings,* X, p. 343.

a new government without dissolving the political bands which had connected them to the British people, under the King of Great Britain; so the right of consent to government became, for them, the right to independence. But every people must have begun with the need to assert this right against other peoples. Every *man* is equal to every other man, and so every *people* is entitled to a "separate and equal station" among the powers of the earth. This consequence is by no means obvious, for it requires a shift from individuals to societies. Men are created equal, but the equality of peoples among the powers of the earth is achieved and protected by the right of men to govern themselves by consent. Equality among societies means independence, and this is a Declaration of Independence. Men are created equal, but they are divided in consequence of this equality into independent peoples. If men did not need government, their equality would not force them to divide themselves into independent peoples who must defend themselves against each other in war and revolution. One must not forget that the Declaration was a statement of reasons for going to war. The equality of men, therefore, has special reference to government: men are equal both in the lack of natural or divinely-appointed rulers and in the need for government.

Thus the Declaration is not chiefly concerned either with the form of government or with defining individual rights against the government. Clearly, men have rights against the government, which the British government had violated in America. But to secure their rights, men must use government as a weapon against offending governments, and so they need it just as much as they must fear it. Liberty is presented in the Declaration not so much in the familiar problem of a free individual versus a free government as it is in the people's right to alter or abolish, and institute, *any* form of government, as long as it rests on consent. In *A Summary View of the Rights of British America,* a proposed statement of instructions to Virginia delegates to the Continental Congress in 1774, Jefferson had said: "From the nature of things, every society must at all times possess within itself the sovereign powers of legislation."[3] The foundation of liberty is the supremacy of the legislative power; and this supremacy is understood not merely as a principle of internal organization but chiefly as the reason for the divisions of human beings into independent peoples. It is through political organization that men are united into a people, and by virtue of their union, divided from other peoples.

That all men are created equal is a "self-evident truth" explained and defended at length in the political philosophy of John Locke. The Declaration,

[3]Thomas Jefferson, *The Papers of Thomas Jefferson,* ed. J. P. Boyd (Princeton, N. J., 1950–1968), I, 132. Hereafter cited as *Papers.*

moreover, implies without saying explicitly that men live as individuals in a state of nature where they have no political relations before they make themselves a people by consenting to government. A "people," it seems, cannot exist except as the consequence of its own political decision, for the American people, though heretofore "connected" to the British, was connected to them by its own consent and hence potentially independent. Yet the necessity to infer a prepolitical state of nature in the principles of the Declaration reveals the importance of politics in that document. It sees obligation in the decision of a people and in men as members of a people, not in unconnected individuals. The reason for this is surely in the circumstances of the Declaration, which describe a people in colonial dependency rather than the state of nature. But it is interesting that the same liberal principles we usually see used to protect individuals against government here defend one people against another people by instituting a government against their government. These circumstances, as we recognize today, are not so rare as they may have seemed to defenders of liberalism writing about established liberal societies. The political philosophy of liberalism is not so incapable in the problem of founding as some of its detractors, and defenders, have assumed.

The Declaration implies that a people is made and can make itself by means of a political act. In this it differs from the doctrine of modern nationalism, which tries to make political divisions conform to pre-existing nations defined according to culture or language. In *A Summary View*, Jefferson said that Americans, like the Saxon ancestors of the British, had used their natural right of "departing from the country in which chance, not choice, has placed them, of going in quest of new habitations, and of there establishing new societies, under such laws and regulations as to them shall seem most likely to promote public happiness."[4] Politics need not be ruled by chance—by the fate of birth in nations; on the contrary, nations—Jefferson usually says "peoples"—can be built by men aware of their natural rights and alive to an opportunity of exercising them. Jefferson was not a nationalist, not even a liberal nationalist. If he had been, he might have had doubts about the justice of displacing the Indian nations in America. Slavery he knew was wrong because it denied the unalienable rights of man, but for this reason, the culture of primitive peoples ignorant of natural right did not deserve respect. Jefferson studied Indian languages because of his interest in the origins of man. He was not a nationalist, but neither was he an internationalist who believes that national differences can be overcome or transcended. For Jefferson, national differences are essentially *political* differences, and mankind is irremediably divided because human liberty takes effect only in the independence of one

[4] *Papers*, I, 121.

people from another. If men were divided merely by the accident of birth in different cultures, one might hope for the institution of international organization by the operation of human choice. But in the Declaration, it is precisely human choice in politics that divides men.

The element of choice in the making of a people is given emphasis in the "patient sufferance" of the American people. "Mankind," the Declaration says, "are more inclined to suffer, while evils are sufferable, than to right themselves by abolishing the forms to which they are accustomed." In the present case, the American colonies have endured "a history of repeated injuries and usurpations," and it is to prove this that the Declaration recites "a long train of abuses and usurpations" by George III. Mankind are slow to anger, and in their deliberateness there is opportunity for deliberation. The Americans show they have in fact made a deliberate choice by submitting facts to a candid world. Their "decent respect to the opinions of mankind" keeps them not merely to a standard of morality but also to a rough standard of prudence in proceeding slowly and perhaps choosing carefully. Government by consent means government by choice rather than whimsy, at least or especially in the fundamental act of making an independent people. In this attempt to make government by consent seem moderate or even wise, Jefferson and his cosigners indicate that government by consent requires a measure of moderation and wisdom in those consenting. A people does not have a right of self-determination merely because it constitutes a separate nation or culture, nor is it likely to make itself independent hastily and regardless of circumstances. Nevertheless, it does have a right of self-determination merely because it may constitute a separate people; and the right of consent is more securely fixed to the nature of man, which is equality, than is the wisdom of those consenting.

Choosing to have a government and hence to be a people comes before the choice of any particular form of government. The Declaration specifies that governments derive their just powers by consent, but it does not specify which governments do that best. It does not even rule out any forms of government, though absolute monarchy seems to be rejected by implication. Limited monarchy, however, such as the existing British government, is apparently included among governments that *could* gain the consent of a people. Otherwise it would have made no sense to list "a long train of abuses and usurpations" in the longest part of the Declaration; it would have been enough to say that monarchy is illegitimate in itself. Apparently all governments must rule by consent, but there is some leeway not only in the details of free government but even in the character or form of the government as a whole. This conclusion, which admittedly we must infer from the Declaration, must be reconciled with the fact that the party Jefferson formed later based itself on "republican principles" and could find nothing more damning to call its opponents than "monarchists." Moreover, the Declaration does not require representative democracy as we practice it today. Specifically, equality in consent does not necessarily imply "one man, one vote," for the former is *the* principle on which free government is founded, while the latter is *a* principle on which it may operate. Jefferson, it may be noted, changed his mind about "one man, one vote"; at first he opposed it, and later favored it. He never wavered in his adherence to the view, apparently indifferent to forms of government, that all government be by consent of the governed.

So much for the strictly political meaning of the self-evident truth that all men are created equal; it does not require democracy and it does require independent peoples. Thus far, however, we have not mentioned the meaning Jefferson himself (as opposed to his cosigners) thought most important. Writing just before his death, he called the Declaration a signal to arouse men to burst the chains of "monkish ignorance and superstition." This, and not "the present King of Great Britain," is cited as the real enemy. Jefferson explained why in memorable words: "All eyes are opened, or opening, to the rights of man. The general spread of the light of science has already laid open to every view the palpable truth that the mass of mankind has not been born with saddles on their backs, nor a favored few booted and spurred, ready to ride them legitimately, *by the grace of God.*"[5]

In this quotation politics and religion are inseparable. A certain religious belief, called "monkish ignorance and superstition," induces men to hold that some men are better than others because they are favored with the grace of God. Holding this political consequence of their religious belief, they give their consent to governments that do not respect the rights of man. They use their right of consent unwisely. The Declaration, therefore, is by no means neutral on religion, but it judges religion by its political consequences, that is, by its conformity to the self-evident truth—the equality of men. Every people, says the Declaration, has a separate and equal station among the powers of the earth by virtue of "the Laws of Nature and of Nature's God." A belief in Nature's God, it seems, is compatible with, or reinforces (but does not seem necessary to) respect for human equality.

"Nature's God" was intended in contrast to a revealed god; so the Declaration (at least in Jefferson's understanding) seems hostile to revealed religion. Revealed religion is revealed only to the godly, and from what Jefferson said in many places against priests, one may suppose that the godly will take advantage of the favor of revelation to demand political power for themselves or their allies. Revelation in its nature, and not merely by its abuse, is opposed

[5]Letter to Roger C. Weightman, June 24, 1826, *Writings*, X, 391–92. The italics are mine.

to the equality of men. On the other hand, "the light of science" is open to man as man and also teaches the equality of men. Of course Jefferson never made himself a crusading deist like Tom Paine; he accommodated himself to a mild Christianity, and tried to make it still milder by compiling a renovated gospel entitled "The Life and Morals of Jesus of Nazareth." As we shall see, he thought that to secure the rights of man, the people must believe either in a revealed religion made harmless to those rights or in Nature's God. But he always promoted the authority of science over the authority of revealed religion. He was himself a scientist in his spare time, making inventions, conceiving explanations, and corresponding with other scientists. Yet though he was greatly interested in science, he was, as a political man, still more interested in the *authority* of science, for he felt that science as opposed to revealed religion supports the vital self-evident truth of human life.

Judged politically, science and natural religion support the equality of man, while revealed religion opposes it. It follows that government which respects the equality of man must secure the support of science and natural religion, while rendering revealed religion harmless. This it can do by separating the churches of revealed religion from the state, for priests cannot then make alliances with governments in which rulers receive divine favor and priests earthly privileges. Because religion and politics are inseparable, church and state ought to be separated. Because free government cannot be indifferent to the character of religion in a free society, it ought to be neutral among the churches of revealed religion.

Thus the Declaration would, after all, discriminate among forms of government to this extent: no government could respect the rights of man if it maintained an established (revealed) religion. But with this inference we go well beyond what the Declaration says explicitly. It does not mention the separation of church and state and does not reproach George III for maintaining an established religion in any of the colonies. Jefferson at this time was beginning his attack on the establishment of the Church of England in Virginia. In one of his bills on disestablishment (offered to the General Assembly of Virginia in 1776), he asserts that a change in form of government makes necessary corresponding changes in laws, since some are "founded on principles heterogeneous to the republican spirit. . . ."[6] This would justify the inference we have made, with Jefferson's suggestion, from the Declaration. But it is safe to say that few who signed the Declaration considered its main intent to attack "monkish ignorance and superstition." This was Jefferson's own gloss, and one may add, a partisan gloss. Jefferson had to fight long and hard for complete disestablishment in Virginia against "Whigs" (that is, parti-

[6]*Papers*, I, 562.

sans of American independence) who did not agree that the self-evident truth of human equality demands separation of church and state. The Declaration harmonized sentiments of the day in favor of independence, but its apparent indifference to forms of government left ground for party conflict over the political consequences of its central, self-evident truth.

NOTES ON VIRGINIA: NATURAL RESOURCES

Jefferson was a one-book author, and his one book, the *Notes on Virginia*, was written in the period 1780–1784 during and after his brief tenure as Governor of Virginia. The *Notes on Virginia* consists of "queries" put by "a Foreigner of Distinction," Francois Marbois, seeking information about America, which Jefferson, through an intermediary, undertook to answer. Thus Jefferson caused his one book to appear as answers to questions in private rather than a voluntary offering to the public. The full title is *Notes on the State of Virginia*. "State" means "condition" as well as "government," and the book contains facts relating to the condition of "Virginia," especially its power among nations in the 1780s and its future potentiality for such power. In the eighteenth century, the term "statistics" was used with a wider meaning than quantitative facts to describe the state of power in a country.

Now this country was of course America, not merely Virginia. Marbois had asked for information about all the states, but Jefferson chose to tell about America through these *Notes on Virginia*. Though in the first Query he gives the exact boundaries of Virginia (then much larger than now) as they were determined by charters and grants from England, he goes on in the second Query to describe all the principal rivers in America westward to the Mississippi. It is as if he wished to indicate how powerless the Old World was to set limits to the New World. Many of his statistics (including the kinds of quadrupeds and of Indians or "aborigines") refer to America rather than Virginia, and his comment shifts with ease from remarks on Virginia to thoughts on America. Perhaps he means to use the meaning of the name, "Virginia." As John Locke once said ". . . in the beginning all the *World* was America," so now Jefferson seems to say America is Virginia, a virgin land in which mankind can make a new beginning.

The *Notes on Virginia* can then be seen as Jefferson's own justification for the Declaration of Independence. Now that the *right* of the American people to independence has been established, their *capability* for independence must be demonstrated. If America were permanently inferior to the Old World, its right to independence would be reduced to an actual subordination. It would be like a newly freed colony in our day that had no basis for independence either in natural resources or in national pride and unity. A former colony lacking the basis for independence can easily become a colony again in fact if not in name. A "declaration" of independence, therefore, is not enough; it must be backed by a proof that this people, the American people, can sustain its independence against nature and against foreign powers.

These two enemies of a people's independence, nature and foreign powers, are taken up separately in the *Notes on Virginia.* The first eleven "Queries" (i.e., chapters) concern the natural environment of Virginia and America; they try to prove, at the least, that contrary to the views of certain French natural philosophers, and to the prejudices of most Europeans, nature has not enlisted herself as a partisan of Europe. The last eleven Queries take up the political and cultural state of America, the conventional environment created by man, and show that America does not suffer from cultural dependence or from what is today called "neocolonialism." The Twelfth Query on counties and towns provides the transition from the natural to the conventional state of the country, for Jefferson there discusses the relative power of nature (by means of rivers) and the laws to decide the existence and importance of towns.[7]

America has natural power in its self-sufficiency. The first eleven Queries show that the New World is not lacking in any natural resource. It has an extensive and well-connected system of rivers, and no sea-ports other than the mouths of its rivers. Thus America is neither forced nor encouraged by nature to have commerce with the Old World; it can trade with itself. Nor does it need "productions, mineral, vegetable and animal" from the Old World, for all can be found in this "extensive country." America has the temperance and variety of climate to support a civilized and independent society. It has a population growing fast enough to double itself every twenty-seven years, and hence has no need of emigrants from the absolute monarchies of Europe, who bring with them either the principles of such governments or their extreme contrary, an "unbounded licentiousness." Even though labor, not land, is scarce in America, Jefferson suggests that it is better to wait patiently for an internal growth that will produce a people "more homogeneous, more peaceable, more durable." This reasoning applies more strongly to the importation of slaves, which has been prohibited "while the minds of our citizens may be ripening for a complete emancipation of human nature."[8]

True to his division of the subject into the natural and cultural environment of America, Jefferson discusses the Indians, not slaves, in the first part of the *Notes on Virginia.* They are called "aborigines" as the inhabitants found in America, not brought there; they have manners rather than laws and they

---

[7]I am indebted for this observation to Jane Johnson Benardete. Marbois had put 22 queries, but Jefferson made them 23 and changed their order; *Papers*, IV, 166.

[8]Thomas Jefferson, *Notes on the State of Virginia*, ed. William Peden (Chapel Hill, North Carolina, 1955), pp. 85, 87. Hereafter cited as *NV.*

use their natural moral sense of right and wrong in place of government. Though they live "principally on the spontaneous productions of nature," they are, again contrary to the view of the Count de Buffon, as brave, enduring, affectionate, sensitive, sexually potent and keen of mind as "Homo sapiens Europaeus."[9] They are, moreover, apparently older than "the red men of Asia," a conclusion Jefferson reached by a calculation of the antiquity of their languages. The American aborigines would then be among the aborigines of mankind.

The Indian stock, developed in America, is as good as European stock. It is in no way stunted as if the Indian were living on a second-rate continent. Perhaps this is why Jefferson (in the sixth Query) chose an Indian chief, Logan, to represent "the Man of America" and in the name of the New World to speak defiance to an English colonial governor, Lord Dunmore. Although Logan had long been a friend of the white man, his family was murdered by a white man, and in revenge he led his tribe to war. After it was defeated, Logan sent a speech worthy of Demosthenes and Cicero (Jefferson says) to Lord Dunmore. "There runs not a drop of my blood in the veins of any living creature," Logan asserted; and having "glutted my vengeance" for the injuries of one man, he now consents and rejoices that his country lives in peace.

Logan is an independent man because he has no ties to other human beings and because he can send his tribe to war on a mission of personal revenge. Jefferson admires his unlettered eloquence, but he also notes that Indians are barbarians for whom force is right. They have a natural moral sense of right and wrong, but they do not know how to apply this in politics to the construction of civilized societies.[10] Logan, in his independence, shows no respect for the self-evident truths that all men are created equal and that government should be by consent of the governed. Natural or aboriginal independence is barbaric; it derives from the power of one's endowments, such as strength or eloquence, and of one's circumstances, such as the resources of the American continent.

The American people has received from nature a golden opportunity for building an independent nation, contrary to the prejudices of Europeans, but Jefferson did not wish to base his case for independence on that fact alone. The "Man of America" is "both aboriginal and emigrant." The emigrant American, as distinguished from the aborigine, has brought his understanding of civil government and natural right from Europe and perfected it on his own. With this great advantage, however, he suffers the great disadvantage of having ties with Europe. His independence is more civilized but more problematic. He

[9]*NV*, pp. 96, 62.
[10]*NV*, pp. 60, 93, 142.

cannot claim, in regard to culture, manners and beliefs, that he has no ties with "any living creature." George Washington, Benjamin Franklin, and David Rittenhouse are the examples Jefferson uses to show that America has contributed its full share of geniuses to the present age, but they must admit comparison to European geniuses and acknowledge an indebtedness to European civilization. They do not have the natural (though savage) independence of Logan: Jefferson himself had to argue the viability of American independence to the French philosophers and other doubters; he could not merely assert it as could Logan.

If Logan speaks for the American Indian, his fate may also be representative. After fierce resistance, he succumbed to the civilized but unjust conqueror, the emigrant American. This American, suppressing the memory of an original immoral deed, must make his independence with a "new political science" (to anticipate the phrase of Alexis de Tocqueville) suited to his natural opportunity and directed to the reform of his cultural inheritance.

NOTES ON VIRGINIA: REFORM

"Human nature is the same on every side of the Atlantic," whatever the greater bounty of nature in land and rivers on this side.[11] The more important difference between the Old World and the New is made by man, for, despite the advantages in natural resources and the equality of human nature, the aborigine is of course far inferior in civilization to both the European and the emigrant American. Now the superiority of the last, according to Jefferson, lay in his very understanding that all men are created equal. When men are understood to be naturally equal, their differences in civilization are attributed to their own striving and making (given the opportunity). But to understand civilization as chiefly man-made, which implies the power of human creation, is a keen incentive to make it better: hence the superiority of those peoples who believe in reform. The power of reform depends on the belief in reform.

Jefferson, it can be said with emphasis, believed in reform, and in this book he tried to teach the American people to do likewise. In the first part of the book, on America's natural state, no proposal for reform can be found, except for a brief discussion of Albino Negroes, who might be taken jokingly for nature's (inadequate) solution to the race problem. But when Jefferson begins to discuss human convention, he urges reform. He no sooner describes the constitution of Virginia in the first Query of the second part than he gives its six major defects and proposes a convention to fix it. Excusing the Virginia constitution, he says it "was formed when we were new and unexperienced

[11]NV, p. 121.

in the science of government."[12] That was in 1776; ten years later he thinks "we"—his fellow Virginians—have achieved maturity in the science of government.

Jefferson's belief in reform is focussed on government. He begins the second part of his book by considering the constitution, and political science seems to be the key science for human improvement. The reason is the connection between human improvement and human equality. To repeat: reform has its full power only when every difference of progress, in a situation of equal opportunity, is attributed to human making; and this requires that men be held naturally equal. The first task of government, then, is to establish and protect the self-evident truth of human equality. To do this, it must secure, in a constitution, the rights of man that follow from the equality of man. Since the constitution of government protects the very possibility of reform, it has, or should have, a special status in a society dedicated to reform. It should not be "alterable by the ordinary legislature." The ordinary legislature can alter the laws, not the constitution; so the belief in reform dictates a distinction between the constitution and the laws.

Jefferson takes up "laws" in the next Query after "constitution" to indicate the *second* task of government, which is to serve as the agent of reform. Before government can reform effectually, it must be set on the only basis that can sustain reform over time, a constitution unalterable by itself. Government can reform the laws on condition that it not be allowed to reform itself, although it may propose constitutional reform.

The people make the constitution under which the government makes ordinary laws. In the rush of revolutionary conflict, Virginia's constitution was not made and ratified by delegates of the people selected for that purpose, and it shows the bad effects of making a constitution by the ordinary method of making laws. The majority is unrepresented in the legislature; the representation of those who do vote is very unequal; the Senate is composed in the same way as the House of Delegates; too much power is concentrated in the legislative body; and the ordinary legislature may alter the constitution itself. The people properly instructed would never have made such a constitution, which is indeed not really a constitution.

For Jefferson, politics is the crucial, but not the ultimate factor in society. The constitution protects the rights of man, but since the people make the constitution, it is they who ultimately protect those rights. The people are "the only safe depositaries" of government. Yet the people do not govern directly; they govern by elections through a constitution. Moreover, under this constitution, the government makes laws that affect the character of the people. To

[12]*NV*, pp. 118, 129.

be safe depositaries of government, Jefferson says that even the people must be *rendered* safe; they are not so when uneducated or corrupted.[13] By means of the distinction between constitution and laws, the people govern and are made fit to govern. By enforcing respect for equality, they make reform possible; and yet by not governing directly themselves, they make it possible for the government to reform the people. Thus even the reformer is reformed. The trick of this recipe for progress is a constitution that is made by men but does not in the ordinary way seem alterable by them. The constitution is a convention above all ordinary conventions by which they may be reformed. It is surely not fixed for a long time, as Jefferson gave each generation the right —even the duty—to make its own fundamental convention. But the constitution must be made with a broader consent than the ordinary laws and on an occasion specially marked for fundamental change.

Jefferson's political science combines two ways of understanding politics that are often thought to be antithetical, the institutional and the sociological. He insists on a special status for the institutions in the constitution, while he also sees them in the context of the interests and manners in society that affect government. But the special status of governmental institutions is connected to a comprehensive social outlook, and for Jefferson the two ways of understanding politics are really one. Institutions must be kept fixed to secure the people's liberties against the ambition of a few, and society must be made republican to protect the people's liberties against their own carelessness and lack of vigilance. Only a republican people can remain free, but only a republican government with a fixed constitution can make the people republican.

Jefferson did not favor unending reform for the purpose of keeping pace with social change. His political science was in the tradition of Montesquieu. In his view politics has a function between the formative power of the Aristotelian regime and the reactive conciliator of social forces argued by modern political sociology. Government derives from the people, where it is "deposited," and yet acts on the people to keep them independent by making them republican.

An independent people must have a republican administration of justice, and Jefferson proposed a revised code for Virginia based on the common law of England but with significant alterations from the existing body of British statutes. Among these was a bill to abolish the importation of slaves, to which was added an amendment to emancipate all slaves, educate them and send them elsewhere in colonies. The bill with this amendment was too radical to succeed, but the occasion gave Jefferson a chance to consider the problem of race in this book. Granted that all men are *naturally* equal, can racial differ-

[13]*NV*, p. 148.

ences among them be disregarded in the *conventions* of human societies? Arguing against the incorporation of blacks into the state, Jefferson seems to conclude (with some present-day theorists of black power) that the difference between black and white is too great to be kept in one free and independent people. It does not follow, then, from human equality that men can be equal members of a racially mixed society.[14] For this unhappy conclusion Jefferson gives political, physical and moral reasons.

Political reasons can be found in the very injustice of slavery: the "deep-rooted prejudices entertained by the whites," and "ten thousand recollections, by the blacks, of the injuries they have sustained." These are sufficient to "divide us into parties, and produce convulsions which will probably never end but in the extermination of the one or the other race."[15] But Jefferson postpones this matter and moves to "physical and moral" considerations.

First among these is the difference of color "fixed in nature" which makes the Negro less beautiful than the white and unable to express his passions by changing color. In addition, the Negro has an inferior mind: an equal memory, but a much inferior reason scarcely capable, for example, of comprehending Euclid, and a dull imagination. To substantiate this judgment Jefferson compares the literary works of American black slaves with those of the Roman slaves who lived in greater misery but excelled in the arts and sciences. In the "endowments of the head," then, nature has been less bountiful to the black. In justice and loyalty, however, the black is fully equal; he steals when he does only because everything is stolen from him. This clear difference of color and supposed difference of faculty (Jefferson offers his opinion of the Negro's mental inferiority "with great diffidence") make it unthinkable in America to mix freed slaves and former masters, even if both should overcome their hatred and distrust of the other.[16] On the other hand, these differences do not justify slavery and do not permit America to perpetuate it indefinitely.

Another factor in the European inheritance is religion, and this also raises the problem of homogeneity in a free people. While men are held apart by the artificial institution of slavery, they are forced together by the establishment of religion. Jefferson fought the establishment of the Anglican church in Virginia for a decade, 1776–1786, in the "severest contests" in which he had ever been engaged. His "Bill for Establishing Religious Freedom," passed in 1786 in modified form, was in his opinion one of the three most notable works of his life, along with the Declaration of Independence and the founding of the University of Virginia. In the *Notes on Virginia,* he supports religious freedom with the argument contained in this famous passage: ". . . it does me no injury for my neighbor to say there are twenty gods, or no god. It neither picks my

[14]*Writings,* I, 68.
[15]*NV,* p. 138.
[16]*NV,* pp. 142–43.

pocket nor breaks my leg." Government can coerce "the acts of the body," not "the operations of the mind," because its legitimate concern is with what is injurious to the body, or by extension, to the purse. When government tries to extend its control to "the operations of the mind," it will establish an error, such as the view that the earth is "as flat as a trencher." If error is undesirable, so is uniformity of opinion; for it prevents the different sects from censoring each other's morals and by repeated persecution succeeds in no more than making "half the world fools, and the other half hypocrites."[17]

This is the argument of Locke's *Essay on Toleration,* and that work reserves the same exception: "the operations of the mind" may have to be coerced in order to protect toleration. Jefferson says, "Difference of opinion is advantageous in religion"; and to this he adds that difference of opinion is harmless in physics and geometry.[18] He does *not* say this of political opinions regarding fundamental principles, the rights of man. Indeed, Jefferson did not regard the rights of man as being founded on mere opinion incapable of demonstration or liable to supercession; they are self-evident truths good for all time. By virtue of these rights, men consent to government to protect their life, liberty and property from injury, and not to improve their souls. If this truth were but an opinion, it could not protect free inquiry into other opinions. The claim of a tyrannical government to abridge religious freedom (or to justify slavery) would stand equally with the demand for religious freedom as a matter of opinion, and the issue would be decided by force, not reason. It seems that civil rights must be defended against religious persecution by *established* political truths; so Jefferson composed a bill for *establishing* religious freedom. Such establishment may not require suppression of error, for reason will defeat error when free to combat it, but the government must instruct the people in their rights.

Moreover, it appears that government, while protecting religious freedom, must favor religion over irreligion. Jefferson agrees that the testimony of the atheist be rejected in a court of law: "reject it then, and be the stigma on him." Then, in a striking return to the political aspect of slavery, he exclaims:

And can the liberties of a nation be thought secure when we have removed their only firm basis, a conviction in the minds of the people that these liberties are of the gift of God? That they are not to be violated but with his wrath? Indeed I tremble for my country when I reflect that God is just.[19]

In a warm climate no man will work who can get a slave to work for him; so in this situation liberty and economic interest are opposed. To overcome the opposition of economic interest, Jefferson implies, liberty needs the sup-

[17] *NV,* pp. 159–60; *Writings,* I, 53.
[18] *NV,* p. 160; *Papers,* II, 546.
[19] *NV,* pp. 159, 163.

port of a religion that professes faith in a just God, benevolent but wrathful. Without such support, Jefferson could not reasonably hope for a total emancipation of slaves by the consent of their masters. This religion seems to be a Judeo-Christian monotheism rendered harmless to liberty by the device of keeping it divided among many sects, whose disputes can be silenced if government takes no notice of them.[20] Religious freedom consists of an established sectarianism in which the necessary minimum of religion receives the support of government in public education and the unwelcome superfluity meets with contempt, fair argument and ridicule. For the sake of liberty, government must support religion in general, but no particular religion.

Although this religion will clearly be predominantly Christian in America, Jefferson quotes from a pagan condemnation of slavery, and nothing from the Bible, in the *Notes on Virginia.* In the natural (or theoretical) part of the book he says regarding natural or Biblical hypotheses: "he is less remote from the truth who believes nothing than he who believes what is wrong." (Query 6). But in the corresponding Query 18 of the political (or practical) part, he says that it is necessary for the people to believe.[21] Religion has a status something like the status of the constitution: as the government needs a constitution above the ordinary laws to check its own ambition, the people need a superhuman source for their natural rights to force them to extend those rights to others when it is against their interest to do so. Jefferson apparently entertained doubts about the truth even of natural religion, but he was willing to use the strength of religion for political purposes. He said: "Truth can stand by itself." This seems to say that truth does not need the support of government. It may mean, however, that government gets its strength from the true rights of man, not the reverse. Then truth uses the strength of government as support when it is opposed by interest. Unwelcome restrictions and unpleasant duties will remain in the new world of the rights of man, and to secure them Jefferson resorted, in his own way, to the traditional method of finding or making a law above law.

Still another problem of human contrivance is education. Nature, we have seen, has provided America with her share of genius, but men of genius do not show themselves by nature. They must be elicited from the people through a system of public education by which "the best geniuses will be raked from the rubbish annually . . ."[22] America must give opportunity to all, because nature has distributed talents among the poor as liberally as among the rich; but in giving favor, it must distinguish between "genius" and "rubbish," so that America can make the best use of its endowment.

[20]*NV*, p. 161.
[21]*NV*, p. 33. Query 18 is on "manners," following Query 17 on "religion."
[22]*NV*, p. 146.

This elitist statement of Jefferson's recalls another still more famous, in an exchange of letters with John Adams: "May we not even say that that form of government is best which provides the most effectually for a pure selection of these natural aristoi into the offices of government?" "These natural aristoi" are members of the "natural aristocaracy" of virtue and talents as opposed to the "artificial aristocracy founded on wealth and birth."[23] They were confused together when the artificial aristocracy characteristic of the Old World was imported to the New, and the problem is to separate them. Jefferson proudly mentions in this letter that laws drawn by himself in the Virginia Revisal abolished entail and primogeniture, "the root of Pseudo-aristocracy." The best way to select the natural aristoi is by the method of free election by the citizens, who will not be corrupted by wealth or blinded by ambition. Yet the people must receive an elementary education and their minds stored, not with the Bible, but with morality and "the most useful facts" of history. History, especially, will make the people "safe . . . guardians of their own liberty," as it teaches them "to know ambition under every disguise it may assume" and to be jealous and suspicious toward their rulers.[24]

Education thus has the double purpose of enabling the people to distinguish the virtuous and the talented from the merely ambitious and of drawing the former from the main body of the people so that they can be prepared for promotion. In nature, men are created equal; in society, their inequalities come to the fore. Jefferson was no democrat in the traditional sense of the term, meaning a partisan of "rule of the people." He was willing to trust the people, not to govern, but to choose their governors. Being uncorrupt, the people will, if well-instructed, choose the best and reject those who are merely well-off; but as they do so, they constitute a kind of impartial judge separated from those whom they judge, who govern them. Their governors are drawn from them in a system of public education that gathers the best geniuses, but in the same act takes these best geniuses away from them. The people, then, are consoled for the loss of their natural equality partly by the principle of equality of opportunity. If they cannot govern themselves, they can be governed by natural aristocrats of popular origin, chosen by themselves—by the men who later were called "Jeffersonians."

These men get a "liberal education" in the Greek and Latin classics as well as in the sciences to make them guardians of the people's liberty. Their virtue is based on the natural moral sense Jefferson thought was in all men, which consists of helping others. They do not have special aristocratic virtues not found in all men, which might distinguish them and make them eager to

[23]Letter to John Adams, October 28, 1813, *The Adams-Jefferson Letters*, ed. L. J. Cappon (Chapel Hill, North Carolina, 1959), II, 388–89. Hereafter cited as *AJ*.
[24]*NV*, p. 148.

distinguish themselves. Jefferson, though a zestful partisan in politics, frowned upon men of ambition. Ambition is a desire to excel in the virtues that raise a few men above the many, and Jefferson wished to use the aristocratic desire to excel in a rivalry to help and defend the people. His natural aristocracy, separated from the people by the system of education, looks back to the needs of the people; the principle of equality of opportunity serves the natural equality of man. He supported that aristocracy which serves the people, and serves them in a cheerful spirit of progress, not with gloomy condescension. He expected, however, that the aristocrats would become corrupt when they governed. His faith in education was limited by his faith in constitutions and elections, which in turn was limited by his faith in revolutions.

Aristocrats are promoted from the people so that they may use their talents for the sake of the people, rather than because they deserve a higher place to use their better talents for the excellence that only they can achieve. This distinction between a utilitarian and an intrinsic view of aristocracy may seem fine, but it allowed Jefferson to retain his belief in the self-evident truth of human equality in the face of many seeming violations of it in the society he helped to found, and enabled him to turn those inequalities to the account of human equality. He may have been guilty of overconfidence to think that public education can so easily find the natural aristocracy and control it, once found.

How should America provide for itself? "The political economists of Europe" were agreed that every state should establish its own manufactures, but the European inheritance, as before, could not answer the question for America. America had a special opportunity from nature, the resources for self-sufficiency and the rivers for internal trade as we have seen, but most important "an immensity of land." Unlike Europe where land was no longer available to support surplus populations, America was so big that it could choose whether to do its own manufacturing. And since America could choose, no doubt existed about how it should choose:

Those who labor in the earth are the chosen people of God, if ever he had a chosen people, whose breasts he has made his peculiar deposit for substantial and genuine virtue. . . . Corruption of morals in the mass of cultivators is a phenomenon of which no age or nation has furnished an example.[25]

The economic question yields to the problem, both moral and political, of keeping a people free. Those who manufacture depend on "the casualties and caprices of their customers," and being dependent, become subservient and venal and live as "the mobs of great cities." Farmers, on the other hand, depend on themselves and on heaven, but not on other men. Their occupation

[25] *NV*, pp. 164–65.

makes the independent character of a free man, and hence of a free people. Instead of the variety of interests found favorable to freedom by *The Federalist*, Jefferson proposed that the farming interest be advanced over the others. He favored a variety of sects, but not of interests, and as we have seen in his immigration policy, he desired a homogeneous people. It was not as if America would have to do without manufactures, for the damage comes from making, not from having, them. "Let our workshops remain in Europe": This will keep Europe weak and corrupt, and America will have the best of both worlds.

Since foreign commerce must make up for the lack of manufacturing, America will not be self-sufficient. It must give up the natural independence allowed by its situation and resources for the sake of moral and political independence. Jefferson later accepted domestic manufacturing when American independence seemed to be endangered by the lack of it, but both views show that he understood a complex truth uncommonly well: that men in remaking their environment remake themselves. Technological progress, therefore, may have unforeseen and untoward moral consequences even in a site so favorable as America, and it is necessary to accept backwardness and dependency in manufacturing in order to protect the cultivated independence of free men. There is more than a hint of Rousseau's *Discourse on the Arts and Sciences* in this exclamation in a letter to John Adams: "And *if* science produces no better fruits than tyranny, murder, rapine and destitution of national morality, I would rather wish our country to be ignorant, honest and estimable as our neighboring savages are."[26] Today we may have to consider Jefferson's praise of the independent farmer as obsolete, but we have reason to share the doubts about the moral and political benefits of scientific progress which were the basis of his praise.

America has "an immensity of land." This means it has enough *new* land so that, in a rising population, every man can have a farm. But how much is enough for this purpose? Jefferson, we have seen, planned for a *rising* population (not merely for the contingency of a surplus) and he nowhere fixed an upper limit beyond which it should not rise. Will not this population need more land? America should remain a society of farmers "while we have land to labor," Jefferson says, clearly asking this question for himself. He seems to have recognized that when an independent people forsakes self-sufficiency, it must seek ways of expansion, not to satisfy an aggressive lust but simply to preserve its own freedom. Jefferson once called America "an Empire of liberty"; he did so when as governor of Virginia in 1780 he commanded George Rogers Clark to undertake an expedition to Detroit from which, among other

---

[26]Letter to John Adams, January 21, 1812; *AJ*, II, 291; cf. II, 332, 458.

things, he hoped to "add to the Empire of liberty an extensive and fertile Country thereby converting dangerous Enemies into valuable friends."[27] With the need for new land in mind, one can understand Jefferson's concern for laws to limit speculation in land. One can also appreciate the overriding motive for his Louisiana Purchase. As so often happens with land, as happened in the case of land bought from the Indians (which Jefferson himself noted), the buyer took advantage of the seller's distress. In the need for new land as understood by Jefferson and later by Jackson, one can see a strong motive for American expansionism from 1780 to 1860.[28]

Such are the problems of founding an independent people on the basis of human equality. In regard to slavery, religion, education and economics it is not sufficient simply to announce the self-evident truth as if its meaning were clear. Even when all believe in human equality, so that Jefferson could assert that the Declaration merely harmonized the sentiments of the day, the meaning of equality is arguable. The *Notes on Virginia* is agreed to be a major work of American political thought, but this is partly for lack of many better works and partly for the eminence of its author. It is in fact a major work, comprehensive and carefully written. In it can be seen every element of Jefferson's later political thought (which appears only in speeches and letters) except his partisanship and the doctrine of states' rights, an instrument of his partisanship. But even Jefferson's party is anticipated in the program of reform he offers for Virginia and America in the *Notes*. Its second part (Queries 13–23) constitutes a commentary of partisan interpretation on the facts of the natural "state of Virginia" given in the first part. We must try to understand why Jefferson thought himself justified in heading a party to establish these reforms.

THE REPUBLICAN PARTY

For all the zeal and success of Jefferson's party, it is surprisingly difficult to discover the chief points of difference with its Federalist opponent, and thus the reason for its existence. It is difficult not because the party was secretive about its aims, but because the announced differences, summed up in the title of the "Republican" party, are difficult to take seriously. Jefferson, though not a framer of the Constitution, was not an Antifederalist opponent of it; he claimed that the republican principles of his party were the "true principles" of the Constitution.[29] As described in *The Federalist* (a book that Jefferson said

---

[27]Letter to George Rogers Clark, December 25, 1780; *Papers*, IV, 237–38. See Julian P. Boyd, "Thomas Jefferson's Empire of Liberty," *Thomas Jefferson: A Profile*, ed. Merrill D. Peterson (New York, 1967), pp. 189–93.

[28]Harry V. Jaffa, "Agrarian Virtue and Republican Freedom," *Equality and Liberty* (New York, 1965), pp. 59–66.

[29]Letter to Edmund Pendleton, February 14, 1799, *Writings*, VII, 355; Letter to John Adams, June 27, 1813, *AJ*, II, 335.

was "in my opinion, the best commentary on the principles of government which ever was written"[30]), the Constitution establishes an entirely new kind of popular government. It is not the popular government of "the petty republics of Greece and Italy" in ancient times, where the people ruled directly over a city. It is modern representative government based on the rights of all men, not just the many, and extended to the breadth of a nation or empire. Yet it is neither the absolute monarchy favored by Hobbes nor the limited monarchy preferred by Locke, the two founding theorists of modern representative government. It is republican, and unlike previous republics that were steadied with hereditary aristocratic or monarchical elements, this republic is to be *completely* popular, its checks and balances contrived entirely by institutions elected or otherwise drawn from the people, with no admixture, however limited, of hereditary monarchy and aristocracy.

On this general conclusion, Jefferson and his opponents were agreed. If there was so much agreement on so much innovation, what then remained to divide them? At the time of the debate over ratification of the Constitution, Jefferson had only two objections. He thought, as did many others, that the Constitution needed a declaration of rights; and this defect was soon remedied by the passage of the first ten amendments. But he also objected to the indefinite eligibility of the president for re-election. He thought that a president, once elected, could contrive his own re-election indefinitely, and so the provision of re-eligibility would actually result in an elective monarchy for life.

That this result could occur, or that it would be harmful if it did, seems an unreasoning fear on Jefferson's part, and has usually been taken for such by historians. Yet he felt this fear, and we must make sense of it if we are to understand his party, its principles and its career. Though after Washington's retirement Jefferson relaxed his belief that the Constitution must prevent the re-election of a president, he described his opponents as "monocrats" and asserted that the Constitution had been "interpreted and administered" like a *"monarchie masquée."* [31] Monarchy was not a casual or temporary danger to him, and to indicate his opposition, he called his party "republican." Why was he so fearful of "monarchy"?

Moreover, since Jefferson was so fearful, why did he tolerate any element of monarchy in the Constitution? For the president, by his own comparison, is an elective monarchy, whether for life or for one term. If he had been motivated by a phobia or exaggerated hatred of the British monarchy, he would have favored abolishing the king altogether, as did the "classical republicans" of the seventeenth century, Sidney and Harrington. Instead, following

[30]Letter to James Madison, November 18, 1788, *Writings*, V, 53.
[31]Letter to Robert R. Livingston, December 14, 1800, *Writings*, VII, 464.

Locke and Montesquieu, he allowed a limited monarchy to be reestablished in America under the name of the "executive power," and he both considered and rejected the possibility of a plural executive.[32] He also would not have praised the British Constitution as the best existing constitution prior to those made by the American colonies, if he had been simply frightened of monarchy.[33] Nor, if he had merely hated the British, would he have asserted that Newton, Bacon and Locke were the three greatest men who ever lived.

As Jefferson's views on monarchy seem to be the cause of his partisanship and the source of his party, they may perhaps be explained by referring to his views on parties. He never collected those views; but he had many occasions and ample time to compose them, for he was rightly accused of having infused American politics with higher party spirit than the Framers thought desirable or even tolerable. What could he say in defense? In letters to Adams after his retirement from the presidency, he began with a premise of considerable scope: "The same political parties which now agitate the U. S. have existed thro' all time . . . in fact the terms whig and tory belong to natural, as well as to civil, history. They denote the temper and constitution of mind of different individuals." By such differences of mind, men form different opinions and by virtue of these opinions divide into parties "in all governments where they have been permitted freely to think and to speak." Jefferson also said that "one of the questions" dividing his Republican party from the Federalists was "on the improvability of the human mind, in science, in ethics, in government etc." But this opinion, which would yield a division into liberal or progressive and conservative parties, does not seem to be responsible for (though it characterizes) the *Republican* party and its opponent. The decisive difference of opinion is a difference about government, whether "the power of the people, or that of the aristoi should prevail."[34]

The difference over who should rule has always agitated free societies, but in describing the American parties Jefferson used significantly altered expressions, and did so consistently on several occasions.

Where a constitution, like ours, wears a mixed aspect of monarchy & republicanism, its citizens will naturally divide into two classes of sentiment, according as their tone of body or of mind, their habits, connections & callings, induce them to wish to strengthen either the monarchial or the republican features of the constitution.[35] (1797)

Both of our political parties . . . agree conscientiously in the same object, the public good: but they differ essentially in what they deem the means of promoting that good.

---

[32]Letter to Destutt de Tracy, January 26, 1811, *Writings,* IX, 306–08; Letter to Marquis de Lafayette, November 4, 1823, *Writings,* X, 280.

[33]Letter to John Adams, September 28, 1787, *AJ,* I, 199.

[34]Letters to John Adams, June 15, 1813, June 27, 1813, *AJ,* II, 332, 335.

[35]Letter to James Sullivan, February 9, 1797, *Writings,* VII, 117.

One side believes it best done by one composition of the governing powers, the other by a different one. One fears most the ignorance of the people; the other the selfishness of rulers independent of them.[36] (1804)

. . . we broke into two parties, each wishing to give a different direction to the government; the one to strenghen the most popular branch, the others the more permanent branches, and to extend their permanence.[37] (1813)

The line of division now is the preservation of State rights as reserved in the constitution, or by strained constructions of that instrument, to merge all into a consolidated government. The tories are for strengthening the executive and general Government; the whigs cherish the representative branch, and the rights reserved by the States, as the bulwark against consolidation, which must immediately generate monarchy.[38] (1823)

In all these formulations, the Whig and Tory parties, which arise by nature and prevail one over the other in all governments but the American, have become aspects, features, powers or branches of the American government. Clearly Jefferson takes for granted a transformation of natural parties in the people to artificial, created parts of the government. He presupposes the existence in America for the first time, of representative government. There was general agreement among the Framers and the political philosophers on whom they relied that representative government was a modern invention to make a large society capable of governing itself freely. "The introduction of this new principle of representative democracy," Jefferson went so far as to say, "has rendered useless almost everything written before on the structure of government . . ."[39]

Under the new principle, it was generally admitted that the purpose of government was to represent and not to impose itself on society, because men were individuals outside government before they created government to serve as an instrument to their ends. In Jefferson's conception, however, the fact that men were once unconnected individuals in the "state of nature" is not so important. What matters is that the people have always been divided and formed into natural parties of "two classes of sentiment," for representative government represents these partisan sentiments rather than individuals. Since it reflects the existence of both natural parties in its branches (which are three, not two), neither natural party can rule over the other in the manner of modern monarchies, on one hand, or of ancient democracies, on the other. Artificial, constitutional government can then be based on the natural mixture of parties in every society, and representative government in this sense, the

[36]Letter to Abigail Adams, September 11, 1804, *AJ*, I, 280.
[37]Letter to John Adams, June 27, 1813, *AJ*, II, 336.
[38]Letter to the Marquis de Lafayette, November 4, 1823, *Writings*, X, 282.
[39]Letter to Isaac H. Tiffany, August 26, 1816, *The Political Writings of Thomas Jefferson*, ed. Edward Dumbauld (New York, 1955), p. 87.

true representative government, is what Jefferson calls republican.[40]

Republican government recognizes and harmonizes the opposite tendencies of government to be found in the people by nature. The natural parties do not quite constitute a natural harmony, for men still need to make government for themselves; but they constitute the natural basis for the artificial harmony that men make. The natural parties are *political* parties, be it noted; they are not economic interests but parties promoting a certain kind of rule. In addition, they have in their natural state a principle on which their artificial harmony can build, the *lex majoris partis*, "that fundamental law of nature, by which alone self-government can be exercised by a society." Jefferson believed that a people must be taught this law. Though it exists by nature, men must learn "the habit of acknowledging" it; and the American Revolution, as compared to the French, succeeded because the American people had learned this habit so well "that with them it is almost innate."[41]

Republican *government* reflects and assures the balance of natural parties in the people, and the Republican *party* promotes republican government. But to do so, it advocates trusting the people for their capability in self-government, which is supported by the balance of natural parties to be found in the people and shown in their habit of obeying the natural law of majority rule. The people are trustworthy because, containing the two natural parties and living under the law of majority rule, they are impartial. Jefferson always said, therefore, that his party was distinguished from its opponent by its republican trust of the people, compared to the antirepublican fear of the people.

There is one party in the government and among the people, the Republican, which restores the balance of both parties, although both parties are natural and have a right to exist both in the people and as powers in the government. The apparent indifference of the Declaration of Independence to forms of government is explained and justified by the impartiality of republican government. But the republican party as the impartial party has by nature a preferred status. That is why Jefferson could admit that "the parties of Whig and Tory, are those of nature," and yet assert in the same place: "The sickly, weakly, timid man, fears the people, and is a tory by nature. The healthy, strong and bold, cherishes them, and is formed a whig by nature."[42] To be a tory is to be the victim of an incurable, congenital disease and the cause of an occasional epidemic in the people, for which the Whigs in a body are the doctor, themselves robust and not too sympathetic to the incurably sick.

When Jefferson, the republican doctor, was elected to the presidency in 1800, he thought it a marvelous event: a revolution comparable to the revolu-

---

[40]Letter to Dupont de Nemours, April 24, 1816, *Writings*, X, 24.
[41]Letter to John Breckenridge, January 29, 1800, *Writings*, VII, 417.
[42]Letter to the Marquis de Lafayette, November 4, 1823, *Writings*, X, 281.

tion that began in 1776, indeed a revolution that for the first time established the principles of 1776. Writing to Joseph Priestley just after his inauguration, Jefferson made no effort to contain his enthusiasm. "We can no longer say there is nothing new under the sun. For this whole chapter in the history of man is new. . . . The mighty wave of public opinion which rolled over [our Republic] is new. But the most pleasing novelty is, its so quickly subsiding over such an extent of surface to its true level again."[43] In his moment of triumph, Jefferson proclaimed the most pleasing aspect of the triumph to be its accomplishment with "order and good sense" and without bloodshed. One is compelled to acknowledge the sincerity of his statement of conciliation in his First Inaugural Address. "But every difference of opinion is not a difference of principle. We have called, by different names, brethren of the same principle. We are all republicans: we are all federalists." The Republican party did not claim victory because it did not aim at a mere party triumph, as had the democrats of old. It aimed, as Jefferson saw it, at the restoration of a republican balance in which the republican party was but one factor, if the preferred factor.

This ambiguity of "republican" entails the ambivalence toward monarchy that we have seen in Jefferson's thought. On the one hand, his party attacked the Federalists above all for favoring monarchy and for being "monocrats"; on the other, it allowed a limited monarchy in the office of the president and even promoted Jefferson to that dignity. The natural tory party has its legitimate representative in the monarchical *power* of modern republican government, and precisely because the tories do have this representative, they need not fear republican government and the people who support it. If they do fear the people nevertheless, if a natural tory such as John Adams or even George Washington receives the office, or if an Alexander Hamilton manages it, then the people may need to give the monarchical power to a partisan republican.

Jefferson seems to have understood the evil of monarchy as one aspect of a more general evil, that of "consolidated government," also described thus: "what has destroyed liberty and the rights of man in every government which has ever existed under the sun? The generalizing and concentrating all cares and powers into one body, no matter whether of the autocrats of Russia or France, or of the aristocrats of a Venetian senate."[44] When monarchy is seen as one of the powers in republican government and the tendency to monarchy as the wider evil of consolidating power, one can make sense of Jefferson's

[43]Letter to Joseph Priestley, March 21, 1801, *Writings*, VIII, 22.

[44]Letter to William Johnson, October 27, 1822, *Writings*, X, 225; letter to Joseph C. Cabell, February 2, 1816, *Political Writings*, ed. Edward Dumbauld, p. 99. Jefferson would have been willing to add "or of the democrats of an Athenian assembly . . ."; Letter to A. Coray, October 31, 1823, *The Life and Selected Writings of Thomas Jefferson*, ed. A. Koch and W. Peden (New York, 1944), p. 111.

seemingly exaggerated fear. It was not that he anticipated the appearance of an exact copy of the British or any other king in America; he was apprehensive that the separation of powers would be violated. Under Hamilton's influence, he thought, the Federalist party in the 1790s was establishing a "paper system," a nexus of bankers and bondholders which constituted the real government behind the mask of formal republican correctness. It had found a way to interpret and administer the Constitution for this purpose in the British policy, founded by the Whigs of 1688 and practiced by the anti-American imperialists of the 1770s, of allying financial and political interests. The task of the Republican party was to take off this mask and expose the British system to the just and effectual indignation of the people.

Jefferson's thought on states' rights arises from the same apprehension as his thought on monarchy. As he feared a consolidation of power in the "more permanent powers" of the national government, so he feared the same in the national government as a whole opposed to the states. He believed that the Federalist system that subverted the principle of separation of powers subverted the principle of federalism at the same time, for the two principles have the same function of representing the natural parties. The executive, the Senate, the judiciary and the national government he considered the more permanent powers; the House of Representatives and the states the more popular.[45] Thus in 1798 Jefferson authored the Kentucky resolutions declaring the Alien and Sedition Acts passed by the Federalist Congress null and void. These acts were aimed at subversion from partisans of the French revolution; they struck the nerve of Jefferson's party, since he expected them to be used against the republican newspapers and editors (some of whom were aliens).

In the Kentucky resolutions, he propounded the theory that the Constitution was a compact of the states, and the "General Government" thus a creature with delegated powers of whose extent the states would have to be the final judge. Without commenting on the accuracy or the later history of this celebrated doctrine, one may remark that it reflects Jefferson's own understanding of representative government.

"Representation" is a method whereby the people are governed by their own choice, but theorists and statesmen who accept this method can differ on how the people should express their choice. Whereas most thought that government could be effective only at a certain distance from the people, so that the people could not lightly or easily change their minds, Jefferson had greater confidence that the people, obeying the natural law of majority rule, could change their minds without turbulence and bloodshed. He thought he saw an example of profound but peaceable revolution in his own election in 1800. The

[45]Letter to the Marquis de Lafayette, November 4, 1823, *Writings*, X, 282.

basis of his confidence, however, was the virtue of the independent farmer. If that basis no longer exists, or never existed, some substitute must be found and his theory rethought.

Jefferson became the founder, or one of the founders, of party government in America (in the contemporary sense), despite his intention. Although he believed that men are naturally divided into two parties, he never intended a public coexistence, permanent establishment and occasional alternation of the two parties. For him, republican balance served the purpose of party government in this sense, and party was a temporary and emergency instrument of the people to correct the abuses of government and to tame the monarchical powers. Thus, though "monarchy" had its necessary place in the government, the only legitimate party was the Republican party, because it was the only party that the people could use. He never ceased to hope that his Republican party, by conciliating its opponents, could safely disappear. We may smile at Jefferson's naïveté, but he would be dismayed to see that American political parties, having become semi-official institutions, now seem as remote from the people as the government they were designed to correct and purge. He once exclaimed: "If I could not go to heaven but with a party, I would not go there at all."[46] This makes it clear that his disgust for partisanship exceeds his attraction to heaven, but it does not say whether he thought party necessary to deal with human corruption. He did think so, and he also thought it necessary, for the public good as well as for partisan success, to keep party temporary by deploring partisanship and by concealing his own partisanship. He once said to a friend on a partisan matter: "Do not let my name be connected with the business"[47]—which could serve as the motto of the modern partisan at work.

The necessity of partisanship diminishes the dignity of politics. This need not be so, it would seem, for a statesman who advances a cause; and Jefferson surely had a cause and advanced it. But his cause was not his own; it was the people's cause. He could appear only as the servant or at best the champion of men who, though in his view honest and industrious, were less remarkable than he. Their cause could never fully be his, since they could share only as beneficiaries and not as participants in the life of science and in the most difficult tasks of politics, such as the making of constitutions and the progress of reform. Jefferson was bound to feel a tension between his sense of his own powers and his understanding of his duty to the people. When shocked and disappointed at unfair criticism of his tenure as governor of Virginia, he could wonder whether the state can command the service of its members to an

---

[46]Letter to Francis Hopkinson, March 13, 1789, *Writings*, V, 76.
[47]Quoted in Noble E. Cunningham, Jr., *The Jeffersonian Republicans* (Chapel Hill, North Carolina, 1957), p. 131.

indefinite extent. "If we are made in some degree for others, yet in a greater we are made for ourselves."

He also said, to the contrary, that "the essence of virtue is in doing good to others. . . ." But what is good to others must be decided by utility: ". . . Nature has constituted *utility* to man, the standard test of virtue."[48] Virtue cannot be precious in itself if it is not precious above all for oneself. In politics, Jefferson devoted his partisanship to an ideal of non-partisanship, an independent, republican people. Where was his place in this people? His political thought as we have explained it centers on the unity of independence and virtue in a people, but he did not provide for the same unity for "natural aristocrats" like himself. In his hands the truth of equality was too abstract; there was not enough justice for himself. His partisanship was based on the self-forgetting of the modern idealist, whose cause is not the public good but always someone else's good. In Jefferson's case, the failure to include himself in republican principles led to overconfidence in the system of republican balance. The problems of equality Jefferson had so well identified, especially the problem of slavery, were lost to sight as men put their faith in Jefferson's institutional solution; for many of the Jeffersonians came to think that slavery had a place in the republican balance itself.

SELECTED SUGGESTED READINGS

The Adams-Jefferson Letters. Edited by L. J. Cappon. 2 vols. Chapel Hill: University of North Carolina Press, 1959. See Jefferson's letters to John Adams.

The Declaration of Independence.

The Life and Selected Writings of Thomas Jefferson. Edited by A. Koch and W. Peden. New York: Modern Library, 1944. See "Draft of the Kentucky Resolutions," "Draft of Statute of Virginia for Religious Freedom," "First Inaugural Address," and selected letters.

Notes on the State of Virginia. Edited by William Peden. Chapel Hill: University of North Carolina Press, 1965.

---

[48]*Papers,* VI, 185; Letter to Thomas Law, June 13, 1814, *Life and Selected Writings,* ed. A. Koch and W. Peden, p. 639.

IST *Martin Diamond*

ı teaching among modern historians of the guiding ideas in the foundation of our government that the Constitution of the United States embodied a reaction against the democratic principles espoused in the Declaration of Independence. This view has largely been accepted by political scientists and has therefore had important consequences for the way American political development has been studied. I shall present here a contrary view of the political theory of the Framers and examine some of its consequences.

What is the relevance of the political thought of the Founding Fathers to an understanding of contemporary problems of liberty and justice? Four possible ways of looking at the Founding Fathers immediately suggest themselves. First, it may be that they possessed wisdom, a set of political principles still inherently adequate, and needing only to be supplemented by skill in their proper contemporary application. Second, it may be that, while the Founding Fathers' principles are still sound, they are applicable only to a part of our problems, but not to that part which is peculiarly modern; and thus new principles are needed to be joined together with the old ones. Third, it may be that the Founding Fathers have simply become irrelevant; they dealt with bygone problems and their principles were relevant only to those old problems. Fourth, they may have been wrong or radically inadequate even for their own time.

Each of these four possible conclusions requires the same foundation: an understanding of the political thought of the Founding Fathers. To decide whether to apply their wisdom, or to add to their wisdom, or to reject it as irrelevant or as unwise, it is absolutely necessary to understand what they said, why they said it, and what they meant by it. At the same time, however, to understand their claim to wisdom is to evaluate it: to know wherein they were wise and wherein they were not, or wherein (and why) their wisdom is unavailing for our problems. Moreover, even if it turns out that our modern problems require wholly new principles for their solution, an excellent way to discover those new principles would be to see what it is about modernity that has outmoded the principles of the Founding Fathers. For example, it is

SOURCE: Martin Diamond, "Democracy and *The Federalist:* A Reconsideration of the Framers' Intent," *American Political Science Review*, LIII (March 1959), 52-68. Reprinted by permission.

possible that modern developments are themselves partly the outcome of the particular attempt to solve the problem of freedom and justice upon which this country was founded. That is, our modern difficulties may testify to fundamental errors in the thought of the Founding Fathers; and, in the process of discerning those errors, we may discover what better principles would be.

The solution of our contemporary problems requires very great wisdom indeed. And in that fact lies the greatest justification for studying anew the political thought of the Founding Fathers. For that thought remains the finest American thought on political matters. In studying them we may raise ourselves to their level. In achieving their level we may free ourselves from limitations that, ironically, they tend to impose upon us, *i.e.*, insofar as we tend to be creatures of the society they founded. And in so freeing ourselves we may be enabled, if it is necessary, to go beyond their wisdom. The Founding Fathers still loom so large in our life that the contemporary political problem of liberty and justice for Americans could be stated as the need to choose whether to apply their wisdom, amend their wisdom, or reject it. Only an understanding of them will tell us how to choose.

For the reflections on the Fathers which follow, I employ chiefly *The Federalist* as the clue to the political theory upon which rested the founding of the American Republic. That this would be inadequate for a systematic study of the Founding Fathers goes without saying. But it is the one book, "to which," as Jefferson wrote in 1825, "appeal is habitually made by all, and rarely declined or denied by any as evidence of the general opinion of those who framed and of those who accepted the Constitution of the United States, on questions as to its genuine meaning." As such it is the indispensable starting point for systematic study.

I

Our major political problems today are problems of democracy; and, as much as anything else, the *Federalist* papers are a teaching about democracy. The conclusion of one of the most important of these papers states what is also the most important theme in the entire work: the necessity for "a republican remedy for the diseases most incident to republican government."[1] The theme is clearly repeated in a passage where Thomas Jefferson is praised for displaying equally "a fervent attachment to republican government and an enlightened view of the dangerous propensities against which it ought to be guarded."[2] *The Federalist*, thus, stresses its commitment to republican or popu-

---

[1] *Federalist*, No. 10, p. 62. All references are to the Modern Library edition, ed. E. M. Earle.

lar government, but, of course, insists that this must be an enlightened commitment.

But *The Federalist* and the Founding Fathers generally have not been taken at their word. Predominantly, they are understood as being only quasi- or even anti-democrats. Modern American historical writing, at least until very recently, has generally seen the Constitution as some sort of apostasy from, or reaction to, the radically democratic implications of the Declaration of Independence—a reaction that was undone by the great "democratic breakthroughs" of Jeffersonianism, Jacksonianism, etc. This view, I believe, involves a false understanding of the crucial political issues involved in the founding of the American Republic. Further, it is based implicitly upon a questionable modern approach to democracy and has tended to have the effect, moreover, of relegating the political teaching of the Founding Fathers to the pre-democratic past and thus of making it of no vital concern to moderns. The Founding Fathers themselves repeatedly stressed that their Constitution was wholly consistent with the true principles of republican or popular government. The prevailing modern opinion, in varying degrees and in different ways, rejects that claim. It thus becomes important to understand what was the relation of the Founding Fathers to popular government or democracy.

I have deliberately used interchangeably their terms, "popular government" and "democracy." The Founding Fathers, of course, did not use the terms entirely synonymously and the idea that they were less than "democrats" has been fortified by the fact that they sometimes defined "democracy" invidiously in comparison with "republic." But this fact does not really justify the opinion. For their basic view was that *popular government was the genus, and democracy and republic were two species* of that genus of government. What distinguished popular government from other genera of government was that in it, political authority is "derived from the great body of the society, not from . . . [any] favoured class of it."[3] With respect to this decisive question, of where political authority is lodged, democracy and republic—as *The Federalist* uses the terms—differ not in the least. Republics, equally with democracies, may

---

[2] *Federalist*, No. 49, p. 327.

[3] *Federalist*, No. 39, p. 244. Here Madison speaks explicitly of the republican form of government. But see on the same page how Madison compares the republican form with "every *other popular* government." Regarding the crucial question of the lodgement of political authority, Madison speaks of republic, democracy and popular government interchangeably. Consider that, in the very paper where he distinguishes so precisely between democracies and republics regarding direct versus representative rule, Madison defines his general aim both as a search for "a republican remedy" for republican diseases and a remedy that will "preserve the spirit and the form of *popular* government." (p. 58.) Interestingly, on June 6 at the Federal Convention, Madison's phrasing for a similar problem was the search for "the only defense against the inconveniences of democracy consistent with the *democratic* form of government," Madison, *Writings*, ed. G. Hunt, Vol. 3 (G. P. Putnam's Sons, New York, 1902), p. 103. Italics supplied throughout.

claim to be wholly a form of popular government. This is neither to deny the difference between the two, nor to depreciate the importance *The Federalist* attached to the difference; but in *The Federalist's* view, the difference does not relate to the essential principle of popular government. Democracy means in *The Federalist* that form of popular government where the citizens "assemble and administer the government in person."[4] Republics differ in that the people rule through representatives and, of course, in the consequences of that difference. The crucial point is that republics and democracies are equally forms of popular government, but that the one form is vastly preferable to the other because of the substantive consequences of the difference in form. Those historians who consider the Founding Fathers as less than "democrat," miss or reject the Founders' central contention that, while being perfectly faithful to the *principle* of popular government, they had solved the *problem* of popular government.

In what way is the Constitution ordinarily thought to be less democratic than the Declaration? The argument is usually that the former is characterized by fear of the people, by preoccupation with minority interests and rights, and by measures therefore taken against the power of majorities. The Declaration, it is true, does not display these features, but this is no proof of a fundamental difference of principle between the two. Is it not obviously possible that the difference is due only to a difference in the tasks to which the two documents were addressed? And is it not further possible that the democratic principles of the Declaration are not only compatible with the prophylactic measures of the Constitution, but actually imply them?

The Declaration of Independence formulates two criteria for judging whether any government is good, or indeed legitimate. Good government must rest, procedurally, upon the consent of the governed. Good government, substantively, must do only certain things, *e.g.*, secure certain rights. This may be stated another way by borrowing a phrase from Locke, appropriate enough when discussing the Declaration. That "the people shall be judge" is of the essence of democracy, is its peculiar form or method of proceeding. That the people shall judge rightly is the substantive problem of democracy. But whether the procedure will bring about the substance is problematic. Between the Declaration's two criteria, then, a tension exists: consent can be given or obtained for governmental actions which are not right—at least as the men of 1776 saw the right. (To give an obvious example from their point of view: the people may freely but wrongly vote away the protection due to property.) Thus the Declaration clearly contained, although it did not resolve, a fundamental problem. Solving the problem was not its task; that was the task for the

[4] *Federalist*, No. 10, p. 58.

Framers of the Constitution. But the man who wrote the Declaration of Independence and the leading men who supported it were perfectly aware of the difficulty, and of the necessity for a "republican remedy."

What the text of the Declaration, taken alone, tells of its meaning may easily be substantiated by the testimony of its author and supporters. Consider only that Jefferson, with no known change of heart at all, said of *The Federalist* that it was "the best commentary on the principles of government which was ever written."[5] Jefferson, it must be remembered, came firmly to recommend the adoption of the Constitution, his criticisms of it having come down only to a proposal for rotation in the presidency and for the subsequent adoption of a bill of rights. I do not, of course, deny the peculiar character of "Jeffersonianism" nor the importance to many things of its proper understanding. I only state here that it is certain that Jefferson, unlike later historians, did not view the Constitution as a retrogression from democracy. Or further, consider that John Adams, now celebrated as America's great conservative, was so enthusiastic about Jefferson's draft of the Declaration as to wish on his own account that hardly a word be changed. And this same Adams, also without any change of heart and without complaint, accepted the Constitution as embodying many of his own views on government.

The idea that the Constitution was a falling back from the fuller democracy of the Declaration thus rests in part upon a false reading of the Declaration as free from the concerns regarding democracy that the Framers of the Constitution felt. Perhaps only those would so read it who take for granted a perfect, self-subsisting harmony between consent (equality) and the proper aim of government (justice), or between consent and individual rights (liberty). This assumption was utterly foreign to the leading men of the Declaration.

II

The Declaration has wrongly been converted into, as it were, a super-democratic document; has the Constitution wrongly been converted in the modern view into an insufficiently democratic document? The only basis for depreciating the democratic character of the Constitution lies in its Framers' apprehensive diagnosis of the "diseases," "defects" or "evil propensities" of democracy, and in their remedies. But if what the Founders considered to be defects *are* genuine defects, and if the remedies, without violating the principles of popular government, *are* genuine remedies, then it would be unreasonable to call the Founders anti- or quasi-democrats. Rather, they would be the wise partisans of democracy; a man is not a better democrat but only a foolish democrat

[5] *The Works of Thomas Jefferson*, ed. Paul L. Ford (The Federal Edition), Vol. 5 (G. P. Putnam's Sons, New York, 1904), p. 434.

if he ignores real defects inherent in popular government. Thus, the question becomes: are there natural defects to democracy and, if there are, what are the best remedies?

In part, the Founding Fathers answered this question by employing a traditional mode of political analysis. They believed there were several basic possible regimes, each having several possible forms. Of these possible regimes they believed the best, or at least the best for America, to be popular government, but only if purged of its defects. At any rate, an unpurged popular government they believed to be indefensible. They believed there were several forms of popular government, crucial among these direct democracy and republican—or representative—government (the latter perhaps divisible into two distinct forms, large and small republics). Their constitution and their defense of it constitute an argument for that form of popular government (large republic) in which the "evil propensities" would be weakest or most susceptible of remedy.

The whole of the thought of the Founding Fathers is intelligible and, especially, the evaluation of their claim to be wise partisans of popular government is possible, only if the words *"disease," "defect,"* and *"evil propensity"* are allowed their full force. Unlike modern "value-free" social scientists, the Founding Fathers believed that true knowledge of the good and bad in human conduct was possible, and that they themselves possessed sufficient knowledge to discern the really grave defects of popular government and their proper remedies. The modern relativistic or positivistic theories, implicitly employed by most commentators on the Founding Fathers, deny the possibility of such true knowledge and therefore deny that the Founding Fathers *could* have been actuated by knowledge of the good rather than by passion or interest. (I deliberately employ the language of *Federalist* No. 10. Madison defined faction, in part, as a group "united and actuated by . . . passion, or . . . interest." That is, factions are groups *not*—as presumably the authors of *The Federalist* were—actuated by reason.) How this modern view of the value problem supports the conception of the Constitution as less democratic than the Declaration is clear. The Founding Fathers did in fact seek to prejudice the outcome of democracy; they sought to alter, by certain restraints, the likelihood that the majority would decide certain political issues in bad ways. These restraints the Founders justified as mitigating the natural defects of democracy. But, say the moderns, there are no "bad" political decisions, wrong-in-themselves, which the majority ought to be restrained from reaching. Therefore, ultimately nothing other than the specific interests of the Founders can explain their zeal in restraining democracy. And inasmuch as the restraints were typically placed on the many in the interest of the propertied, the departure of the Constitution is "anti-democratic" or "thermidorean." In short, according to this view, there cannot be what the Founders claimed to possess, "an *enlightened* view of the dangerous propensities against which [popular government] . . . ought to be guarded," the substantive goodness or badness of such propensities being a matter of opinion or taste on which reason can shed no light.

What are some of the arrangements which have been considered signs of "undemocratic" features of the Constitution? The process by which the Constitution may be amended is often cited in evidence. Everyone is familiar with the arithmetic which shows that a remarkably small minority could prevent passage of a constitutional amendment supported by an overwhelming majority in the thirty-seven most populous states. But let us, for a reason to be made clear in a moment, turn that arithmetic around. Bare majorities in the thirty-eight least populous states can pass amendments against the opposition of overwhelming majorities in the twelve most populous states. And this would mean in actual votes today (and would have meant for the thirteen original states) constitutional amendment by a minority against the opposition of a majority of citizens. My point is simply that, while the amending procedure does involve qualified majorities, the qualification is not of the kind that requires an especially large numerical majority for action.

I suggest that the real aim and practical effect of the complicated amending procedure was not at all to give power to minorities, but to ensure that passage of an amendment would require a *nationally* distributed majority, though one that legally could consist of a bare numerical majority. It was only adventitious that the procedure has the theoretical possibility of a minority blocking (or passing) an amendment. The aim of requiring nationally distributed majorities was, I think, to ensure that no amendment could be passed simply with the support of the few states or sections sufficiently numerous to provide a bare majority. No doubt it was also believed that it would be difficult for such a national majority to form or become effective save for the decent purposes that could command national agreement, and this difficulty was surely deemed a great virtue of the amending process. This is what I think *The Federalist* really means when it praises the amending process and says that "it guards equally against that extreme facility, which would render the Constitution too mutable; and that extreme difficulty, which might perpetuate its discovered faults."[6] All I wish to emphasize here is that the actual method adopted, with respect to the numerical size of majorities, is meant to leave all legal power in the hands of ordinary majorities so long as they are national majorities. The departure from simple majoritarianism is, at least, not in an oligarchic or aristocratic direction. In this crucial respect, the amending procedure does conform strictly to the principles of republican (popular) government.

Consider next the suffrage question. It has long been assumed as proof of

[6] *Federalist*, No. 43, p. 286.

an anti-democratic element in the Constitution that the Founding Fathers depended for the working of their Constitution upon a substantially limited franchise. Just as the Constitution allegedly was ratified by a highly qualified electorate, so too, it is held, was the new government to be based upon a suffrage subject to substantial property qualifications. This view has only recently been seriously challenged, especially by Robert E. Brown, whose detailed researches convince him that the property qualifications in nearly all the original states were probably so small as to exclude never more than twenty-five per cent, and in most cases as little as only five to ten per cent, of the adult white male population.[6a] That is, the property qualifications were not designed to exclude the mass of the poor but only the small proportion which lacked a concrete—however small—stake in society, *i.e.*, primarily the transients or "idlers."

The Constitution, of course, left the suffrage question to the decision of the individual states. What is the implication of that fact for deciding what sort of suffrage the Framers had in mind? The immediately popular branch of the national legislature was to be elected by voters who "shall have the qualifications requisite for electors of the most numerous branch of the State Legislature." The mode of election to the electoral college for the presidency and to the Senate is also left to "be prescribed in each State by the legislature thereof." At a minimum, it may be stated that the Framers did not themselves attempt to reduce, or prevent the expansion of, the suffrage; that question was left wholly to the states—and these were, ironically, the very hotbeds of post-revolutionary democracy from the rule of which it is familiarly alleged that the Founders sought to escape.[7]

In general, the conclusion seems inescapable that the states had a far broader suffrage than is ordinarily thought, and nothing in the actions of the Framers suggests any expectation or prospect of the reduction of the suffrage. Again, as in the question of the amending process, I suggest that the Constitution represented no departure whatsoever from the democratic standards of the Revolutionary period, or from any democratic standards then generally recognized.[8]

[6a] *Middle Class Democracy and the Revolution in Massachusetts, 1691–1780.* (Cornell University Press, Ithaca, 1955).

[7] Madison must have thought that he had established this point beyond misinterpretation in *The Federalist*, No. 57. "Who are to be the electors of the federal representatives? Not the rich, more than the poor; not the learned, more than the ignorant; not the haughty heirs of distinguished names, more than the humble sons of obscurity and unpropitious fortune. The electors are to be the great body of the people of the United States. They are to be the same who exercise the right in every State of electing the corresponding branch of the legislature of the State." (p. 371.)

[8] This is not to deny the importance of the existing property qualifications for the understanding of the Founders' political theory. The legal exclusion from the franchise of even a very small portion of the adult population may have enormous significance for the politics and life of a

What of the Senate? The organization of the Senate, its term of office and its staggered mode of replacement, its election by state legislatures rather than directly by the people, among other things, have been used to demonstrate the undemocratic character of the Senate as intended by the Framers. Was this not a device to represent property and not people, and was it not intended therefore to be a non-popular element in the government? I suggest, on the contrary, that the really important thing is that the Framers thought they had found a way to protect property *without* representing it. That the Founders intended the Senate to be one of the crucial devices for remedying the defects of democracy is certainly true. But *The Federalist* argues that the Senate, as actually proposed in the Constitution, was calculated to be such a device as would operate only in a way that "will consist . . . with the genuine principles of republican government."[9] I believe that the claim is just.

Rather than viewing the Senate from the perspective of modern experience and opinions, consider how radically democratic the Senate appears when viewed from a pre-modern perspective. The model of a divided legislature that the Founders had most in mind was probably the English Parliament. There the House of Lords was thought to provide some of the beneficial checks upon the popular Commons which it was hoped the Senate would supply in the American Constitution. But the American Senate was to possess none of the qualities which permitted the House of Lords to fulfill its role; *i.e.*, its hereditary basis, or membership upon election by the Crown, or any of its other aristocratic characteristics.[10] Yet the Founding Fathers knew that the advantages of having both a Senate and a House would "be in proportion to the dissimilarity in the genius of the two bodies."[11] What is remarkable is that, in seeking to secure this dissimilarity, they did not in any respect go beyond the limits permitted by the "genuine principles of republican government."

Not only is this dramatically demonstrated in comparison with the English House of Lords, but also in comparison with all earlier theory regarding the division of the legislative power. The aim of such a division in earlier thought is to secure a balance between the aristocratic and democratic elements of a polity. This is connected with the pre-modern preference for a *mixed* republic, which was rejected by the Founders in favor of a *democratic*

---

country. This is obvious in the case of a racial, ethnic or religious minority. And the exclusion of otherwise eligible adult males on the grounds of poverty may be equally important. The property qualification clearly praises and rewards certain virtues, implies that the voter must possess certain qualities to warrant his exercise of the franchise, and aims at excluding a "rabble" from the operations of political parties. But important, therefore, as the property qualification was, it does not demonstrate that the Founding Fathers departed radically from the most important aspects of the principle of majority rule.

[9] *Federalist*, No. 62, p. 403.
[10] *Federalist*, No. 63, p. 415.
[11] *Federalist*, No. 62, p. 403.

republic. And the traditional way to secure this balance or mixture was to give one house or office to the suffrages of the few and one to the suffrages of the many. Nothing of the kind is involved in the American Senate. Indeed, on this issue, so often cited as evidence of the Founders' undemocratic predilections, the very opposite is the case. The Senate is a constitutional device which *par excellence* reveals the strategy of the Founders. They wanted something like the advantages earlier thinkers had seen in a mixed legislative power, but they thought this was possible (and perhaps preferable) without any introduction whatsoever of aristocratic power into their system. What pre-modern thought had seen in an aristocratic senate—wisdom, nobility, manners, religion, etc.— the Founding Fathers converted into stability, enlightened self-interest, a "temperate and respectable body of citizens." The qualities of a Senate having thus been altered (involving perhaps comparable changes in the notion of the ends of government), it became possible to secure these advantages through a Senate based wholly upon popular principles. Or so I would characterize a Senate whose membership required no property qualification and which was appointed (or elected in the manner prescribed) by State legislatures which, in their own turn, were elected annually or biennially by a nearly universal manhood suffrage.

The great claim of *The Federalist* is that the Constitution represents the fulfillment of a truly novel experiment, of "a revolution which has no parallel in the annals of society," and which is decisive for the happiness of "the whole human race."[12] And the novelty, I argue, consisted in solving the problems of popular government by means which yet maintain the government "wholly popular."[13] In defending that claim against the idea of the Constitution as a retreat from democracy I have dealt thus far only with the easier task: the demonstration that the constitutional devices and arrangements do not derogate from the legal power of majorities to rule. What remains is to examine the claim that the Constitution did in fact remedy the natural defects of democracy. Before any effort is made in this direction, it may be useful to summarize some of the implications and possible utility of the analysis thus far.

Above all, the merit of the suggestions I have made, if they are accurate in describing the intention and action of the Founders, is that it makes the Founders available to us for the study of modern problems. I have tried to restore to them their *bona fides* as partisans of democracy. This done, we may take seriously the question whether they were, as they claimed to be, wise partisans of democracy or popular government. If they were partisans of democracy and if the regime they created was decisively democratic, then

[12] *Federalist*, No. 14, p. 85.
[13] *Ibid.*, p. 81.

they speak to us not merely about bygone problems, not from a viewpoint—in this regard—radically different from our own, but as men addressing themselves to problems identical in principle with our own. They are a source from within our own heritage which teaches us the way to put the question to democracy, a way which is rejected by certain prevailing modern ideas. But we cannot avail ourselves of their assistance if we consider American history to be a succession of democratizations which overcame the Founding Fathers' intentions. On that view it is easy to regard them as simply outmoded. If I am right regarding the extent of democracy in their thought and regime, then they are not outmoded by modern events but rather are tested by them. American history, on this view, is not primarily the replacement of a predemocratic regime by a democratic regime, but is rather a continuing testimony to how the Founding Fathers' democratic regime has worked out in modern circumstances. The whole of our national experience thus becomes a way of judging the Founders' principles, of judging democracy itself, or of pondering the flaws of democracy and the means to its improvement.

III

What was the Founding Fathers' view of the good life? Upon what fundamental theoretical premises did that view of the good life depend? How comprehensive was their understanding of the dangers against which popular government was to be guarded? How efficacious were their remedies and what may have been the unanticipated costs of those remedies? These questions are clearly too vast to answer here and now. What follows is only a series of notes which bear upon the problems raised, and which I think may serve as general guides to what it is important to seek in studying the Founding Fathers.

The Federalist does not discuss systematically, as would a theoretical treatise, the question of the ends or purposes of government. That is, it does not deal systematically with philosophical issues. This is not to say that its authors did not have a view in such matters. But what that view was, and what are its implications for the understanding of the Constitution, is a subject on which I find it difficult to speak with confidence. I must still regard as open the question whether the authors of *The Federalist*, or the other leading Founders, had themselves fully reflected on these matters, or whether they treated them as settled by thinkers like Locke and Montesquieu, or whether crucial premises in their thought were unreflectively taken for granted. But men cannot act on a political scale so vast as they did without having and employing a view of the politically fundamental; and it is this view which provides the crucial perspective for the understanding of their particular actions and thoughts.

Perhaps the most explicit fundamental utterance of *The Federalist* is the statement regarding

the great principle of self-preservation . . . the transcendent law of nature and of nature's God, which declares that the safety and happiness of society are the objects at which all political institutions aim, and to which all such institutions must be sacrificed.[14]

But self-preservation, it is made clear, includes more than mere preservation. This passage, which interestingly echoes the Declaration of Independence on the "laws of nature and of nature's God," emphasizes that preservation includes "happiness" as well as "safety." That is, *The Federalist* is aware of and explicitly rejects the kind of regime that would follow from a narrower view of self-preservation. For example, *The Federalist* seems explicitly to be rejecting Hobbes when, in another context, it rejects the view that "nothing less than the chains of despotism can restrain [men] from destroying and devouring one another."[15] But while it rejects the "chains of despotism," *i.e.*, the Hobbesean solution to the problem of self-preservation, it nonetheless seems to accept the Hobbesean statement of the problem. As it were, the primary fears of *The Federalist* are Hobbesean, that is, fears of "foreign war and domestic convulsion." Rejecting a despotic solution, the great aim of *The Federalist* is to supply a liberal and republican solution to the same problem. But while there is a great difference, never to be underestimated, between a liberal and a repressive, a republican and a monarchical solution, it may be that in making the same dangers and their solution *the* desideratum for the structure and functions of government much of the Hobbesean view is preserved.

The main object of *The Federalist* was to urge the necessity of a firm and energetic Union. The utility of such a Union, and therefore the chief ends it will serve, is that is will strengthen the American people against the dangers of "foreign war" and secure them from the dangers of "domestic convulsion." These functions of government are the most frequently discussed and the most vehemently emphasized in the whole work. To a very great extent, then, *The Federalist* determines the role of government with reference only, or primarily, to the extremes of external and internal danger. It is to avoid the pre-civil forms of these dangers that men form government and it is the civil solution of these dangers which, almost exclusively, determines the legitimate objects of government. But again. *The Federalist* repeatedly emphasizes that a "novel" solution is at hand. The means now exist—and America is uniquely in a position to employ them—for a republican solution which avoids the extremes of tyranny and anarchy. But notice that, on this view, liberalism and republicanism are not the means by which men may ascend to a nobler life; rather they are simply instrumentalities which solve Hobbesean problems in

---

[14] *Federalist*, No. 43, p. 287.
[15] *Federalist*, No. 55, p. 365.

a more moderate manner. It is tempting to suggest that if America is a "Lockean" nation, as is so often asserted, it is true in the very precise sense that Locke's "comfortable preservation" displaces the harshness of the Hobbesean view, while not repudiating that view in general.

To be sure, *The Federalist* does make other explicit statements regarding the ends of government. For example: "Justice is the end of government. It is the end of civil society."[16] But this statement, to the best of my knowledge, is made only once in the entire work; and the context suggests that "justice" means simply "civil rights" which in turn seems to refer primarily to the protection of economic interests. That justice has here this relatively narrow meaning, as compared with traditional philosophical and theological usage, is made more probable when we take account of the crucial statement in *Federalist* No. 10. There the "first object of government" is the protection of the diverse human faculties from which arise the "rights of property" and the unequal distribution of property. The importance of this statement of the function of government is underscored when it is recalled how large a proportion of *The Federalist* deals with the improvements in "commerce" made possible by the new Constitution. For example, in a list of the four "principal objects of federal legislation,"[17] three (foreign trade, interstate trade, and taxes) deal explicitly with commerce. The fourth, the militia, also deals with commerce insofar as it largely has to do with the prevention of "domestic convulsion" brought on by economic matters.

The very great emphasis of *The Federalist* on commerce, and on the role of government in nurturing it, may not be at all incompatible with the theme of "happiness" which is the most frequently occurring definition of the "object of government." The most definite statement is the following:

A good government implies two things: first, fidelity to the object of government, which is the happiness of the people, secondly, a knowledge of the means by which that object can be best obtained.[18]

The Federalist is not very explicit in defining happiness. But there are firm indications that what it had in mind has little in common with traditional philosophical or theological understandings of the term. At one place, *The Federalist* indicates that happiness requires that government "provide for the security, advance the prosperity, [and] support the reputation of the commonwealth."[19] In another, happiness seems to require "our safety, our tranquility, our dignity, our reputation."[20] Part of what these words mean is made clear by the fact that they summarize a lengthy indictment of the Articles of Confed-

[16]*Federalist*, No. 51, p. 340.
[17]*Federalist*, No. 53, p. 350–51.
[18]*Federalist*, No. 62, p. 404.
[19]*Federalist*, No. 30, p. 186.
[20]*Federalist*, No. 15, p. 88.

eration, the particulars of which deal in nearly every case with commercial shortcomings. Happiness, "a knowledge of the means" to which *The Federalist* openly claims to possess, seems to consist primarily in physical preservation from external and internal danger *and* in the comforts afforded by a commercial society; which comforts are at once the dividends of security and the means to a republican rather than repressive security.

What is striking is the apparent exclusion from the functions of government of a wide range of non-economic tasks traditionally considered the decisive business of government. It is tempting to speculate that this reduction in the tasks of government has something to do with *The Federalist's* defense of popular government. The traditional criticism of popular government was that it gave over the art of government into the hands of many, which is to say the unwise. It would be a formidable reply to reduce the complexity of the governmental art to dimensions more commensurate with the capacity of the many. I use two statements by Madison, years apart, to illustrate the possibility that he may have had something like this in mind. "There can be no doubt that there are subjects to which the capacities of the bulk of mankind are unequal."[21] But on the other hand, "the confidence of the [Republican party] in the capacity of mankind for self-government"[22] is what distinguished it from the Federalist party which distrusted that capacity. The confidence in mankind's capacities would seem to require having removed from government the subjects to which those capacities are unequal.

IV

So far as concerns those ends of government on which *The Federalist* is almost wholly silent, it is reasonable to infer that what the Founders made no provision for they did not rank highly among the legitimate objects of government. Other political theories had ranked highly, as objects of government, the nurturing of a particular religion, education, military courage, civic-spiritedness, moderation, individual excellence in the virtues, etc. On all of these *The Federalist* is either silent, or has in mind only pallid versions of the originals, or even seems to speak with contempt. The Founders apparently did not consider it necessary to make special provision for excellence. Did they assume these virtues would flourish without governmental or other explicit provision? Did they consciously sacrifice some of them to other necessities of a stable popular regime—as it were, as the price of their solution to the problem of

----

[21]Letter to Edmund Randolph, January 10, 1788.
[22]Letter to William Eustis, May 22, 1823. The letters to Randolph and Eustis were brought to my attention by Ralph Ketcham's article, "Notes on James Madison's Sources for the Tenth Federalist Paper," *Midwest Journal of Political Science*, Vol. 1 (May, 1957).

democracy? Or were these virtues less necessary to a country when it had been properly founded on the basis of the new "science of politics"? In what follows I suggest some possible answers to these questions.

The Founding Fathers are often criticized for an excessive attention to, and reliance upon, mechanical institutional arrangements and for an insufficient attention to "sociological" factors. While a moderate version of this criticism may finally be just, it is nonetheless clear that *The Federalist* pays considerable and shrewd attention to such factors. For example, in *Federalist* No. 51, equal attention is given to the institutional and non-institutional strengths of the new Constitution. One of these latter is the solution to the "problems of faction." It will be convenient to examine *Federalist* No. 10 where the argument about faction is more fully developed than in No. 51. A close examination of that solution reveals something about *The Federalist's* view of the virtues necessary to the good life.

The problem dealt with in the tenth essay is how "to break and control the violence of faction." "The friend of popular governments never finds himself so much alarmed for their character and fate, as when he contemplates their propensity to this dangerous vice." Faction is, thus, *the* problem of popular government. Now it must be made clear that Madison, the author of this essay, was not here really concerned with the problem of faction generally. He devotes only two sentences in the whole essay to the dangers of *minority* factions. The real problem in a popular government, then, is *majority* faction, or, more precisely, *the* majority faction, *i.e.*, the great mass of the little propertied and unpropertied. This is the only faction that can "execute and mask its violence under the forms of the Constitution." That is, in the American republic the many have the legal power to rule and thus from them can come the greatest harm. Madison interprets that harm fairly narrowly; at least, his overwhelming emphasis is on the classic economic struggle between the rich and the poor which made of ancient democracies "spectacles of turbulence and contention." *The* problem for the friend of popular government is how to avoid the "domestic convulsion" which results when the rich and the poor, the few and the many, as is their wont, are at each others' throats. Always before in popular governments the many, armed with political power, invariably precipitated such convulsions. But the friend of popular government must find only "a republican remedy" for this disease which is "most incident to republican government." "To secure the public good and private rights against the danger of . . . [majority] faction, and at the same time to preserve the spirit and the form of popular government, is then the great object to which our inquiries are directed."

Without wrenching Madison's meaning too greatly, the problem may be put crudely this way: Madison gave a beforehand answer to Marx. The whole of the Marxian scheme depends upon the many—having been proletarianized—causing precisely such domestic convulsion and usurpation of property as Madison wished to avoid. Madison believed that in America the many could be diverted from that probable course. How will the many, *the* majority, be prevented from using for the evil purpose of usurping property the legal power which is theirs in a popular regime? "Evidently by one of two [means] only. Either the existence of the same passion or interest in a majority at the same time must be prevented, or the majority, having such co-existent passion or interest, must be rendered, by their number and local situation, unable to concert and carry into effect schemes of oppression." But "we well know that neither moral nor religious motives can be relied on" to do these things. The "circumstance principally" which will solve the problem is the "greater number of citizens and extent of territory which may be brought within the compass" of large republican governments rather than of small direct democracies.

Rather than mutilate Madison, let me complete his thought by quoting the rest of his argument before commenting on it:

The smaller the society, the fewer probably will be the distinct parties and interests composing it; the fewer the distinct parties and interests the more frequently will a majority be found of the same party; and the smaller the number of individuals composing a majority, and the smaller the compass within which they are placed, the more easily will they concert and execute their plans of oppression. Extend the sphere and you take in a greater variety of parties and interests; you make it less probable that a majority of the whole will have a common motive to invade the rights of other citizens; or if such a common motive exists, it will be more difficult for all who feel it to discover their own strength, and to act in unison with each other.

I want to deal only with what is implied or required by the first of the two means, *i.e.*, preventing the majority from having the same "passion or interest" at the same time. I would argue that this is the more important of the two remedial means afforded by a large republic. If the majority comes to have the same passion or interest and holds to it intensely for a period of only four to six years, it seems certain that it would triumph over the "extent of territory," over the barriers of federalism, and separation of powers, and all the checks and balances of the Constitution. I do not wish to depreciate the importance of those barriers; I believe they have enormous efficacy in stemming the tide Madison feared. But I would argue that their efficacy depends upon a prior weakening of the force applied against them, upon the majority having been fragmented or deflected from its "schemes of oppression." An inflamed Marxian proletariat would not indefinitely be deterred by institutional checks or extent of territory. The crucial point then, as I see it, is the means by which a majority bent upon oppression is prevented from ever forming or becoming firm.

Madison's whole scheme essentially comes down to this. The struggle of classes is to be replaced by a struggle of interests. The class struggle is domestic convulsion; the struggle of interests is a safe, even energizing, struggle which is compatible with, or even promotes, the safety and stability of society. But how can this be accomplished? What will prevent the many from thinking of their interest as that of the Many opposed to the Few? Madison, as I see it, implies that nothing can prevent it in a small democratic society where the many are divided into only a few trades and callings: these divisions are insufficient to prevent them from conceiving their lot in common and uniting for oppression. But in a large republic, numerous and powerful divisions will arise among the many to prevent that happening. A host of interests grows up "of necessity in civilized nations, and divide[s] them into different classes, actuated by different sentiments and views." "Civilized nations" clearly means here large, commercial societies. In a large commerical society the interest of the many can be fragmented into many narrower, more limited interests. The mass will not unite as a mass to make extreme demands upon the few, the struggle over which will destroy society; the mass will fragment into relatively small groups, seeking small immediate advantages for their narrow and particular interests.

If the Madisonian solution is essentially as I have described it, it becomes clear that certain things are required for the solution to operate. I only mention several of them. First, the country in which this is to take place will have to be profoundly democratic. That is, all men must be free—and even encouraged—to seek their immediate profit and to associate with others in the process. There must be no rigid class barriers which bar men from the pursuit of immediate interest. Indeed, it is especially the lowly, from whom the most is to be feared, who must feel most sanguine about the prospects of achieving limited and immediate benefits. Second, the gains must be real; that is, the fragmented interests must from time to time achieve real gains, else the scheme would cease to beguile or mollify. But I do not want to develop these themes here. Rather, I want to emphasize only one crucial aspect of Madison's design: that is, the question of the apparently narrow ends of society envisaged by the Founding Fathers. Madison's plan, as I have described it, most assuredly does not rest on the "moral and religious motives" whose efficacy he deprecated. Indeed there is not even the suggestion that the pursuit of interest should be an especially enlightened pursuit. Rather, the problem posed by the dangerous passions and interests of the many is solved primarily by a reliance upon passion and interest themselves. As Tocqueville pointed out, Americans employ the principle of "self-interest rightly understood."

The principle of self-interest rightly understood is not a lofty one, but it is clear and sure. It does not aim at mighty objects, but it attains . . . all those at which it aims. By its admirable conformity to human weaknesses it easily obtains great dominion; nor is that dominion precarious, since the principle checks one personal interest by another, and uses, to direct the passions, the very same instrument that excites them.[23]

Madison's solution to his problem worked astonishingly well. The danger he wished to avert has been averted and largely for the reasons he gave. But it is possible to question now whether he did not take too narrow a view of what the dangers were. Living today as beneficiaries of his system, we may yet wonder whether he failed to contemplate other equally grave problems of democracy, or whether his remedy for the one disease has not had some unfortunate collateral consequences. The Madisonian solution involved a fundamental reliance on ceaseless striving after immediate interest (perhaps now immediate gratification). Tocqueville appreciated that this "permanent agitation . . . is characteristic of a peaceful democracy,"[24] one might even say, the price of its peace. And Tocqueville was aware of how great might be the price. "In the midst of this universal tumult, this incessant conflict of jarring interests, this continual striving of men after fortune, where is that calm to be found which is necessary for the deeper combinations of the intellect?"[25]

V

There is, I think, in *The Federalist* a profound distinction made between the qualities necessary for Founders and the qualities necessary for the men who come after. It is a distinction that bears on the question of the Founding Fathers' view of what is required for the good life and on their defense of popular government. Founding requires "an exemption from the pestilential influence of party animosities";[26] but the subsequent governing of America will depend on precisely those party animosities, moderated in the way I have described. Or again, founding requires that "reason" and not the "passions," "sit in judgment."[27] But, as I have argued, the society once founded will subsequently depend precisely upon the passions, only moderated in their consequences by having been guided into proper channels. The reason of the Founders constructs the system within which the passions of the men who come after may be relied upon.

Founders need a knowledge of the newly improved "science of politics" and a knowledge of the great political alternatives in order to construct a durable regime; while the men who come after need be only legislators who

---

[23]*Democracy in America*, ed. Phillips Bradley (Knopf, New York, 1951) Vol. 2, pp. 122–23.
[24]*Ibid.*, p. 42.
[25]*Idem.*
[26]*Federalist*, No. 37, p. 232.
[27]*Federalist*, No. 49, p. 331.

are but interested "advocates and parties to the causes they determine."[28] *The Federalist* speaks, as has often been observed, with harsh realism about the shortcomings of human nature, but, as has not so often been observed, none of its strictures can characterize the Founders; they must be free of these shortcomings in order to have had disinterested and true knowledge of political things. While "a nation of philosophers is as little to be expected as the philosophical race of kings wished for by Plato,"[29] it is tempting to speculate that *The Federalist* contemplates a kind of philosopher-founder, the posthumous duration of whose rule depends upon "that veneration which time bestows on everything,"[30] and in particular on a regime well-founded. But once founded, it is a system that has no necessary place and makes no provision for men of the founding kind.

It is clear that not all now regarded as Founding Fathers were thought by the authors of *The Federalist* to belong in that august company. Noting that "it is not a little remarkable" that all previous foundings of regimes were "performed by some individual citizen of pre-eminent wisdom and approved integrity,"[31] *The Federalist* comments on the difficulty that must have been experienced when it was attempted to found a regime by the action of an assembly of men. I think it can be shown that *The Federalist* views that assembly, the Federal Convention, as having been subject to all the weaknesses of multitudes of men. The real Founders, then, were very few in number, men learned in the new science of politics who seized upon a uniquely propitious moment when their plans were consented to first by a body of respectable men and subsequently, by equally great good fortune, by the body of citizens. As it were, America provided a rare moment when "the prejudices of the community"[32] were on the side of wisdom. Not unnaturally, then, *The Federalist* is extremely reluctant to countenance any re-opening of fundamental questions or delay in ratifying the Constitution.

This circumstance—wisdom meeting with consent—is so rare that "it is impossible for the man of pious reflection not to perceive in it a finger of that Almighty hand."[33] But once consent has been given to the new wisdom, when the government has been properly founded, it will be a durable regime whose perpetuation requires nothing like the wisdom and virtue necessary for its creation. The Founding Fathers' belief that they had created a system of institutions and an arrangement of the passions and interests, that would be

[28]*Federalist*, No. 10, p. 56.
[29]*Federalist*, No. 49, p. 329.
[30]*Ibid.*, p. 328.
[31]*Federalist*, No. 38, p. 233.
[32]*Federalist*, No. 49, p. 329.
[33]*Federalist*, No. 38, p. 231.

durable and self-perpetuating, helps explain their failure to make provision for men of their own kind to come after them. Apparently, it was thought that such men would not be needed.

But does not the intensity and kind of our modern problems seem to require of us a greater degree of reflection and public-spiritedness than the Founders thought sufficient for the men who came after them? One good way to begin that reflection would be to return to their level of thoughtfulness about fundamental political alternatives, so that we may judge for ourselves wisely regarding the profound issues that face us. I know of no better beginning for that thoughtfulness than a full and serious contemplation of the political theory that informed the origin of the Republic, of the thought and intention of those few men who fully grasped what the "assembly of demi-gods" was doing.

SELECTED SUGGESTED READINGS

The Federalist. Nos. 1, 6, 9–10, 14–15, 23, 31, 33, 37–39, 44, 47–49, 51, 62–63, 68, 70, 72, 78, 81, 84.

"James Madison to Thomas Jefferson," October 24, 1787, *The Writings of James Madison.* Edited by Gaillard Hunt. 9 vols. New York: G. P. Putnam's Sons, 1900–1910, V, 17–41.

"James Madison to Thomas Jefferson," October 17, 1788, *The Writings of James Madison.* Edited by Gaillard Hunt. 9 vols. New York: G. P. Putnam's Sons, 1900–1910, V, 269–74.

The Records of the Federal Convention of 1787. Edited by Max Farrand. 4 vols. New Haven: Yale University Press, 1966. See volumes one and two.

"Thomas Jefferson to James Madison," December 20, 1787, *The Life and Selected Writings of Thomas Jefferson.* Edited by A. Koch and W. Peden. New York: Modern Library, 1944, pp. 436–41.

★ JOHN MARSHALL *Robert K. Faulkner*

Marshall's is not American political thought in the usual sense. John Marshall was great in the law, and his best thought is legal thought. He is "the great Chief Justice," first, with no one second. As leader of the Supreme Court from 1801 to 1835, he conceived his fundamental duty to be, "the Expounder of the Constitution." Marshall's greatest deeds take the form of decisions and opinions in constitutional law. Even the purposes, principles, and general reflections guiding his decisions appear as legal fundamentals, verging on jurisprudence rather than political philosophy. Still, who would deny that Marshall's great constitutional opinions were decisively political in tenor and impact? He was guided by law, but the fundamental law is an essentially political law. It erects a powerful government for the new nation implicit in the Preamble's aspiration for "a more perfect union." Marshall himself called the coming of the new government a "political revolution." It was a revolution achieved essentially by consent or agreement, not force. The Constitution was the instrument of agreement. In construing that law, then, Marshall as judge defined the kind and extent of the country's political revolution: the many states made one, their policies, powers, and regimes made subordinate to the pervasive national government and the individual liberty and free enterprise it authorized. Informing Marshall's constitutional construction there was, as there had to be, a deep political understanding.

Marshall's doctrine of legal construction clarifies the point. His general rule was: Respect for the letter of the law must be combined with a devotion to its "spirit" or intent. "The intention of the instrument must prevail." That intention, however, "is to be collected chiefly from its words," and this requires careful attention to the "common sense" meaning of a legal provision. Marshall always pondered the words of the law. By distinguishing their "natural and common import," he settled on the most likely interpretation or interpretations. This is insufficient to decide difficult cases, however. Often one must consult the intent of the whole law to clarify a part: . . . "The same words in different connexion have a different import."[1] Such attention

NOTE: This chapter draws on my *The Jurisprudence of John Marshall* (Princeton University Press, 1968). In that book may be found more extensive citation of authorities.

[1] See *Ogden* v. *Saunders,* 12 Wheaton (U.S.) 332 (1827); *Sturges* v. *Crowninshield,* 4 Wheaton

ided especially by a constitution. A summary of a whole government s inevitably that "only its great outlines should be marked, its important ects designated, and the minor ingredients which compose those objects be educed from the nature of the objects themselves." Thus particular powers, over wages or hours or rates, must be deduced from general powers, such as those of Congress "to regulate commerce . . . among the several states." These general objects or powers are stated in the Preamble and body of the American Constitution. They are not, however, defined. Construing the Constitution requires, then, some grasp of the defining principles of the American political order. Guided by the words of the Constitution, the American judge at his highest needs finally a wise understanding of the American government and nation.

Marshall was the first Chief Justice to construe the Constitution according to such a masterful understanding, and perhaps his was the most masterful. For both reasons he too was a founder, not indeed of our Constitution, but of our constitutional law. He framed not the document but the most authoritative statements of what the document means. His thought reveals, then, the political implications of the American rule of law, the political philosophy at the core of American jurisprudence. It shows especially the distinctive contribution of law, legal doctrines, and judges to the American experiment in liberal republicanism.

The Chief Justice's constitutional opinions are of three kinds. *Marbury* v. *Madison,* alone of its kind, sets forth comprehensively the essentials of the American rule of law. It provides for judicial supervision of executive and legislature alike. Their deeds are to be kept faithful to applicable statutes, to the Constitution, and finally to "general principles" of law protecting individual rights and to "certain principles" delimiting the functions of each department. Second, a series of cases secures private rights, especially the right of contract, against state and general governments. *United States* v. *Burr, Sturges* v. *Crowninshield, Fletcher* v. *Peck,* and *Dartmouth College* v. *Woodward* had a profound effect upon civil liberties, free commercial exchange, and industrial development. Finally, one must mention Marshall's famous endeavors to establish the national government's powers and protect them from state encroachments. *McCulloch* v. *Maryland* is best known, sustaining the federal authority to charter a bank and, generally, to enjoy a broad discretion as to means. *Gibbons* v. *Ogden, Brown* v. *Maryland, Cohens* v. *Virginia,* and *Osborne* v. *Bank of the United States* might also be singled out.

(U.S.) 202–03 (1819); *Pennington* v. *Coxe,* 2 Cranch (U.S.) 52 (1804); *King* v. *Delaware Insurance Co.,* 6 Cranch (U.S.) 80 (1810); *Shore* v. *Jones,* 1 Brockenbrough 289 (1814).

THE LIBERAL NATION AND ITS GOVERNMENT

The thought guiding Marshall's work had as its touchstone human liberty, understood in the sober manner of the Framers' classical liberalism. Government should attend to the basic needs and thus the natural rights of men: protecting the lives, the liberties, the property, of as many people as possible. With his generation, Marshall seemed to think that politics and law should rest upon a more restricted and stable basis than aspirations for human excellence. Liberty should be "rational liberty." It must be understood in a "realistic" manner to accord with the legitimate if not especially noble "interests" of most men. Returning from a sobering diplomatic foray to France in 1797 and 1798, Marshall delivered a speech cautioning the people of Richmond against "visionary" foreign views:

> To a citizen of the *United States,* so familiarly habituated to the actual possession of liberty, that he almost considers it as the inseparable companion of man, a view of the despotism, which borrowing the garb and usurping the name of freedom, tyrannizes over so large and fair a proportion of the earth, must teach the value which he ought to place on the solid safety and real security he enjoys at home.[2]

"Real security" means safety of person first of all. On the Court and off, Marshall had always sought for government those powers, and those limits on power, which could assure domestic tranquillity without endangering the citizen's life. Consider especially his leniency in conducting the trial for treason of Aaron Burr. The former vice president, nearly president in place of Thomas Jefferson, was in effect prosecuted by Jefferson himself. Dominating the Circuit Court, Marshall "came between Burr and death" through a rigorous construction of the Constitution's requirements for a treason conviction. The relevant constitutional definition of treason was "levying war." This must be understood, Marshall said, as involving actual perpetration, not planning nor even procuring the act perpetrated. Only those engaged bodily in warring against the nation, by means of visible acts to which two witnesses might testify, could receive the dire penalties for this worst of political crimes. Marshall admitted that the procurers and planners, "in truth the chief traitors" as he himself allowed, might thus go scot-free. But here, as elsewhere, he adhered to the principle that "penal laws" afflicting life and liberty should be strictly construed. In criminal trials the defendant should be treated "with as much liberality and tenderness as the case will admit."[3] Marshall's concern for

---

[2]"General Marshall's Address to the Citizens of Richmond, Virginia," reprinted in Albert J. Beveridge, *Life of John Marshall* (Boston, 1919), II, 572.

[3]David Robertson, *Reports of the Trials . . . of Aaron Burr . . . for Treason* (Philadelphia, 1808), II, 534, 440, 436–37; Cf. I, 178, 196.

security of person did not extend, however, to Jefferson's almost obsessive horror at the infliction of bodily pain or his doubts as to the rightness of capital punishment.

Security of the individual required that he enjoy liberty of speech and opinion as well as freedom from bodily arrest. In his *History of the Colonies*, Marshall repeatedly castigated the Puritans' persecutions as violations of "religious liberty" and the "rights of conscience." But his reasons for favoring liberty of opinion should not be confused with the present-day faith in progress by free struggle of ideas in the "competition of the market," as Justice Oliver Wendell Holmes put it. Marshall favored free speech because the opposite easily encouraged a dangerous despotism, especially a theocratic despotism. He favored also, however, the limits on speech and opinion which decency, good order, and individual security itself, demanded. He defended, for example, the constitutionality of the Sedition Act of 1798, which authorized the national government to prosecute those using false, malicious slander to rouse the people against their government. Morals generally, even the triter sort assuring domestic tranquillity, are "defended solely by opinion." A nation's best institutions and soundest customs must even be "cherished" by opinion. If the Constitution's "necessary and proper clause" authorized punishment of actual resistance to law, did it not also authorize provision for punishment of those acts criminal under the common law of libel, "and which obviously lead to and prepare resistance"?[4]

Of the several rights of the individual, that to property is the one by which Marshall is best known and least understood. Speech has replaced property as the freedom officially central in our constitutional galaxy, and Marshall's classical liberalism now seems downright "conservative." But it is clear from the Constitutional Convention and *The Federalist* that the protection of property rights was viewed by our framers as central to a liberal order, even, James Madison said, as "the first object of government." Marshall's judicial opinions clarify what the right is and why it is so important.

Observe that his relevant decisions do not typically involve "property" as such. They protect "vested rights," or the "rights of contract." These are claims to ownership which come to exist, or "vest," in one party, simply by his undertaking, or contracting, with another. It is the doctrine of "vested rights" that was called by Professor Edward S. Corwin the "basic doctrine of American constitutional law." Marshall thought that the right to property obtained by contract stems from nature itself, "from the right which every man retains to acquire property, to dispose of that property according to his

[4]John Marshall, *Address of the Minority in the Virginia Legislature* . . . (Richmond, 1799), pp. 11–14.

own judgment, and to pledge himself for a future act. These rights are not given by society, but are brought into it."[5] Nature dictates that men are to be protected in what they acquire by contract, that is, by voluntary exchange. In effect, nature authorizes free exchange, that is, commerce.

Observe also that the authority for gain by commerce is deduced from a more fundamental authority for gain: it results "from the right which every man retains to acquire property." In short, the basic right to property is the right to acquire property. Possessions are protected less as such than as *products* of the acquisitive faculty. Madison says in *Federalist* No. 10 that the first object of government is the protection of "the different and unequal faculties of acquiring property." And the key ability is that to work or labor. "Every man," as Marshall puts it in the case of *The Antelope*, "has a natural right to the fruits of his own labor." In short, one has less the right to possess than the right to possess what one has worked for. The import of this is immense. What is fundamentally protected is the incentive to work, acquire, and trade, and thus a dynamic force for production. What is served is not as much the leisurely property of the aristocrat as the restless enterprise of the business man. The property right affords legal warrant to the economy of free enterprise, moving men to incessant work by an anxious and acquisitive search for profit. And here one must ask: why is this private right in the interest of society at large?

The reconciliation of private property and the public welfare is but the most controversial part of that perennial task of the liberal statesman: the reconciliation of individual rights generally with the needs of a nation. Whatever the difficulties in practice, however, Marshall understood that the solution in principle was part of liberalism itself. The rights of the individual served his legitimate interest. And by protection of private interest, public interest too could be served. "In this country," Marshall remarked at the Virginia Ratifying Convention, "there is no exclusive personal stock of interest. The interest of the community is blended and inseparably connected with that of the individual. When he promotes his own, he promotes that of the community. When we consult the common good, we consult our own."[6] Complementary to the safety, freedom, and gain sought by private citizens was the "public interest": peace within, defense from without, and continual progress in what we now call the Gross National Product.

This political foundation in "self-interest rightly understood," as Alexis de Tocqueville was to call it, works even with respect to each man's concern for safety, and freedom of movement and opinion. Such rights protected, some

[5]*Ogden* v. *Saunders*, 12 Wheaton (U.S.) 346 (1827).
[6]Jonathon Elliot, *The Debates in the Several State Conventions on the Adoption of the Federal Constitution* (Philadelphia, 1836), III, 232.

powerful causes of civil strife are avoided. With the property right, however, the solid basis of liberal politics comes into its own. To begin with, safe property contributes to the individual's security, so far as his activities are bound up with his property. A safe shop serves the safety of the shopkeeper. In what came to be called "the acquisitive society," or "a nation of shop-keepers," that means much. Also, a certain general peaceableness is encouraged. The protection of contractual rights mitigates that perennial cause of civil war, the struggle between "haves" and "have-nots." The haves are secure in what they possess, but the road to having is opened to the have-nots by a fundamental protection of acquiring, not possessing. In addition, commerce promotes mutual dependence and hence mutual helpfulness and civility.

Above all, protection of the fruits of private labor is a reliable incentive for economic development. In his *History of the Colonies,* Marshall criticizes the community ownership of early Jamestown and Plymouth. An identical and "constant" difficulty plagued both colonies: "The public supplies were generally inadequate to the public necessities." The cause was "their adherence to the pernicious policy of a community of goods and of labor." The solution lay in giving "industry its due reward," "exclusive property in the product of its toil." When this was partly granted at Jamestown, "a sudden change was made in their appearance and habits. Industry, impelled by the certainty of recompense, advanced with rapid strides, and the inhabitants were no longer in fear of wanting bread. . . ."[7]

Vested rights, then, serve a dynamic public good. The basic doctrine of American constitutional law is a cause of the basic American accomplishment: the fabulous increase of the means of production. Marshall saw economic accomplishment as true to constitutional intent.

"[The] great and visible economic improvement occurring around 1790 [was in part due to] the influence of the Constitution on habits of thinking and acting, [which] though silent, was considerable. In depriving the states of the power to impair the obligations of contracts, or to make anything but gold and silver a tender in payment of debts, the conviction was impressed on that portion of society which had looked to the government for relief from embarrassment, that personal exertion alone could free them from difficulties; and an increased degree of industry and economy was the natural consequence of this opinion."[8]

It is important to understand that Marshall's version of "private interest, public gain," does not amount to the unleashing of crude acquisitiveness usually associated with that maxim. As Tocqueville stressed, "self-interest"

    [7]John Marshall, *A History of the Colonies,* reprinted as Volume I of *The Life of George Washington* (Fredericksburg, 1926), pp. 42–43, 45–46, 77–79. Henceforth cited as *History.*
    [8]John Marshall, *The Life of George Washington* (Philadelphia, 1839), II, 192. Henceforth cited as *Life.*

must be "rightly understood." Proper "habits of thinking and acting" are required, as Marshall himself put it. Safety and mutual security require peaceableness, benevolent humanity, and tolerance of others' character and opinions. Similarly, acquisitiveness would degenerate into monopoly, speculation, and exploitation were it not made responsible by "industry" and "private faith," and sobered by "economy." The desire for gain results in real production only when accompanied by hard work, honesty in exchange, and saving rather than spending.

Private interest properly channeled breeds prosperity, and wealth breeds power, in the nation as in the wealthy. There are then political as well as economic benefits. Marshall foresaw for the United States a "legitimate greatness" in wealth, population, extent, and arms. More accurately, its greatness would lie in increasing these, in the "progress" prized by the enlightenment. "In arts, in arms, and in power, [the United States] have advanced, and are advancing, with unexampled rapidity." This "vast republic" was to be "a great, powerful, and independent nation," "extending from the St. Croix to the Gulph of Mexico, from the Atlantic to the Pacific." He foresaw, in short, a "widespreading, rising empire."[9]

Yet the country was not imperial in its aim. The glory of conquest was not its end. Marshall thought that the United States should take only its legitimate place among the nations, a place defined by the law of nations. He was, indeed, as much the founder of the American version of the law of nations as of the country's constitutional law. The law of nations was to be regarded as part of the law of the land, as authoritative. As were the other laws of the country, it was to be interpreted according to "the great and immutable principles of equity and natural justice," "the simple and natural principles." Since natural rights belong to man as man, Marshall believed America should defer to all other nations equally, recognizing their legitimate needs and engaging in mutual commerce. Marshall's grand opinions on the law of nations were humanitarian in tenor. They promoted the "humane, civilized" and "modern" trend encouraging commerce, lessening the rigors of war on the persons and property of neutrals and belligerents, and removing by adjudication some of the occasions for strife.

Law was not enough, however. Power was needed as well. If not an empire in its aims, he felt that the United States must nonetheless pile up imperial means. "The nature of man forbids us to conclude that we are in no danger from war . . . A defenseless country cannot be secure." Sustaining Marshall's preoccupation with producing ever greater wealth, population and arms, is fear of unmeasurable dangers to come. "The exigencies of nations have

[9]See, for example, *McCulloch* v. *Maryland*, 4 Wheaton (U.S.) 408 (1819); *Life*, II, 440, 64.

been generally commensurate to their resources."[10] Marshall's political science urges incessant preparation for those necessities which, in the general run of things, may be expected eventually to show themselves. Thus the decisive function of acquisitiveness liberated: It yields an ever-increasing pile of the means of defense. Enlightenment is at bottom acquaintance with the first necessity of men and of the means of meeting it. At the basis of the acquisitive society is apprehension, the fear of future dangers.

Yet there is a nobler strand in Marshall's understanding: his republicanism. The nation was not simply a union in public means for private ends. Its political life reflected a worthy end in itself, republican self-government. The citizen's privileges of occupying office and choosing office holders are "the choicest rights of humanity." America's political life was then dedicated to "a national faith," holding as "the most sacred of deposits—the right of self-government."[11] Still, it will be shown that republicanism occupies but a subordinate place in Marshall's understanding of the American nation. Fundamentally, although not exclusively, the nation comprised a union in public power for private security. And the crucial power was political, not economic; the public governor, not the resources piled up by private endeavor. Americans had made a union by subordinating themselves jointly to their new protective government.

Government is that public representative with force enough to provide for the common needs of private individuals: "an investment of power for the general advantage, in the hands of agents selected for that purpose." Entering civil society men do not surrender their rights to life, liberty, and property. They do, however, give up that of enforcement. ". . . This original and natural right of coercion . . . would be incompatible with general peace, and is, therefore, surrendered. Society . . . gives in its place a more safe and certain remedy."[12] The "safe and certain" home of liberty is within the walls provided by liberal government. Secure liberty is civil liberty, but civil liberty is a rare plant. Law in most countries is not oriented above all to securing the individual's safety and prosperity. Marshall's understanding of what makes of government liberal government, and of law liberal law, is therefore of considerable interest.

The character of the Constitution itself is of course crucial, according to Marshall. Government is itself governed by the fundamental law. In all its parts, barring those few grudging concessions made to the existing institution of slavery, that law aims to provide for liberty. Its provision is two-fold: in-

[10]Elliot, *Debates*, III, 235, 237.
[11]Marshall as envoy, United States, *State Papers*, Foreign Relations, II, 176, 170; cf. 177; *History*, pp. 86–87, cf. p. 428.
[12]*Ogden* v. *Saunders*, at p. 350; *Gibbons* v. *Ogden*, 9 Wheaton (U.S.) 189 (1824).

direct, by raising a political instrument, and direct. The direct means are themselves two-fold: express limits on government and, more important, an implicit continuation of the English common law.

The common law comprised chiefly those "unwritten" principles of justice that had been accepted by courts: "human reason applied by courts, not capriciously, but in a regular train of decisions, to human affairs, for the promotion of the ends of justice."[13] The "ends of justice" were the rights of individuals. As the most authoritative of the many expositions of the common law, Marshall deferred to William Blackstone's *Commentaries on the Laws of England,* published from 1765 to 1769. Blackstone understood the laws of England, its old common law especially, to have their basis in man's "absolute rights" to "personal security," "personal liberty," and "all his acquisitions." It seems that Blackstone sought to render politic and habitual the promising, but corrosive and calculating, individualism of Locke. He sought to weave the natural rights of man into a legal and political fabric comprising traditional British laws, customs and institutions, all subtly reinterpreted. The key to Blackstone's scheme was a rebirth in suitably redefined form of the old common law. The rights of Englishmen were equated with the rights of the individual: natural, universal, "absolute." It was to the ends of justice thus understood that Marshall deferred. He presumed "the common or unwritten law which pervades all America" to be the "substratum of our laws," despite minor differences from state to state. Thus the basic customs governing interpretation of the laws were understood as attuned to individual rights.

The Constitution went further than suppositions. It also put express limits on state and national governments. There was provided in Article I, Section 10, what Marshall called "a bill of rights for the people of each state," as well as the better known Bill of Rights for the nation. Occasionally, the Constitution varied from common law, as in its strict provisions regarding treason convictions. Usually it merely made explicit common law maxims, as it forbade to the states laws impairing the obligation of contracts, and to both states and nation *ex post facto* laws and bills of attainder (depriving a man of all civil rights and capacities to sue, to inherit, etc.). The harmony of unwritten with written law is nicely illustrated by Marshall's opinion for the Supreme Court in the leading contract clause case, *Fletcher* v. *Peck.* Georgia's revocation of a grant under which legal estates have vested is void, as Marshall summed up the course of his argument, "either by general principles which are common to our free institutions, or by the particular provisions of the Constitution of the United States."

With legal safeguards for individual liberty went the Constitution's princi-

---

[13] *Livingston* v. *Jefferson,* 1 Brockenbrough 20 (1811).

pal endeavor: establishing a government. Marshall's views accord with the Framers' understanding of the new government: a pervasive authority, vested in a system of distinct powers duly separated and balanced. By its machinery of government, and by an ingenious mechanical arrangement setting ambition against ambition, it would protect against dangers to the individual without being itself dangerous.

Two kinds of powers, serving the individual in different ways, are distinguished by Marshall. Legal or judicial power is vested in the courts, political power in the law-making and law-executing departments. The *locus classicus* of Marshall's explication is the first two parts of *Marbury* v. *Madison,* prior to the concluding discussion of judicial review. William Marbury had been appointed a justice of the peace in the frenetic last moments of the outgoing Federalist administration. President John Adams signed his commission, conferring the authority. But Marshall, then Secretary of State, neglected to deliver it. Finding the stack of Federalist commissions, Thomas Jefferson ordered his own Secretary of State, James Madison, not to convey them. Claiming his office, Marbury sued Madison.

Chief Justice Marshall determined, first, that Marbury had a right, according to statute, to his commission; second, that he might obtain legal remedy in the shape of a *mandamus,* a writ of command, from the courts to the executive. He had to meet the arguments that delivery of the commission lay within the president's political discretion, and that, in any event, the president as an independent political officer was not subject to a court order. The gist of Marshall's reply is this: Indeed, "the president is invested with certain important political powers, in the exercise of which he is to use his own discretion, and is accountable only to his country in his political character and to his own conscience . . . The subjects [of such powers] are political. They respect the nation, not individual rights, and being entrusted to the executive," his decision is conclusive. "But where a specific duty is assigned by law, and individual rights depend upon the performance of that duty, it seems equally clear that the individual who considers himself injured, has a right to resort to the laws of his country for a remedy." Duties assigned by law are here sharply distinguished from the discretion appropriate to the political branches. In these two sections is established the president's duty to obey a valid law, and his subjection to the courts' enforcement of rights vesting under such a law. For, "the question whether a right has vested or not, is, in its nature, judicial, and must be tried by the judicial authority." Here, shorn of complications and difficulties, is a goodly portion of the American doctrine of the rule of law and, correspondingly, of the rationale for the courts' eminence in America.

The judicial authority is to construe laws as they apply to individuals. The legislature with the president makes law, the judges construe it as civil or criminal cases require. Not unmindful of Jefferson's attacks on the judges, Marshall repeated frequently that "the judiciary department of every government is the rightful expositor of its law." He extolled "the great political principle . . . that the legislative, executive, and judicial powers of every well constructed government are co-extensive with each other."[14] Despite the vast implications of this authority, Marshall was wont to deny emphatically that it was political in nature. The judiciary's power over "the rights of individuals" concerns "objects unconnected with government." This is very hard to understand, for how can the prerogatives of citizens be "unconnected with" the government that cares for them? The solution seems to be this. Courts protect individuals in rights given ultimately not by government but by nature, while the political powers protect individuals *en masse* with the indirect "policies" invented or devised by government itself.

The courts' duties do not involve policy or will. "Courts are the mere instruments of the law, and can will nothing. When they are said to exercise a discretion it is a mere discretion . . . to be exercised in discerning the course prescribed by law."[15] Yet Marshall grants at various times that the prescriptions of law are often vague and uncertain, requiring interpretation. Does not such interpretation amount to "discretion" without the guidance of law? In such a case, Marshall says in *United States* v. *Burr,* the court is "to be guided by sound legal principles." Here is the key premise. Even while deciding upon interpretations of law and custom, judges are not willful because their choice is ultimately guided by "sound legal principles," that is, by a higher law. These principles are precisely the same maxims of universal and natural justice which we saw embraced by the common law. It is true then that judges "merely" construe the laws. Their constructions, however, shape the law in accord with those individual rights which all laws are assumed to respect and protect. This is the judicial function by nature, so to speak. Courts are "by definition," Marshall writes in *Fletcher* v. *Peck,* "those tribunals which are established for the security of property and to decide on human rights." One might say that as natural private rights vest under private contract, so a kind of natural judicial power vests under the social contract.

There are endless illustrations of the courts' distinctive role, including every case this chapter mentions. Wherever the federal courts applied common law, Constitution, statutes, or law of nations, they were to construe it in light of the "tenderness" for men and their property that law was presumed to wish. Perhaps the most interesting of Marshall's remarks occur as he inter-

[14] *Osborne* v. *Bank of United States,* 9 Wheaton (U.S.) 818–819 (1824); *Bank of Hamilton* v. *Dudley's Lessee,* 2 Peters (U.S.) 807 (1829).

[15] *Osborne* v. *Bank of United States,* at p. 866.

prets a treaty in *The American Insurance Co.* v. *Canter.* The fundamental orientation to liberty is visible, while the limitations on liberty posed by the necessities of political life are also given their due. Treaties are ticklish arrangements involving "great national concerns." Their letter is then to be closely followed. "The rights of parties," so solicitously attended to in "mere private cases," may even be ignored if the words of the treaty require. If the letter is unclear, however, Marshall would emphatically presume a treaty to embody "that security to private property which the laws and usages of nations would, without stipulation, have conferred. No construction which would impair that security further than the positive words require would be admissible." Although liberty is to be protected where possible, we see that the qualification of possibility poses real limits in this world of harsh necessities. Private security must bow to the means of collective security. It is hemmed in especially by the political powers raised to assure commerce, peace, safety. Even "a bill of rights is merely recommendatory," Marshall remarked in the Virginia Ratifying Convention. "Were it otherwise, the consequence would be that many laws which are found convenient would be unconstitutional."

Political power is distinguished from legal power by both its end and its means. If courts deal with "objects unconnected with government," legislature and executive engage in "an exercise of sovereignty without affecting the rights of individuals." Both powers serve finally the individual, but the service of the political branches is indirect. They attend not to rights, the claims of each, but to policy, plans for the safety and interrelation of all. They clear away obstacles to a commercial system, assure order within, fend off dangers from without. Corresponding to the difference in task is a difference in means: the political branches are to enjoy a broad discretion. They are not strictly governed by law. Even in *Marbury* v. *Madison* Marshall remarks that the president might "use his own discretion" in exercising his "important political powers."

The political powers are indeed limited to what the Constitution grants and enumerates. Marshall disavowed Alexander Hamilton's endeavor to deduce a plenary legislative power from the authority in Article I, Section 8, "to pay the debts and provide for the common defense and general welfare of the United States."[16] Still, the enumerated powers must be understood to encompass the full panoply of necessary means. They cannot benefit from the literal interpretation appropriate to a "legal code." "The power being given," Marshall writes in *McCulloch* v. *Maryland,* "it is the interest of the nation to facilitate its exercise." This reflects the premise that Hamilton puts forth in *Federalist* No. 31 as the first of the "axioms" of government: "A government ought to contain in itself every power requisite to the full accomplishment of the objects committed to its care." In modern (and Hamiltonian) language:

[16]Letter to Timothy Pickering, March 18, 1828 (Massachusetts Historical Society.)

government must be *effective*. Safety for the people requires measures decisive, pervasive, unhindered. "It can never be their interest, and cannot be presumed to have been their intention, to clog and embarrass" the "execution" of the government's powers "by withholding the most appropriate means." This is the thought guiding *McCulloch* v. *Maryland*, a kind of short practical treatise on the American doctrine of sovereignty.

That opinion exhibits also why such "energy" is necessary: great and inevitable dangers must be anticipated. Marshall evokes the spectre of future "exigencies," urgent but sudden crises. Since their extent and hour cannot be foreseen, although their inevitability can, the government must possess the power to master them as they occur. The Chief Justice argued in 1819 for the authority of Congress to charter a national bank. "Throughout this vast republic . . . from the St. Croix to the Gulph of Mexico, from the Atlantic to the Pacific, revenue is to be collected and expended, armies are to be marched and supported. The exigencies of the nation may require that the treasure raised in the north should be transported to the south . . . Is that construction of the constitution to be preferred which would render these operations difficult, hazardous, and expensive?" Preoccupation with political power, as with economic power, comes from a preoccupation with future dangers, especially of war. To a considerable extent, Marshall's political understanding amounts to a long preparation in the name of peace for inevitable war.

In providing for domestic order, Marshall's views follow *The Federalist*. The chief problem lay in more or less democratic "factions." The strong new judiciary would help in promoting liberal order by protecting the rights of each, especially the property rights of creditors. More was needed, especially "vigor" in the executive. Marshall extolled the overwhelming force with which Washington and Hamilton cowed the Whiskey Rebellion of 1794.

The power over commerce, the greatest warrant for federal intervention in domestic activities, was understood by Marshall as chiefly a means of removing the obstacles to free trade. Authorization of commerce was unnecessary; the natural right to acquire had as a consequence the right to trade. "The right of intercourse between State and State," as Marshall wrote in *Gibbons* v. *Ogden*, ". . . derives its source from those laws whose authority is acknowledged by civilized man throughout the world." "Regulation" was needed, however, to clear away hindrances. Marshall personally favored more positive steps. He promoted in his native Virginia such "improvements" as roads and canals. It seems, however, that he read the enumerated powers as confining the general government to a "power to make [internal improvements only] for military purposes or for the transportation of the mail." He recognized, however, that such might serve the purposes of commerce as well.[17] In any event his inter-

---

[17]Letter to Timothy Pickering, March 18, 1828 (Massachusetts Historical Society).

pretations went far to sweep away obstacles to a national free market.

The classic case will always be *Gibbons* v. *Ogden,* decided in 1824. It broke the steamboat monopoly authorized since 1808 by New York State law. In effect, as Albert J. Beveridge showed in his *Life of Marshall,* it opened up the rivers of the whole country to the thriving competition of innumerable boats. In a remarkable opinion Marshall read a federal act licensing ships engaged in the coasting trade, to contradict and thus void the New York grant of exclusive privilege. From a mere coasting license he deduced a federally authorized "right to trade," inconsistent with a state grant of monopoly. The argument is typical. Great powers are granted to accomplish great objects. A narrow interpretation would defeat the object: the words in question must be otherwise construed. Thus a nation is raised. Barriers of state, section, and custom are breached by individual enterprise, a national flow of trade, and the bonds of mutual interests which follow. A government is fitted for great efforts of direction and coercion. Over the once-independent state sovereignties is erected the new and superior protective umbrella of the national sovereign, limited in its tasks, supreme in all means needed for their accomplishment.

This mixture of sovereignties, the American system of "federalism," renders the country's politics peculiarly complicated. Marshall often indicated the "novel," "rare and difficult," "complex," character of this scheme, presenting "for many purposes an entire nation, and for other purposes several distinct and independent sovereignties." In his own reconciliation of state and nation, he tried above all to protect the federal government's great powers from what the Framers had most feared: the encroachments of the states, older and more strongly entrenched in the people's affections. He sought so to interpret the law that a series of bulwarks might sustain the national authority, and bar the jealous counter-measures of its rivals. Thus he cut down state attempts to relax the duties of the private debtor, to interfere by taxation or otherwise with a national instrument or with the national flow of trade, and, crucially, to evade review by the federal courts of state court decisions involving federal questions. The legitimate policies of the general government were to predominate over contrary policies of the states. This very predominance enforced a fundamental unity. State governments could be independent only within the limits of policy and principle permitted by the national government. The nation and its purposes were supreme.

Still, Marshall saw that more had to be said. It would be foolish to authorize the primacy of every national act over every contrary state act. The core of useful local projects would often be sacrificed to the trivial implications of a national measure. The Chief Justice held, to begin with, that "in our complex system" the national authority should not be extended beyond the purpose of the power in question. More to the point, he understood the purposes of state and general governments to be complementary—as parts of a larger national whole by whose common good each might be measured and limited.

Marshall's remarks on the functions served in a great liberal nation by state and local governments are disturbingly slight compared to Jefferson's. He does presume in *Gibbons* v. *Ogden* that the states are to regulate "internal commerce" and "domestic police," whereas the national government is concerned with matters "general in their nature, which interest all America, which are connected with the general safety." To the extent that the two kinds of government act for complementary purposes, they are not independent of one another in the decisive sense. The state governments are decisively subordinate, not sovereign. The role of each is defined by the needs of the whole, and the general government has final say as to what those needs are. No fundamental conflict of purpose can in principle exist, and a conflict of policy under complementary purposes can be resolved by allowing the measure required, on balance, by the good of the whole (which includes the good of its parts). This thought guides implicitly some of Marshall's sensible adjustments of state and nation, as, for example, *Willson* v. *Blackbird Creek Marsh Company.* It never becomes explicit, however. Marshall remained true to the key doctrine distinguishing American federalism from a central government acting through provincial departments: the supposition of two kinds of governments, state and federal, not only distinct but independent within their sphere.

THE REPUBLIC

More than once we have alluded to Marshall's republicanism. He was a "votary" of the cause of republican liberty sweeping the Western world, dominating America. With those of his generation, he understood republican or free government as popular government through representatives. This is a noble end in itself, the free man's privileges of choosing officers and holding office, of political participation, being "the choicest rights of humanity." Republicanism qualifies and to some extent ennobles the pedestrian jurisprudence oriented to "solid safety and real security." Republican government is, however, a problem. It was a question for Marshall, as for the Founders, whether republican institutions could really govern. Could they perform the necessary tasks for which government, by the very nature of its powers, was erected? Prior to the founding Marshall had begun to doubt. Shays' Rebellion in Massachusetts, and debtor politics elsewhere, "cast a deep shade over that bright prospect which the revolution in America and the establishment of our free governments had opened to the votaries of liberty throughout the globe. I fear, and there is no opinion more degrading to the dignity of man, that these have truth on their side who say that man is incapable of governing himself."[18]

[18]John Marshall to James Wilkinson, January 5, 1787, *American Historical Review*, XII (January 1907), 347–48.

Whatever his doubts in 1787, they did not then ripen to certainties. Indeed, the new national government was itself an attempt to prove the possibility of republican government. By Marshall and the Framers alike, it was seen as a republican "experiment" in the modern science of politics.

Marshall watched the experiment's progress from the inauguration of George Washington to Andrew Jackson's war upon the "monster Bank." So long as he believed the American majority could be lightly reined by the new Constitution into acquiescence in sound government, he remained a devoted republican. When that belief ebbed, his enthusiasm for popular rule receded as well. His description of Washington's politics is also the best compression of his own principles. "In speculation, he was a real republican, devoted to the Constitution of his country, and to that system of equal political rights on which it is founded. But between a balanced republic and a democracy, the difference is like that between order and chaos. Real liberty, he thought, was to be preserved, only by preserving the authority of the laws, and maintaining the energy of government."[19]

Among the many difficulties threatening the experiment's success, two were inseparable from the country's republicanism. Those qualities of judgment and character needed for sound citizens and statesmen were threatened by an increasingly pervasive devotion to mere place and gain, to "success." Much larger in Marshall's mind loomed the second problem: the dangers posed by the tumultuous growth of democratic control, inspired by Jefferson, consummated by Jackson.

Marshall thought the American character needed more than the utilitarian virtues of benevolence, toleration, industry, honesty, and economy. He urged his fellow citizens to aspire to "the exalted character of freemen." His remarks on the subject do not rival Jefferson's in extent. It is evident, nonetheless, that Marshall too admired such traits as courage, endurance, and a patriotic devotion to republican liberties. He would emphasize, what Jefferson did not, "discipline," and a proper deference to the community's better men. These would be distinguished above all by "talents and virtues." The peak of excellence was Washington himself. Washington was the highest of republican citizens, with moral and intellectual qualities that could even found the republic. Scattered throughout Marshall's *Life of Washington* are tributes to the magnanimous dignity and generosity, the courage in battle, the moderate ambition in peace, distinguishing the father of his country. Above all is praised Washington's statesmanlike practical judgment, "perhaps the most rare, and . . . certainly the most valuable quality of the human mind."[20] As the

[19] *Life*, II, 447.
[20] *Life*, II, 446.

years passed, however, Marshall came to wonder whether the qualities exemplified by the gentleman-statesman were not discouraged or at least eroded by the characteristic tendencies among his countrymen. "Does there exist," he ruminated in a letter to his old friend John Randolph, "any cause lurking beneath our institutions which so influences the education, the early habits of youth as to relax the great principles which form the foundation of national prosperity & happiness, as to substitute superficial showy acquirements for that substantial and real knowledge which is to be acquired only by labor, & which is essential to the formation of a statesman?"[21]

It seems that Marshall was alarmed by the pursuit of success without excellence: gain without respectable competence, and, especially, position without judgment and honor. He was in the habit of contrasting to his friend Joseph Story the "party politicians" of the 1820s and 1830s with the great "statesmen and patriots" of the founding. There is no evidence, however, that Marshall delved deeply into the problematic relation between his aspirations for republican excellence, and the basis in private interest of the jurisprudence he espoused. The superior man of Washingtonian stamp despises a pettily ambitious career pursuing place and gain. The citizen guided by private interest lives that way. If Marshall did not penetrate to the roots of the problem, however, he did at least display distinct practical concern for a remedy, worrying that his country would suffer by a "carelessness in performing the great duty of impressing on the youthful mind lessons of religion and morality."[22]

Marshall thought that religion should receive the encouragement of statesmen for its moral effects, whatever its higher consequences. Washington had been "a truly devout man"; "principles of religion" had much to do with his steadfast character. It is true that Marshall's concern for "liberty of conscience" had led him to approve disestablishment of the Virginia church. He favored nonetheless a compulsory tax supporting religion in general (as opposed to any particular church), "each individual being at liberty to declare the person to whom his contribution should be paid."[23]

The forming of the young by education was peculiarly important to a republic like America's. "It is more indispensable in governments entirely popular than in any other, that the mass of the people should receive that degree of instruction which will enable them to perform with some intelligence the duties which devolve on them." "Primary schools" are therefore of "greater interest" than our "colleges and universities." Still, Marshall wished also that the more prominent leaders of our complicated government and

[21]June 26, 18?? (Virginia Historical Society).
[22]John Marshall to James M. Garrett, December 17, 1830 (Virginia Historical Society).
[23]John Marshall to the Reverend William B. Sprague, July 22, 1828 (John Marshall Papers, Earl Greg Swem Library, The College of William and Mary in Virginia).

society should be instructed in such crucial modern subjects as constitutional jurisprudence and political economy. He was especially delighted at an abridgment for law students of Story's *Commentaries on the Constitution.* "The vast influence which the members of the profession exercise in all popular governments, especially in ours, is perceived by all, and whatever tends to their improvement benefits the nation." "I have finished reading your great work," wrote Marshall to his friend at the *Commentaries'* first appearance, "and wish it could be read by every statesman, and every would-be statesman in the United States."[24]

Probably the best illustration of Marshall's thoughts on political education is his own *Life of Washington.* The book's lessons are complicated. Essentially, however, it combines commendation of the solid system of strong government, free commerce, and sound credit, with a eulogy of austere and even noble republican statesmen. Always before the reader's eyes is the character of Washington, which will, the book concludes, furnish "a lesson well meriting the attention of those who are candidates for political fame." It is not accidental that Marshall, after his seventy-fifth year, condensed the work into a schoolbook. True enlightenment of a republican people induces them to emulate or at least revere the greatest of their statesmen.

That deference the American people increasingly declined to pay. Their recalcitrance symbolized the second and more massive problem in the republic: the growth of political democracy. The difficulty was simple, obvious, critical. The majority refused to play the circumscribed republican role for which they had been cast by Marshall. America, like any republic, was to be "administered according to the public will by representatives chosen to administer it."[25] Still, the necessary public tasks had to be performed there as in any government: the "public will" only *administers* the *government,* rather than ruling in any manner it might wish. Moreover, not the public at large, but "representatives" do the administering. The "people" embrace man as man, but man as Lockean individualism conceives of him, with many of the desires and features associated with the modern middle class. They are supposed to wish the law, order, and protection which only a government free of direct popular control can provide. Marshall's "government of the people" is less of, by, and for the people than from, on, and for the people. While the people would elect, directly or indirectly, all of their representatives, they were to

[24]John Marshall to Joseph Story, July 31, 1833 (Massachusetts Historical Society); letter to Joseph Story, June 3, 1833, *Massachusetts Historical Society, Proceedings,* 2nd series, XIV (1900), 358; henceforth cited as *Proceedings:* John Marshall to Charles Mercer, April 7, 1827 (courtesy of the Trustees of the Boston Public Library).

[25]John Marshall to the Secretary of State, September 15, 1787, *William & Mary Quarterly,* XII (October 1955), 637–38.

select the community's better men—"our most virtuous and able citizens"—
and to leave matters of policy to their enlightened judgment. This system of
representation allowed the electors a negative check to preclude particular
oppressions. It was not to yield a positive control over general policies. Discretion in both senses should belong to the people's representatives, then, to
whom the remainder of the country ought to defer.

Now this subordination did not come naturally to the American populace.
Experience under the Articles of Confederation had taught that. Struggles
between debtors and creditors had become, Marshall writes in the *Life of
Washington,* "the more animated, because, in the state governments generally,
no principle had been introduced which could resist the wild projects of the
moment, give the people time to reflect, and allow the basic good sense of the
people time for exercise." The constitutional "experiment" sought to provide
that principle, without being non-republican. It checked popular excesses by
basically popular means. It introduced "some principles into the political system, which might correct the obvious vices, without endangering the free
spirit of the existing institutions."[26] At the Virginia Ratifying Convention
Marshall went so far as to call the Constitution "democratic." Taken with some
other remarks of his, this seems to reflect his belief in the fundamental harmony between the people's proper political role, and their will as lightly
checked by the Constitution.

The Constitution relied on the legal check of judicial review, to be discussed later, and two political checks. Representation would continue to refine
the people's desires and opinions, as the better citizens were chosen. Moreover,
the new departments would be "balanced" so that the more sober and settled
Senate and president could together counter the more democratic House.
Thus the "real and deliberate sentiments of the people" would prevail over
their "prejudices and gusts of passion."[27] In this balance the president's role
was central. Marshall repeatedly praises Washington's "firmness of resolution"
as crucial to the government's successful inauguration. "Though prizing popular favour as highly as it ought be prized, he never yielded principle to obtain
it, or sacrificed his judgment on its altar. This firmness of character added to
his acknowledged virtue enabled him to stem a torrent which would have
overwhelmed almost any other man, and did, I believe, save his country."[28]

In Marshall's eyes, the country's democratic tendency turned out to be
not an occasional if dangerous wave, but an overwhelming "torrent." The
mounting popular pressure on Washington's administration is a theme second

[26] *Life,* II, 105, 103.
[27] *Life,* II, 446–47.
[28] John Marshall to Timothy Pickering, March 15, 1827, *Proceedings,* XIV, 322–23.

only to the hero himself in Marshall's concluding volume. An ever-growing "torrent of public opinion" threatened to overthrow representation with the founding of "democratic societies" for "watching the conduct of their rulers," bitter resentment of secrecy in government, and violent outbursts on issues like the Jay Treaty and the hereditary order of the Cincinnati. Still, the basically representative arrangements persisted. Yet they did not filter as Marshall had expected. "In a popular government," Marshall weighed developments in the years from 1789 to 1796, "the representatives of the people may generally be considered as a mirror, reflecting truly the passions and feelings which govern their constituents."[29] This assimilation of representative to constituent was aggravated by the growth of political parties: candidates were elected according to their views or "platform." The old deference to superior character and judgment was disappearing. Conversely, the strife of party leaders was transmitted to the people, coarsening civil life as well as political debate.

Despite his distaste for factional controversy, Marshall naturally allied himself with the Washingtonian Federalists in support of the new national institutions. In the *Life of Washington* the Federalists are described as those who had long favored strict enforcement of contracts, alleviation of distress by personal industry, and, "by a natural association of ideas," a strong national government. The Republicans are identified with the old democratic and debtor party. They had, however, been "more numerous and more powerful" even under the Articles. Only with "infinite difficulty" had the Constitution been ratified: a majority of citizens was almost surely opposed. There was needed "a concurrence of extrinsic circumstances to force on minds unwilling to receive the demonstration, a conviction of the necessity of an effective national government, and to give even a temporary ascendancy to that party which had long foreseen and deplored the crisis to which the affairs of the United States were hastening."[30] Extreme prudence was then required of the ruling Federalists. It was not forthcoming. Marshall thought their Sedition Act (not to mention the disastrous split between Hamilton and Adams) a classic political mistake, however constitutional. It opposed the dominant if often foolish democratic passion for freedom, especially from restraints on speech. ". . . An act operating on the press in any manner, affords to its opposers arguments which so captivate the public ear, which so mislead the public mind that the efforts of reason to correct false impressions will often fail of success."[31] During Washington's last term, the Senate itself fell from Federalist

[29]*Life*, II, 293, 269, 73, 144–46, 322, 324, 365, 447.
[30]*Life*, II, 77, 103, 127, 126, 181, 206–7.

control. The influence of the House increased correspondingly. Even the executive branch was threatened: "Almost any other man" than Washington would have capitulated to the torrent. The capture of the presidency in 1800 by the Jeffersonian Republicans marked the political defeat of Marshall's cause.

Marshall feared the Republican following. He feared more the leader. The reason was in good part "the general cast" of Jefferson's "political theory." It tended to weaken the aloof and distant general government in favor of the more easily watched states, and subject it to more democratic control. In 1832, as several southern states sought to "nullify" laws of the nation, Marshall wrote, "We are now gathering the bitter fruits of the tree . . . planted by Mr. Jefferson, and so industriously and perseveringly cultivated by Virginia."[32] On the eve of the election of 1800 Marshall had written that Jefferson will "embody himself with the House of Representatives. By weakening the office of president, he will increase his personal power. He will diminish his responsibility, sap the fundamental principles of the government, and become the leader of that party which is about to constitute the majority of the legislature."[33] Jefferson's "revolution" prepared the way for Jackson. Democratic liberalism came to rule without apology, with one of its own finally supplanting the Virginia and New England gentry. Then the presidential office had gone full circle, from check upon the *demos* to tribune of the *demos*. Marshall himself had come to think that it might "break down and trample on every other department of government." He then favored reduction of its power, limitation of the president's tenure to but one term, even his selection by lot from among the senators.

It was Marshall's awakening to the power and direction of the American public that caused him to doubt finally republican self-government. He doubted the people's "basic good sense." Retaining his views as to their interests, he ceased to believe that they would, even under the Constitution's reins, voluntarily pursue them. He came to call his early republicanism "wild and enthusiastic democracy." He had learned from experience, he thought. If the generality of citizens would act soundly, he wrote to William Gaston, "a republic would indeed be the utopia which enthusiasm has painted, but which experience has too often shown to be so coloured by the hand of the artist as scarcely to resemble the original."[34]

---

[31]John Marshall to Timothy Pickering(?) January 8, 1799. Quoted by permission of the Harvard College Library.

[32]John Marshall to Joseph Story, December 25, 1832, *Proceedings*, XIV, 353–54.

[33]John Marshall to Alexander Hamilton, January 1, 1801, *The Works of Alexander Hamilton*, ed. John C. Hamilton (New York, 1851), VI, 502.

[34]July 22, 1832 (from the William Gaston Papers in The Southern Historical Collection in the University of North Carolina Library, Chapel Hill, North Carolina).

JUDICIAL REVIEW

With the demise of political buffers protecting public powers from the popular will, legal checks became all the more important. In essence these amounted to the Supreme Court's enforcement of the written Constitution upon the other, elective, branches.

Marshall interpreted the Constitution as law, not merely plan, authority over government, not merely sketch. "The powers of the legislature are defined, and limited," he wrote in the third portion of *Marbury* v. *Madison*, "and that those limits may not be mistaken, or forgotten, the Constitution is written." It was because of the permanence thus given the government's fundamentals that Marshall deemed a written constitution "the greatest improvement on political institutions." Similarly, he construed the amending power as but another way of assuring "immortality to [the framers'] work." It allowed the variations in detail which are a politic response to changing circumstances. In short, the people were supposed to have essentially exhausted their own exercise of sovereignty with establishment of the Constitution. The great institutions then established are forever.

That the people have an original right to establish for their future government, such principles as, in their opinion, shall most conduce to their own happiness, is the basis, on which the whole American fabric has been erected. The exercise of this original right is a very great exertion; nor can it, nor ought it be frequently repeated. The principles, therefore, so established, are deemed fundamental. And as the authority, from which they proceed is supreme, and, can seldom act, they are designed to be permanent.[35]

The result is a republican check of the first order: the liberal government at the core of popular government is to be made permanent in the face of the popular will. The Constitution, it will be remembered, was framed not by the majority, but by the "enlightened statesmen and patriots" of the Federal Convention. When in doubt Marshall always followed their intentions, rather than the divided and occasionally more democratic thoughts expressed in the ratifying conventions. Nor was the Constitution ratified by the people at large. "The best talents of the several states" acting in convention, the people's representatives in Marshall's republican sense, acquiesced.[36]

For this great legal check to be made actual, however, it had to be enforced. Hence the importance of judicial review. By the judiciary's innocuous-sounding "maintenance of the principles established in the constitution," it held up the liberal government, and with it the republic. Marshall emphatically

---

[35] *Marbury* v. *Madison*, 1 Cranch (U.S.) 176 (1803).
[36] *Gibbons* v. *Ogden*, 9 Wheaton (U.S.) 202 (1824).

disclaimed any political authority for the court he made the grandest political court in the world. "Questions in their nature political, or which are, by the constitution and laws, submitted to the political departments, can never be made in this court." There is a trap, however. The courts might not meddle in the political sphere. They alone determine, however, how far the forbidden sphere extends. By their authority to construe finally what the Constitution allows, they control the sphere of law-maker and law-executor alike.

The reasoning which supports this great and unprecedented power occurs in the third and final part of *Marbury* v. *Madison*. There are grounds for thinking that Marshall seized a doubtful occasion to solidify the Court's position in Jeffersonian America. Whatever doubts surround the particular case, the convictions there expressed are those he had long held. As early as the Virginia Ratifying Convention he had contended that "a law not warranted by any of the powers enumerated" would be considered by the judges as "an infringement of the constitution which they are to guard" and, hence, "void."

The argument of *Marbury* v. *Madison* is this: It is the province of the judiciary to say what the law is. Where laws conflict, the judges must decide which one to apply. As the supreme law, the Constitution must be applied by courts in preference to any conflicting law of the legislature. Not to do so would have the political effect of making the Constitution "alterable when the legislature shall please to alter it," and thus an absurd attempt "to limit a power in its own nature illimitable."

Who reading *Marbury* v. *Madison* can deny the rhetorical compulsion of this reasoning? There are, however, difficulties dwelled upon by commentators to this day. Are not the judges' views also susceptible of conflict with the Constitution, of being unconstitutional? Marshall's argument proceeds by pointing to the horrors of "legislative omnipotence." Only inconspicuously are the courts given a potency such that, as mouth of the ruling Constitution, they rule. It won't do to simply affirm that it is the province of courts to construe the law. There is warrant even in Marshall's own views for application of this prerogative only to ordinary or "civil" law, not to great "political laws" like treaties or constitutions. Marshall himself had in *McCulloch* v. *Maryland* distinguished the Constitution from "an ordinary legal code." The judges' authority as to individual rights, after all, does not justify a similar authority as to political fundamentals. If any department must be authoritative on such matters, commentators say, it should be the legislature. The legislature is accustomed to determine matters of policy, is not obliged to wait upon the hazards of private suits, is itself subject to a check: popular election.

There, however, is the rub. The Framers had feared excesses of the legislature, precisely because it of all departments was most influenced by the democratic majority. Indeed the state legislatures had been accustomed to deciding political matters—but too often contrary to individual rights and the public interest. With the excesses under the Articles in mind, it was more "rational," as Hamilton wrote in *Federalist* No. 78, "to suppose that the courts were designed to be an intermediate body between the people and the legislature, in order, among other things, to keep the latter within the limits assigned to their authority." Thus the republicanism implicit in Marshall's argument for judicial review.

For the courts' unique political role they enjoyed unique political advantages. Their selection was by appointment, their tenure for good behavior. All his life Marshall tried to make the judges "perfectly and completely independent." But the dangers to the federal judiciary in Jeffersonian America dictated more than institutional provisions. The courts and especially the Supreme Court had to present a united front. "The harmony of the bench will, I hope & pray, never be disturbed," Marshall wrote to Story in 1821. "We have external & political enemies enough to preserve internal peace."[37] Marshall's deeds in such circumstances bespeak the thoughts never made public.

Frequent rotation of membership, which had dogged the Court before Marshall, ceased. Having had three Chief Justices in eleven years, the Court had Marshall for thirty-four. The Associate Justices' terms also lengthened markedly, if not so strikingly. Most important of all, a stop was put to *seriatim* judgments—whereby each of the justices gave a separate opinion in each case. The significance of this was grasped by Jefferson, who sought all of his life to restore the old way. Also, dissents declined in number, perhaps by Marshall's example. As a rule he would "acquiesce silently" in his brethren's views where different from his own. Henceforth the Court spoke with one strong voice.

Usually the voice was Marshall's. He delivered almost all of the Court's opinions during his first five years as Chief Justice, three fourths during the next seven years, nearly half of all the opinions—and almost all of the greatest constitutional decisions—given during his whole tenure, the longest of any Chief Justice. Those constitutional opinions, political in import if legal in form, were designed as much for political education as for the particular decision. In this new republic, framed according to the best visions of the modern enlightenment, "much of the public happiness" depended on "rescuing public opinion from those numerous prejudices" about it. Marshall's was the legal rhetoric of public enlightenment. "All wrong, all wrong," John Randolph is supposed to have cried despairingly of one Marshallian opinion, "but no man in the United States can tell why or wherein."

[37]*Proceedings*, XIV, 328.

Marshall's most obvious rhetorical theme is the authority, even the sanctity, of law. His grave and deliberate respect for the letter of the law rises to a magisterial reverence where some provision of the Constitution is involved. He repeatedly calls the document "sacred." A similar progress toward awe is evident in his respectful treatment of legislators and especially "those wise and patriotic statesmen and patriots" who framed the Constitution. He gave no hint of noticing Jefferson's thought that ". . . laws and institutions must go hand in hand with progress of the human mind." America could not expect more than the framers gave her. Their work was to be venerated, not controverted. Marshall is in good part responsible for the Americans' reverence for their fundamental law and "Founding Fathers,"—and even for "the cult of the robe." There is one peculiarly telling illustration of his art. The Chief Justice was confronted in one case with a rather ambiguous provision of the Constitution. So strongly did he desire to protect law and Framers from any imputation of error, that he ascribed to the fault itself responsibility for its own appearance. "I feel no diminuition of reverence for the Framers of this sacred instrument, when I say that some ambiguity has found its way into this clause."[38]

There is a deeper lesson in Marshall's rhetoric. It comprises instruction in the whole protective shield of purposes, principles, and judgments which would assure, so far as rhetoric can, a judicious interpretation of our new and complicated institutions. He pointed beyond the law to the justice, and the political and economic system, in the light of which the Constitution must be construed. In *Gibbons* v. *Ogden* he summed up the reason, in an America so influenced by Jefferson's variant of republican enlightenment, for his opinion's length: "Powerful and ingenious minds, taking, as postulates, that the powers expressly granted to the government of the Union are to be contracted by construction into the narrowest possible compass . . . may . . . explain away the constitution of our country, and leave it, a magnificent structure, indeed, to look at, but totally unfit for use. They may . . . obscure principles, which were before thought quite plain, and induce doubts where, if the mind were to pursue its own course, none could be perceived. In such a case, it is peculiarly necessary to recur to safe and fundamental principles to sustain those principles. . . ."

Probably *Marbury* v. *Madison* illustrates Marshall's judicial rhetoric at its most shrewd. His argument presupposes a republican suspicion of excesses by the more democratic legislature—but that suspicion is never explicit. Marshall may indeed be following Hamilton's argument in *Federalist* No. 78. He selects only the most legal portion of No. 78, however, simply affirming interpreta-

---

[38] *United States* v. *Maurice*, 2 Brockenbrough 100 (1823).

tion of the law to be the province of courts. He never calls attention to "ill humours . . . among the people themselves." Why the brevity, the confident brevity, for which Marshall's opinion has occasionally been criticized? "It seems only necessary to recognize certain principles," he writes, "supposed to have been long and well established to decide" the question. Part of the reason surely lies in Marshall's caution before Jeffersonian democracy. He was confronted with a public of various tendencies, favorable and unfavorable. He built his argument into the favorable or liberal side, thus reducing the other or democratic side in spite of itself. The task did not call for the exhaustive discussion which would rouse the democrat's suspicions. It needed simply the memorable inculcation of those principles requiring public belief in order that judicial review be sustained.

It is then the combination of practical judgment and a certain theoretical wisdom that distinguishes Marshall's political thought. This is as it should be. Marshall was a statesman, not a political philosopher. Yet he was a statesman in a regime founded on the doctrines of political philosophers. He guided a practical Court compelled to apply wisely the peculiarly theoretical basis of the first "new nation." The legal form of his thought may even afford the truest perspective for understanding American political thought, revolving as it does about the public law, and the private law, dictated by nature itself.

SELECTED SUGGESTED READINGS

"Answers to Freeholder's Questions," in Albert J. Beveridge, *The Life of John Marshall.* 4 vols. Boston: Houghton, Mifflin, 1916–1919, II, 575–77.

An Autobiographical Sketch. Edited by J. S. Adams. Ann Arbor: University of Michigan Press, 1937.

The Debates in the Several State Conventions on the Adoption of the Federal Constitution. Edited by Jonathan Elliot. 5 vols. Philadelphia: J. B. Lippincott, 1836–1859, III, 222–36, 419–21, 551–62. John Marshall's speeches on the ratification of the Constitution are included in these pages.

The Life of George Washington. 2 vols. Philadelphia: James Crissy and Thomas Cowperthwaite, 1839. See especially the portions treating 1788–1799.

See also the following United States Supreme Court decisions:
   Marbury v. *Madison,* 1 Cranch (U.S.) 137 (1803).
   Fletcher v. *Peck,* 6 Cranch (U.S.) 87 (1810).
   McCulloch v. *Maryland,* 4 Wheaton (U.S.) 316 (1819).
   Dartmouth College v. *Woodward,* 4 Wheaton (U.S.) 518 (1819).
   Cohens v. *Virginia,* 6 Wheaton (U.S.) 264 (1821).

Gibbons v. *Ogden*, 9 Wheaton (U.S.) 1 (1824).
Ogden v. *Saunders*, 12 Wheaton (U.S.) 213 (1827).
Brown v. *Maryland*, 12 Wheaton (U.S.) 419 (1827).
Worcester v. *Georgia*, 6 Peters (U.S.) 515 (1832).
Barron v. *Baltimore*, 7 Peters (U.S.) 243 (1833).

★ JOHN C. CALHOUN   *Ralph Lerner*

The reputation of John C. Calhoun is not an enviable one. Some of his biographers have dealt harshly with him, viewing him with a mixture of awe and disgust. People who know little about him associate his name (not incorrectly) with the defense of slavery, the cry for nullification, and the movement toward secession—none of them honorable causes. Nor do his portraits reveal a sympathetic or congenial character; there is something gloomy, unbending, austere about him. Yet it is not only by virtue of his prominence as a political actor that Calhoun's name commands attention. A further and greater claim to fame is presented in the form of his *Disquisition on Government,* that rarity in American political thought, a work that explicitly declares itself to be a theoretical study of politics. By purporting to give a comprehensive and systematic account, by claiming to have explored new territory beyond the range of American discoveries, Calhoun in effect put his *Disquisition* in a class of which it is almost the sole example: an American political theory.

But this claim to esteem and originality has been disputed; and in the subsequent debates among his interpreters, we have yet to find a satisfactory solution to the problem that Calhoun represented in such clear form. Those who have rated him as a statesman and thinker—be that assessment high or low—and those who have accepted or denied his claim to originality have all failed to solve the peculiar problem of how to study and interpret the writing of a man of theory-and-practice. Until that problem is met, our understanding of the *Disquisition* is not clear and we remain without a way of evaluating Calhoun's merits and originality. How, then, ought Calhoun's *Disquisition,* or his high theoretical pretensions in general, best to be understood? Reducing his theory to practice, or saying in effect that the *Disquisition* was only another string to his pro-slavery bow, forecloses the question of what Calhoun can teach us. Reducing his practice to theory places what is almost a superhuman burden upon a man who was at or near the center of the national political stage for forty tumultuous years. A more moderate procedure would seem to be indicated. The *Disquisition* should be examined as the work of political theory it claims to be. At the same time, free use ought to be made of the practical

SOURCE: Ralph Lerner, "Calhoun's New Science of Politics," *American Political Science Review,* LVII (December 1963), 918–32. This essay has been revised by the author especially for this volume.

political arguments and positions Calhoun adopted over a lifetime of political activity as further indications of his intention and meaning. Following this procedure may help in assessing his stature as a political theorist.

In advancing his claim to the rank of political theorist, Calhoun proposed not only to transcend the practical, but to transcend conventional political theory as well. He would make of politics a science modelled after astronomy: the solid foundation must be some fundamental law, standing in relation to human nature as gravitation does to the material world. This astronomical political science is concerned with facts, with the way in which humans actually behave. In fact, humans behave in a manner that testifies to the primacy of interest or selfishness or self-preservation. That men behave in such a manner is for him the decisive consideration; the praise or blame that we may attach to this behavior is, strictly speaking, beside the point. We legislate, not for man in the abstract or for men in general, but for a particular portion of mankind. The guide for the legislator is not what he thinks men ought to do, but rather his shrewd perception of what actually moves men to act. "We must take human nature as it is, and accommodate our measures to it, instead of making the vain attempt to bend it to our measures."[1] It is, above all, in his *Disquisition,* wherein he hoped to "lay a solid foundation for political Science," that Calhoun strove hardest to emulate his avowed models: Newton, Laplace, Galileo, and Bacon. Calhoun's science is not to be mistaken for an ethics or a particularistic empiricism or an arid "scholastic refinement"; but it may be called metaphysics, if by that we mean as he did the mind's power of reducing a complexity to its elements and of combining these into one harmonious system. The test of a theorist that Calhoun would have applied to himself is the extent to which he can prepare the way for a *science* of politics, one that goes beyond "a mere observation of insulated facts." He will have met the severest test—and, incidentally, have laid claim to "the highest attribute of the human mind"—if, heedless of the "senseless cry of metaphysics," he succeeds in formulating scientific laws adapted to "the high purpose of political science and legislation."

But what precisely is that purpose? The analogy to astronomy fails us. Calhoun spoke of the latter as "that noble science which displays to our admiration the system of the universe." But for Calhoun, as for any man not utterly removed from the stuff of political life, the end of his theorizing about

[1]References are to *The Works of John C. Calhoun,* ed. Richard K. Crallé (6 vols.; Columbia, S. C., and New York, 1851–55), I, 1, 3; II, 182 (1817), 648 (1837). Hereafter cited as *Works.* Volume I consists of *A Disquisition on Government* and *A Discourse on the Constitution and Government of the United States,* two posthumously published writings on which Calhoun worked intermittently during the last few years of his life. Where the reference is to the other five volumes of this edition, I have added the year of publication or delivery, since Crallé's order is not strictly chronological. Unless otherwise noted, all italics in quotations are in the original.

politics was not a theory that displays to our admiration the system of the political universe, but rather a theory that directs itself to political practice. It is without any sense of self-contradiction or confusion that Calhoun could begin with a political science, patterned after astronomy or chemistry and whose first premise is the self-interested behavior of men, and end by asserting that enlisting "the individual on the side of the social feelings to promote the good of the whole, is the greatest possible achievement of the science of government."[2] How did he move between these two points?

I

The beginning of political science lies in a fundamental understanding of the "matter" of politics—human nature. Calhoun began by making two assumptions, regarding both as incontestable. First, that man's "inclinations and wants, physical and moral, irresistibly impel him to associate with his kind; and he has, accordingly, never been found, in any age or country, in any state other than the social." Second, that "while man is so constituted as to make the social state necessary to his existence and the full development of his faculties, this state itself cannot exist without government. The assumption rests on universal experience." Calhoun suggested that man's association with his fellows is due at least in part to a subrational drive. In any event, neither society nor government is a matter of choice for man. Both are necessary for the bare existence, let alone the perfection or full development, of the human kind; they are "equally of Divine ordination." Man's natural state is social or, rather, political.[3]

The question remains: why is the existence of society and government no more a matter of volition than is breathing? How does the nature of man dictate such arrangements? Calhoun does say that man has natural feelings of sympathy for his fellows, but these social feelings are subordinate to his selfish feelings. In the *Disquisition* (though not in the *South Carolina Exposition* of 1828), he avoided the expression "selfish feelings" because, "as commonly used," it carries an inference of "something depraved and vicious." For Calhoun, however, "selfish" did not connote vice. Like the Framers of the American Constitution, who "understood profoundly the nature of man and of government," Calhoun recognized that our nature remains "unchanged by change of condition." Selfishness, like gravitation, is one of the facts of the world and hence part of that science which would explain the world. There

[2] *Works*, I, 70; II, 232–33 (1833). "Correspondence of John C. Calhoun," ed. J. Franklin Jameson, *Annual Report of the American Historical Association for the Year 1899*, Vol. II (Washington, 1900), p. 768 (1849). Hereafter cited as *Correspondence*.
[3] *Works*, I, 2, 5, 8; IV, 509–10 (1848).

are, to be sure, exceptions—"few," "extraordinary" exceptions—but these only prove the rule. A mother's subordination of her individual feelings to those of her infant is due to one of those "peculiar relations"; then, again, there are "peculiar constitutions" over which education and habit have singular effect. A science may admit of such exceptions without undermining the generality and force of its most fundamental law: the predominance of "the selfish passions of our nature," which are "planted in our bosom for our individual safety." We have, in fact, arrived at a law not merely of human life, but of all animated existence, throughout its entire range, so far as our knowledge extends. It would, indeed, seem to be essentially connected with the great law of self-preservation which pervades all that feels, from man down to the lowest and most insignificant reptile or insect. In none is it stronger than in man.[4]

The fundamental fact of human life is not distinctively human; the law upon which a science of politics will be erected points to man's subrational part, to the part that makes him brother to the beast. If man has foresight, its effect is to enable him to fear more and hence to be more, and more intelligently, concerned with self-preservation than any lower animal could be. Calhoun allowed that, given certain preconditions, men's social feelings might grow. In no case, however—even assuming safety, abundance, and "high intellectual and moral culture"—could this "all-pervading and essential law" of self-preservation be overpowered. The social feelings, as indeed the very conditions in which they thrive, are of only limited effect. There is a passing suggestion that Calhoun found it easier to conceive of a human devoid of any social feeling than to imagine one in whom sympathy for his fellows outweighed or perhaps even equalled his selfish feelings. The predominance of selfishness is seen as necessary for the preservation of a being such as man with "limited reason and faculties." Of this, at least, Calhoun was certain: that "self-preservation is the supreme law, as well with communities as individuals." In developing both his theoretical teaching and his practical program, he always bore in mind what he took to be "the strongest passions of the human heart,—avarice, ambition, and rivalry."[5]

In the course of a long digression that interrupts the *Disquisition's* discussion of liberty and governmental power, the argument is made that a pre-social state is "purely hypothetical." "Instead of being the natural state of man, it is, of all conceivable states, the most opposed to his nature—most repugnant to his feelings, and most incompatible with his wants."[6] We are hardly surprised, however—considering Calhoun's "psychology"—to find many, if not all, of

---

[4] *Works*, I, 2–4; II, 63 (1814); VI, 53 (1828).

[5] *Works*, I, 4–5, 10, 47; VI, 202 (1832). However, there appear to be such things as "too concentrated" affections and too predominant a regard for self-interest. See Calhoun's condemnation of Webster and of the Northern states. *Works*, III, 287 (1838); IV, 386 (1847).

[6] *Works*, I, 58; see also *Works*, IV, 509–10 (1848); VI, 221–22 (1843); *Correspondence*, p. 758 (1848).

the inconveniences of the state of nature appearing in the social, pre-governmental stage of human development. Our natural inclination to give greater weight to our selfish feelings than to "what affects us indirectly through others"[7] produces "the tendency to a universal state of conflict, between individual and individual; accompanied by the connected passions of suspicion, jealousy, anger and revenge,—followed by insolence, fraud and cruelty." Unchecked, the result of such a tendency can only be the destruction of social life and of the "ends for which it is ordained." For Calhoun, we may say, society was intended to secure not mere life, but a fully human life. In analogous, but subordinate, fashion, government seeks not only to "preserve" or "protect" society, but to "perfect" it. Both society and government, as already noted, are divinely ordained, and in the assignment of such states to man, Calhoun saw another manifestation of the Creator's "infinite wisdom and goodness."[8] But if the easy necessity that impels man to seek his own kind and to form government is a sign of God's goodness, the difficult option of controlling the governors through some kind of constitution is perhaps a sign that God's goodness is incomplete.[9] The governors, Calhoun believed, are no better than those they govern and for that very reason require a check upon their tendency to aggrandize themselves at the expense of their fellows. The ultimate perfection of God's handiwork lies in the hands of man.

On first thought, we might suppose that the need for this ultimate perfection is limited. Savages require government, but hardly stand in need of that government which perfects society, namely constitutional government. Simple societies, with the requisite political intelligence and while still in a relatively natural and undifferentiated condition, can control their governors through the operations of simple majorities. What "has thus far exceeded human wisdom, and possibly ever will"—a perfect constitution holding the government to its proper ends—does not appear to be a need of every place and every age. This supposition, however, is undermined by Calhoun's reexamination of the problem. Governmental powers necessarily entail opportunities for private aggrandizement. Men's finite capacities and great diversities,[10] and various other causes, lead to the formation of independent

---

[7] *Works*, I, 2–3, 4. Such is Calhoun's careful circumlocution for sympathetic or social feeling. Our regard for others is ultimately a regard for self.

[8] The emphatic distinction of social and political states replaces the "state of nature—civil society" dichotomy of the modern natural rights teachers. At this stage of the argument one can only suspect that Calhoun wrought this change less with a view to building a doctrine that vested associations of men with a right of revolution than to avoiding the premise of natural egalitarianism.

[9] Calhoun used such terms as "the Creator" or "the Infinite" or "Providence" in the *Disquisition*. The sole mention of "God" there occurs when the concurrent voice of a people is called *"the voice of God." Works*, I, 39. On Calhoun's avoidance of this name, see Gerald M. Capers, *John C. Calhoun—Opportunist: A Reappraisal* (Gainesville, Florida, 1960), p. 17 (note).

[10] In this connection Calhoun mentioned "language, customs, pursuits, situation, and complexion." This is the only direct reference to color in the *Disquisition. Works*, I, 9.

communities. Among these communities there is the same "tendency to a universal state of conflict" that Calhoun discovered in the ungoverned human association. For Calhoun, as for Publius, it was "a sort of axiom in politics, that vicinity, or nearness of situation, constitutes nations natural enemies."[11] Because war is always a possibility, domestic aggrandizement is always a possibility. The community's self-preservation takes precedence over "every other consideration." A government that must be strong enough to ward off foreign dangers, by that very fact forms a domestic danger. The need for constitutional government is one that necessarily develops out of human society.[12]

However persistent the need for constitutional government might be, its founding and perpetuation are matters of the greatest difficulty and rarity. Calhoun never tired of reiterating his contention that chance and circumstances are of decisive importance. An insufficient regard for the prerequisites of constitutional government might lead to the subversion of such a government as had been formed "by some good fortune." This is not to say that a sufficient regard for the prerequisites of constitutional government would be enough to establish such a government. Neither is it to say that theoretical understanding is superfluous. Indeed, it would be difficult to understand the intention, form, and style of the *Disquisition* on any such premise. But it is to maintain that Calhoun's highest political teaching rests on or presupposes "some fortunate combination of circumstances." Two of the hallmarks of constitutional governments, setting them apart from the various absolute forms, are "complexity and difficulty of construction." In even more marked form than Burke—"the wisest of modern statesmen"—Calhoun belittled the efficacy of human understanding in meeting and solving major political problems. He saw but two ways in which constitutional governments, of whatever form, might be constructed, and in neither instance was as much due to wisdom and patriotism as to "favorable combinations of circumstances." In most cases, constitutional governments are the unforeseen result of the struggles of warring interests; thanks to "some fortunate turn," an unremitting civil war is avoided and each of the belligerent parties is given "a separate and distinct voice in the government." Necessity prevails where human sagacity fails.

The other, less frequent way in which such governments have been formed is not essentially different from the first: "fortunate circumstances, acting in conjunction with some pressing danger," have compelled men to adopt constitutional governments with their eyes open as a desperate move to avoid chaos. Even if we grant that it is within the grasp of the human mind

---

[11] *The Federalist*, ed. Jacob E. Cooke (Cleveland, 1961), No. 6, p. 35.
[12] *Works*, I, 2, 4–10, 42–43, 52.

or human minds to know thoroughly the character, needs, and interests of a particular advanced community and to construct a suitable constitutional government for that people, its adoption by that people is problematic. Necessity prevails where the persuasive power of wisdom fails. The conclusion remains: "Such governments have been, emphatically, the product of circumstances."[13] If Calhoun, like a proud Bacon, now grasped a truth that others had only on occasion stumbled upon, he also, like an unpresumptuous Burke, ultimately had to rely upon the workings of fortunate historical accidents.

Not only is Fortune's realm expanded, but there is also some contraction in the task assigned or assignable to education. We have already noted Calhoun's judgment that it is only in men of "peculiar constitutions" that education and habituation have sufficient force to enable social feelings to overpower selfish ones. The general rule is unshaken. The deepest stratum of human nature remains unchanging and unchangeable, beyond the reach of education or, indeed, of civilization. A free press, for example, may do much to enlighten men and meliorate society; "far less power" may be needed for governing as men learn that they can safely enlarge their social feelings and restrain their individual feelings. But men would not be changed in the most fundamental sense: men still would need governing, and governing still would require power. It is this power over men that forms the core of the political problem. In the absence of a constitutional check to the exercise of political power—that is, in the absence of some form of concurrent majority rule—the mere use of such power is corrupting. "Neither religion nor education can counteract the strong tendency of the numerical majority to corrupt and debase the people."

Calhoun developed an elaborate argument in support of a system of peaceable and effective resistance to the abuse of power. Not the least part of that argument is the attempt to show the whole train of consequences for public and private morals that follows from the alternative modes of organizing government. Calhoun looked forward to a governmental structure that would reinforce, or at least not undermine, the formation of good character. "For of all the causes which contribute to form the character of a people, those by which power, influence, and standing in the government are most certainly and readily obtained, are, by far, the most powerful." The "talented and aspiring" crave for these objects, take due note of the means of securing them, and "assiduously" cultivate those means. The alternative paths to the desired respect and admiration are marked with Calhoun's favorite colors—white and

---

[13] *Works,* I, 13, 31, 77–79; III, 591 (1841). For similar judgments of the American Constitution, see *Works,* I, 199; IV, 99 (1842), 417 (1848). The establishment of the Roman tribunate is called both "wise" and "fortunate." In neither Rome nor Britain did the warring interests have "any conception of the principles involved, or the consequences to follow, beyond the immediate objects in contemplation." *Works,* I, 96, 104.

black. Knowledge, wisdom, patriotism, and virtue contend with cunning, fraud, treachery, and party devotion. There is no indication that the "youths who crowd our colleges" would find anything as convincing as a formula for success that works. Virtue appears to be almost entirely imitative; its utility may be persuasive, but hardly its beauty.[14] "The great principle of demand and supply governs the moral and intellectual world no less than the business and commercial."[15] What the science of politics has to teach is not so much edifying as useful. Calhoun's science takes men as they are and then proceeds to lead them, indeed not directly to the goal of an enlightened and civically virtuous populace actively laboring for the public good, but indirectly— through a balance of powers—to the regulated actions and controlled consequences that to some extent free men from their baser impulses.

The clearest evidence that Calhoun thus deliberately narrowed the scope of political science merits full quotation:

. . . By what means can government, without being divested of the full command of the resources of the community, be prevented from abusing its powers?

The question involves difficulties which, from the earliest ages, wise and good men have attempted to overcome;—but hitherto with but partial success. For this purpose many devices have been resorted to, suited to the various stages of intelligence and civilization through which our race has passed, and to the different forms of government to which they have been applied. The aid of superstition, ceremonies, education, religion, organic arrangements, both of the government and the community, has been, from time to time, appealed to. Some of the most remarkable of these devices, whether regarded in reference to their wisdom and the skill displayed in their application, or to the permanency of their effects, are to be found in the early dawn of civilization;—in the institutions of the Egyptians, the Hindoos, the Chinese, and the Jews. The only materials which that early age afforded for the construction of constitutions, when intelligence was so partially diffused, were applied with consummate wisdom and skill. To their successful application may be fairly traced the subsequent advance of our race in civilization and intelligence, of which we now enjoy the benefits. For without a constitution . . . there can be little progress or permanent improvement.

In answering the important question under consideration, it is not necessary to enter into an examination of the various contrivances adopted by these celebrated governments to counteract this tendency to disorder and abuse, nor to undertake to treat of constitution in its most comprehensive sense. What I propose is far more limited,—to explain on what principles government must be formed, in order to resist, by its own interior structure,—or, to use a single term, *organism,*—the tendency to abuse of power. This structure, or organism, is what is meant by constitution, in its strict and more usual sense. . . . It is in this strict and more usual sense that I propose to use the term hereafter.[16]

---

[14]Compare Alexis de Tocqueville, *Democracy in America,* II, Part ii, Chapter 8.

[15]*Works,* I, 3, 50–51, 74–75; III, 116–17 (1837). In the context of the last citation, the banking system is attacked for "concentrating in itself most of the prizes of life—wealth, honor, and influence—to the great disparagement and degradation of all the liberal, and useful, and generous pursuits of society. The rising generation cannot but feel its deadening influence."

[16]*Works,* I, 10–11.

Calhoun kept his word: the other four devices are not themes of the *Disquisition.* The core of Calhoun's science of government—indeed, by far its largest part—is what he called an "organic arrangement." Let us return, however, to the quoted paragraphs, some of whose most striking features are also the most puzzling. We had at first entertained the supposition that a perfect constitution was a luxury of sorts, that only men in a highly civilized, that is, "artificial," condition stood in need of it. That suggestion seemed to be untenable in view of the accumulation of power—and hence possibilities for the abuse of power—made necessary by the omnipresent threat of external danger. Now we learn that the concern with a perfect constitution has occupied the thoughts of the wise and the good "from the earliest ages." The devices and applications most worthy of note are located "in the early dawn of civilization," before the darkness of barbarism had been dissipated and while intelligence was the preserve of a few. We marvel at these ancient lawgivers, whose names Calhoun either did not know or would not disclose.[17] Their success may have been partial, but they apparently were successful. We are puzzled by their success. Did the founders of these "celebrated governments" succeed because of, or in spite of, the rude character of their people? If the latter, there are perhaps some valuable lessons yet to be gleaned from their institutions.[18] If the former, we owe them a nod of thanks and little more. Calhoun's procedure in the *Disquisition* leaves us in no doubt of what his answer was. He did not find it necessary to even "enter into an examination" of these "remarkable" devices of remote antiquity. The success of the ancient legislators depended as much upon the general backwardness of the times as upon the legislators' wisdom and skill. Accordingly, our interest in them can be little more than antiquarian. True, our progress beyond those ancient peoples is due in no small part to them, but the very success of the early lawgivers has made obsolete most of the devices to which they had recourse.[19] Today's man-in-the-street is more knowing than his forefather in the woods. Superstition, ceremonies, education, and religion

---

[17]Calhoun went to some lengths to avoid using any individual's proper name in the *Disquisition.* Consider, for example, the highly abstract account of English history. *Works,* I, 99–100.

[18]*The Federalist* reached back to Minos (see No. 38); Calhoun cast his net wider, but never mentioned the Greeks in the *Disquisition.* The Romans, from whose institutions lessons *are* drawn, apparently belong to a later stage.

[19]Now, as always, a disproportionately large share of wealth is given to the nonproducing classes. But the "brute force and gross superstition of ancient times" have been supplanted by the "subtle and artful fiscal contrivances of modern." *Works,* II, 631 (1837). A reversion to barbarism is out of the question for Calhoun. While commerce diffuses the blessings of civilization and printing preserves and diffuses knowledge, the military applications of steam and gunpowder have "for ever" assured the ascendancy of civilized communities. *Works,* I, 62, 87–88. On the relation of manufacturing to the moral and political progress of civilization, see *Works,* IV, 103 (1842), 184 (1842), 283–84 (1846); VI, 92 (1831). One of the two examples of impiety mentioned in the *Disquisition* is doubting that the discoveries and inventions of technology will "greatly improve the condition of man ultimately." *Works,* I, 89.

cannot deter him from the shrewd perception of his selfish interest in the market place of ambition. His manners are less rude, but he is cagier.

For Calhoun, no less than for Publius, the science of politics was susceptible to great improvement. Publius saw that progress in the moderns' understanding of various principles "which were either not known at all, or imperfectly known to the ancients." At the same time, he was far from rejecting the use of devices that Calhoun seemed to consider as no longer of consequence.[20] For Calhoun, man's progress consists less in the discovery of wholly new principles of political life than in the outgrowing of some old devices of governance and the adaptation of another. What first appears as a sloughing off of outmoded and outgrown restrictions turns out to be a more complex and artificial elaboration of the "old and clumsy, but approved mode of checking power, in order to prevent or correct abuses."[21]

This mechanistic device of resisting power by power and tendency by tendency, on which Calhoun's entire system rested, cannot be instituted in a mechanical fashion. There are prerequisites to the formation of constitutional government, and of these Calhoun held the principal to be the right of popular suffrage. "When this right is properly guarded, and the people sufficiently enlightened to understand their own rights and the interests of the community, and duly to appreciate the motives and conduct of those appointed to make and execute the laws," suffrage may suffice to control the governors.[22] The psychological premises of the *Disquisition* do not require that the degree of popular enlightenment be very great. It suffices that the people understand that irresponsible rulers endanger what affects them directly (private rights) and what affects them indirectly through others (community interests).

But while suffrage is effective in holding rulers to account, it does not even begin to solve the problem of oppressive government for any but "small communities, during the early stages of their existence," while these are still in a relatively natural—that is, poor, unrefined, simple—condition. In all other

---

[20] *The Federalist*, No. 9, p. 51; No. 49, p. 340.

[21] *Works*, I, 10–11, 42; VI, 85 (1831).

[22] Calhoun's firm adherence to the language of rights deserves at least passing notice. While he denied that a numerical majority could conclude for an entire people, he was far from denying the "rights, powers, and immunities of the whole people" or that "the people are the source of all power; and that their authority is paramount over all." *Works*, I, 30; VI, 226 (1843). If one regards man in "what is called the state of nature," he will be found to have rights and duties deduced from the faculties and endowments common to the human race as a whole. "All natural rights are individual rights, and belong to them as such. They appertain neither to majorities nor minorities. On the contrary, all political rights are conventional." This is the teaching of "Locke, Sydney, and other writers on the side of liberty," whose doctrines "fortunately for us . . . became the creed of our ancestors." When *"the right of revolution"* is properly invoked, it is a case of individuals resuming their natural rights, "which, however restricted or modified they may be, in the political state, are never extinguished." *Works*, VI, 138 (1831), 221–22 (1843), 226 (1843), 230 (1843), 269 (1846).

cases, where the motives for the oppressive use of governmental power are considerably enhanced, the "organism" of concurrent consent is needed to complete, or rather to form, constitutional government.[23] Such an organism presupposes "the different interests, portions, or classes of the community, to be sufficiently enlightened to understand its character and object." The *Disquisition on Government* might be said to be a work of popular enlightenment in this sense. It is hardly far-fetched to surmise that Calhoun believed the United States of 1850 to stand in "some pressing danger" that might force the adoption of what he defined to be constitutional government.[24] If his estimate of the shortcomings of human sagacity in coping with chance and circumstance was correct, it nonetheless did not preclude his own desperate efforts. Fortune seemed most apt to smile on men standing at the precipice's edge.

II

The *Disquisition on Government* consists of a critique and a proposal. The full dimensions of the proposal can be perceived only in the light of the critique. In its barest formulation, the critique is this: representative government, when most perfectly realized, partakes of all the vices of a pure democracy. This is precisely the point denied by the defenders of the American Constitution; indeed, the contrary proposition was, in their eyes, one of the Constitution's most considerable advantages. "The true distinction between [the ancient republics] and the American governments, lies *in the total exclusion of the people in their collective capacity* from any share in the *latter. . . .*"[25] One senses the full measure of Calhoun's undertaking when one recognizes that he was calling not so much for the reform of constitutional government in America as for its refounding. Stated most radically, the United States have not yet had a fully constitutional government. If such a government, strictly understood, would once have been an unnecessary complication, that hardly could be said to be the case today (1850). The critical fact of political life is the diversity of interests within the community. "It is so in all; the small and the great,—the poor and the rich,—irrespective of pursuits, productions, or degrees of civilization. . . ." As a result of such diversity, governmental actions, however equitable "on their face," necessarily have unequal effects. This inequality is a universal phenomenon; it is only the degree of inequality and oppressiveness that varies.

---

[23]"The numerical majority, *perhaps*, should *usually* be one of the elements of a constitutional democracy. . . ." *Works*, I, 45. Italics supplied. In the Senate, Calhoun said that he did not object to the preponderance of the numerical majority in the American government, but to its "subjecting the whole, in time, to its unlimited sway." *Works*, IV, 92 (1842). The *Disquisition's* argument, though cautiously stated, spells out the implications of these earlier remarks.

[24] *Works*, I, 12–13, 26, 42–43, 78–79.

[25] *The Federalist*, No. 63, p. 428.

A necessary consequence of the ordinary operations of government is that the community as a whole is divided into tax-payers and tax-consumers. In effect, these "portions," "classes," "interests," "divisions," or "orders" are at war. Under the best of circumstances, the one's gain is the other's loss. What, then, can be expected from the ordinary unchecked actions of men as they are if not systematic aggrandizement by one group or party at the expense of the other? Publius' statelier prose exactly conveys Calhoun's own position: "If the impulse and the opportunity be suffered to coincide, we well know that neither moral nor religious motives can be relied on as an adequate control."[26]

The traditional distinctions between government of the one, the few, and the many are irrelevant here: in the absence of a constitution (in Calhoun's sense), all rulers oppress their subjects. Restated in purely American terms, Calhoun's critique was an extensive commentary upon, and correction of, *The Federalist's* remedy for the "diseases most incident to republican government." It is a characteristic of popular government that natural groupings are allowed to assume political importance; there is no veneer of artificial classes or orders to conceal the natural variety of interests "resulting from diversity of pursuits, condition, situation and character of different portions of the people,—and from the action of the government itself." Publius seized upon this fact and developed safeguards that work, if anything, too well. He diagnosed the critical disease to be majority faction and prescribed a specific for it. But in seeking to eliminate one strain of the tyrannical virus—the unmitigated rule of the natural majority—he disarmed the community in the face of another strain—the unmitigated rule of the artificial majority centering about the control of government itself. No provision had been made for the disease of party.[27]

Calhoun's reputation as a political theorist rests largely on his analysis of the problem posed by party and his proposed solution of it. His consideration of political parties led him, on the one hand, to develop his views within the larger context of the problem of identifying the common good and, on the other, to pay especial attention to the particular question of class conflict. While the *Disquisition* offers alternative suggestions of the ways in which parties arise, in each case the concept of party remains the same. For Calhoun, the political party was simply an instrument by which men sought to capture the control of the government and its patronage. His first explanation traces the genesis of party to that natural diversity of interests and consequent conflict which he saw as the critical and universal fact of social life. Where the control of government is determined solely by the right of suffrage, the strug-

---

[26] *The Federalist*, No. 10, p. 61.
[27] *Works*, I, 13–15, 19–25, 37, 43, 61, 80.

gle of interests takes the form of alliances to create or maintain a majority. Party conflict is thus the inevitable consequence of government by numerical majority.

A more radical formulation is then suggested. Even if one were to posit an entirely homogeneous community, without any diversity of interests or inequality of condition, the mere fact of numerical majority rule would suffice to bring parties into existence. "The advantages of possessing the control of the powers of the government, and, thereby, of its honors and emoluments, are, of themselves, exclusive of all other considerations, ample to divide even such a community into two great hostile parties." Governmental action or, what was its equivalent for Calhoun, the advantage of possessing governmental power leads to conflict and finally to the formation of parties. The principle of concurrent majority rule rests on this unavoidable diversity of interests, from which even our hypothetical homogeneous community is not immune. There are *always* at least two portions or interests in the community: the ins and the outs.

Calhoun also traced the origin of parties to the need, "in the present condition of the world," for protection against external dangers.[28] The threat of such dangers gives rise to large defense establishments and even bigger government. The result is "sufficient to excite profoundly the ambition of the aspiring and the cupidity of the avaricious." It is not surprising that Calhoun saw unremitting and violent party conflict as the ultimate result, considering that he regarded these "most powerful passions of the human heart" as being beyond the reach of time, reflection, reason, discussion, entreaty, or remonstrance. Nor is there cause to wonder that he regarded the handiwork of the Founding Fathers as being deficient in the decisive respect. Calhoun's message seems to be that even if the poor should not always be with us, the same cannot be said of patronage and the pork barrel. Until the problem of "party-usage" is met and solved, none of the auxiliary protections and parchment barriers will prove of any avail. The task remains to form a constitutional government.[29]

It may be granted that the mere possession of governmental power creates an interest and party in opposition to those who have none. And yet the question remains: would such a government party interest suffice to keep the ins in? Would not an appeal have to be made, beyond an even numerous group of job-holders, to a still larger constituency? To embrace a majority of the whole electorate, would not the ruling party have to adopt a policy of system-

---

[28]Even here Calhoun successfully resisted using the word "nation."

[29]*Works,* I, 16–18, 28, 33–34, 47; II, 245–46 (1833); VI, 202 (1832). Calhoun believed that the Americans are "greatly distinguished by the love of acquisition—I will not call it avarice—and the love of honorable distinction." The causes of these propensities are traced in an interesting speech in favor of increased compensation for members of Congress. *Works,* II, 182 (1817).

atic favoritism to a coalition of interests with something in common (say, a desire to promote home manufactures), with the consequent chance to exploit a minority with an opposite interest? Calhoun's notion of a governmental policy that benefits a majority at the expense of a minority seems to presuppose two elements of society so differently circumstanced that such a policy, in matching one set of interests, necessarily crosses the other. Underlying Calhoun's majorities and minorities are some grand divisions of society; party organizations do not simply supersede these natural divisions. If this is the case, Calhoun's critique of *The Federalist* may be restated. Publius assumed that a large republic splinters interests, so that none can rule solely in its own behalf. He erred in this, for the splinters—amounting to a majority—will discover a common interest that was really there all the while, but temporarily obscured by lesser differences. This majority will quickly discover a common interest that *government can promote* at the expense of the rest of society.

The case against party conflicts and numerical majority rule that is presented in the *Disquisition* appears to be quite independent of the bitter sectional disputes of the 1840s and 1850s. At least we must concede that the arguments cut deeper than the dominance of the North in the American political system. The right of a minority to transform itself into a majority and turn the rascals out was, Calhoun argued, only the right to be aggrandized and to aggrandize in turn. The contingency that marks one party's monopoly of power, far from moderating its tendency to be abusive, only heightens it.[30] In an effort to retain its advantages as long as possible, a party will "concentrate the control over its movements in fewer and fewer hands." Government by party leads inexorably to government by party leaders. Partisan fidelity and zeal are secured by party organization, caucuses, and discipline, but above all by patronage, "on which, in turn, depends that powerful, active and mercenary corps of expectants, created by the morbid moneyed action of the Government." In time, political parties must degenerate into factions, competing with one another in "gross appeals to the appetites of the lowest and most worthless portions of the community." Social sympathies are destroyed, and the good of the party places the good of the community in total eclipse. Finally, party strife is nothing less than *the* corrupter of communal life, poisoning the very wells of public and private morality. Not even what Calhoun admitted to be "a new and important political element"—a free press devoted to both edifying and reflecting public opinion—could counteract the baneful effects of party.[31]

Calhoun spoke often and clearly—and at length—about "the different interests, portions, or classes of the community," and occasionally, but ob-

---

[30] *Works*, I, 23–24. This important proposition is asserted, but not defended or elaborated.
[31] *Works*, I, 40–42, 47–50, 73–76; VI, 200 (1832).

scurely, about "the common interests of the whole." Parties are condemned, not because they promote the interests of the part over the whole, or because they cater to man's selfish rather than social feelings, but because they do so excessively, unreasonably, perhaps even unnaturally. A party does ill when the mere machinery of getting and holding power dictates its objects and procedures, or when it may with impunity prescribe a governmental policy that unjustly overrides the claims of other parties, or when it embitters conflicts to the point that men no longer recognize any minimal common grounds. One cannot help being puzzled by Calhoun's notion of the common good. While it is the criterion by which he justified his proposed solution of the problem of party—the system of concurrent consent—it is by no means certain what he understood by the good or interest of the community or, for that matter, by the community itself, "Where the organism is perfect, every interest will be truly and fully represented, and *of course* the whole community must be so."[32] The community's interest is the sum of all its particular interests: the whole appears to be defined in terms of its parts. We wonder how the parts themselves are defined; we wonder what constitutes an "interest."

Calhoun rejected an infinite regress by which the sense of every portion would be determined by the concurrent majority of *its* parts. Within each portion the numerical majority would rule.[33] This is not to assume internally homogeneous portions, but rather the presence of an interest that overrides many lesser interests. Whatever diversity of interests there may be within a given minority portion, all the people of that portion have the same interest "against that of all others, and, of course, the government itself." Just as control of the government in order to determine a line of policy dictates a combination of kindred interests into a single ruling majority, so does effective opposition dictate a combination of kindred elements left out of the government (and adversely affected by it) into one or a few counterforces. Political power is to be won or lost. With those alternatives before them, the lesser interests are forced to distinguish between minor wishes and essentials. The presumed hostility of every other portion serves to delimit the area within which a set of interest groups and individuals might trust the rule of a numerical majority "with confidence" that their several interests will not be abused. For Calhoun there was no whole transcending its parts. He went even further. Speaking of the larger community, he suggested that the requirements of constitutionalism (as he understood it) would largely be met if the concurrent consent were limited to "a few great and prominent interests only." Here again there is

[32]*Works*, I, 26, 69. Italics supplied.
[33]However, in his *Discourse on the Constitution and Government of the United States*, Calhoun did suggest a way of taking the concurrent consent of "the more strongly marked interests" of each of the several states. *Works*, I, 397.

assumed a kind of combined partial interest that overrides many lesser interests.[34] It is surely remarkable that Calhoun studiously avoided carrying this
line of reasoning to what others chose to call "the nation." The only exception
is when the larger community's very existence must be defended; then, and
only then, must "every other consideration" yield.[35] The sole suggestion of an
overarching common interest concerns the preservation of a system that allows particular interests to express themselves. It appears that men are to be
prepared to lay down their lives, not for a nation, but for a process of government.

The principle by which constitutional governments are said to be preserved is compromise. In this they are distinguished sharply from all forms of
absolute government, whose conservative principle, according to Calhoun, is
force. It is clear that in constitutional governments each interest or portion has
a negative by which it can protect itself against the predatory designs and
interests of others. What is not clear is the source of the various groups' desire
to compromise. The answer Calhoun offered is simple, if not altogether satisfying. The effect of the various groups' possession of a veto power is to cause
them

to desist from attempting to adopt any measure calculated to promote the properity
of one, or more, by sacrificing that of others; and thus to force them to unite in such
measures only as would promote the prosperity of all, as the only means to prevent the
suspension of the action of the government;—and, thereby, to avoid anarchy, the
greatest of all evils. . . .
    It would, perhaps, be more strictly correct to trace the conservative principle of
constitutional governments to the necessity which compels the different interests, or
portions, or orders, to compromise,—as the only way to promote their respective
prosperity, and to avoid anarchy,—rather than to the compromise itself. No necessity
can be more urgent and imperious, than that of avoiding anarchy. It is the same as that
which makes government indispensable to preserve society; and is not less imperative
than that which compels obedience to superior force. Traced to this source, the voice
of a people,—uttered under the necessity of avoiding the greatest of calamities, through
the organs of a government so constructed as to suppress the expression of all partial
and selfish interests, and to give a full and faithful utterance to the sense of the whole
community, in reference to its common welfare,—may, without impiety, be called *the
voice of God*. To call any other so, would be impious.[36]

We may wonder at the aplomb with which compromise, so understood,
is contrasted with force. Does not this compromise, too, rest on a kind of force?
A dread of impending anarchy compels the groups to compromise and forces
them to unite. (This is not to deny that there is a difference—and an important
one—between an absolute government's force, which acts solely *from* the

---

[34]The principal safeguard of these lesser interests appears to be their pettiness, because of
which they can never be desirable objects of plunder.
[35]*Works*, I, 10, 26–28, 36–37, 60.
[36]*Works*, I, 37–39.

separate interest of one side *on* the interest of the other, and the necessity that forces to a compromise, making *each* party sacrifice part of its purpose for an object that *both* recognize as valuable to themselves.) We may be totally incredulous on learning now that constitutional government suppresses the expression of partial interests while giving voice to the sense of the whole community. Has Calhoun not taught us that the sense of the whole community is nothing but the sum of all partial and selfish interests? Calhoun's system rests upon the expression, not the suppression, of these interests; he was very far from "making the vain attempt" to bend human nature to his measures. If he expected government by the concurrent majority to produce harmony rather than discord, it was because under that system a great deal of controversial business would be removed from central control. In an effort to check encroachments on local concerns, lesser interests within a minority will find a common ground of resistance: the preservation and enlargement of the sphere of individual rights and liberties. The effect is to restrict the government to "its primary end,—the protection of the community," the business of internal and external security. The latter, of course, is precisely the kind of activity concerning which we might expect to find a compelling common interest and a reasonable prospect of compromise.[37]

The old science of politics, while not unaware of the important and even profound differences that divided men, never ceased emphasizing those interests that all men in the community shared and the common good that they esteemed. This traditional teaching is identified in the *Disquisition* as the erroneous premise of numerical majority rule and the remote cause of the eclipse of the common good. By mistakenly regarding all men as sharing the same interests and then offering the control of the government as the grand prize, the system of numerical majority rule *insures* that men's desire for honors and emoluments will turn them into bitter rivals "waging, under the forms of law, incessant hostilities against each other." The new science of politics starts from the opposite premise. By regarding all men as being interested, above everything else, in preserving what is peculiarly their own, the system of concurrent majority rule places men in a position where they can afford to conciliate one another. On second thought, they cannot afford *not* to conciliate. "Each [interest or portion] sees and feels that it can best promote its own prosperity by conciliating the good-will, and promoting the prosperity of the others." Out of the mass of particular and conflicting interests, there emerges a true community of interests; "there would be patriotism, nationality,[38] harmony, and a struggle only for supremacy in promoting the common

[37] *Works,* I, 36–37, 59–61; II, 648 (1837).
[38] "Nationality" is mentioned twice again in the *Disquisition,* when praising the Roman and British constitutions. *Works,* I, 104–5.

good of the whole." Love emerges as a by-product of a "process." Love emerges for that which makes it possible for each interest to preserve itself comfortably—namely, a process of government. It is that process which turns out to be the common interest, the common good.

Calhoun went to some pains to show that the process of concurrent majority rule was not impracticable. More narrowly, the question is whether one does well to rely upon a disposition to harmonize that is said to lead to unanimity. Calhoun's answer is that "when something *must* be done,—and when it can be done only by the united consent of all,—the necessity of the case will force to a compromise." The principal example is that of a petit jury: the jurors are under the necessity of reaching some common opinion after giving a fair and impartial hearing to both sides. Guided by this necessity and a love of truth and justice, a jury usually reaches a verdict.[39] "Far more urgent," much more "imperious" and "overpowering," is the necessity that impels men to compromise in constitutional governments. And, we may add, far more difficult to reach is such a compromise, since the interests that are involved are our own.[40]

Yet Calhoun was convinced—if not convincing—that the impulse to compromise would be well-nigh irresistible. A fear of anarchy that would attend the suspension of governmental action, bolstered by "an ardent love of country" or "an exalted patriotism," would induce each portion to take an enlarged and public-spirited view of whatever sacrifice it might have to make.

But to form a juster estimate of the full force of this impulse to compromise, there must be added that, in governments of the concurrent majority, each portion, in order to advance its own peculiar interests, would have to conciliate all others, by showing a disposition to advance theirs; and, for this purpose, each would select those to represent it, whose wisdom, patriotism, and weight of character, would command the confidence of the others. Under its influence,—and with representatives so well qualified to accomplish the object for which they were selected,—the prevailing desire would be, to promote the common interests of the whole; and, hence, the competition would be, not which should yield the least to promote the common good, but which should yield the most. It is thus, that concession would cease to be considered a sacrifice,—would become a free-will offering on the altar of the country, and lose the name of compromise.[41]

In these lines we catch a glimpse of a common good that is truly common to all concerned, and not a mere composite of *n* interests. We can only surmise

---

[39] It hardly requires noting that opposing counsel try to enhance the likelihood of a fair hearing by rejecting potential jurors who have an *interest* in the trial's outcome, to say nothing of the fact that a jury's failure to find a verdict rarely entails dire consequences for the jurymen. Calhoun also referred to the Polish *liberum veto* to show that even in its most extreme form the principle of concurrent majority rule was both practicable and compatible with "great power and splendor." *Works,* I, 71–72. Has any other political thinker held that constitution to be a model of good government?

[40] *Works,* I, 47–49, 64–68. This necessity was precisely what stamped the work of the Constitutional Convention of 1787 with "so much fairness, equity, and justice." *Works,* I, 195–96.

[41] *Works,* I, 68–70.

—for Calhoun did not declare himself unambiguously—that *this* common good is more or less identical with the effects of the Roman and British constitutions, with whose celebration the *Disquisition* concludes:

to unite and harmonize conflicting interests;—to strengthen attachments to the whole community, and to moderate that to the respective orders or classes; to rally all, in the hour of danger, around the standard of their country; to elevate the feeling of nationality, and to develop power, moral and physical, to an extraordinary extent.[42]

A calculating concern for others' interests becomes, somehow, a genuine concern for the common interests of the whole. Calhoun did not explain with sufficient clarity how this might be expected to come about. He had, however, all but maintained that a predominance of social feelings, or even an equality between social and individual feelings, is an impossibility. In the light of his psychological premises, we are justified in doubting whether these confidence-inspiring men are in a position to sacrifice their peculiar interests. Rather, are these not confidence men, making a *show* of concern for others? I suggest this interpretation: Calhoun believed that love of country comprehends, "within itself, a large portion both of our individual and social feelings." He believed that "few motives exert a greater sway." Satisfying some of *those* motives enables men to act as patriots. The selfishness that takes the form of warring interests is not eradicated, but it is tamed and possibly even civilized.[43] By giving selfish interest its due as a fact of life—one might almost say, as a law of nature—it is possible to transcend it. Calhoun's system appears to elicit—perhaps even to require—men's thinking about the common good, or at least a kind of self-interest, so guided by very indirect considerations, that barely can be distinguished from genuine public-spiritedness.[44]

If Calhoun's discussion of the common good sheds light on a wide range of issues related to the problem of partisanship, it is not a very strong light. His treatment of class conflict has a narrower focus and in some respects is more illuminating. The inevitability of class divisions and the tendency of labor and capital to conflict are persistent themes in Calhoun's speeches and writings, from the *South Carolina Exposition* to the *Disquisition on Government.* He saw in the system of protective tariffs a mighty instrument for erecting an

---

[42] *Works*, I, 104.

[43] "For the very nature of the group process (which our government shows in a fairly well-developed form) is this, that groups are freely combining, dissolving, and recombining in accordance with their interest lines. And the lion when he has satisfied his physical need will lie down quite lamb-like, however much louder his roars were than his appetite justified." Arthur F. Bentley, *The Process of Government* (Chicago, 1908), p. 359.

[44] *Works*, I, 5, 68; see also VI, 68 (1831). The manner in which the President is elected makes him "look more to *the interest of the whole* [and] soften sectional feelings and asperity." Even aspirants to that office find it easier "to be more of a patriot than the partisan of any particular interest." *Works*, IV, 87–88 (1842). Consider the discussion in Tocqueville, *Democracy in America*, II, Part ii, Chapter 4.

chy. This system's tendency is, as the experience of Europe bears less,

make the poor poorer, and the rich richer. Heretofore, in our country, this tendency as displayed itself principally in its effects, as regards the different sections,—but the time will come when it will produce the same results between the several classes in the manufacturing States. After we [the staple states] are exhausted, the contest will be between the capitalists and operatives; for into these two classes it must, ultimately, divide society.[45]

Calhoun was not prone to belittle the unique splendors of the United States. But in this respect, he believed the American government—"perfectly distinct from all others which have preceded it—a government founded on the rights of man; resting, not on authority, not on prejudice, not on superstition, but reason"—could claim no providential dispensation. While the Americans had "wisely exploded" the artificial distinctions of social classes, they had not thereby secured an exemption from the threat of oligarchy. Calhoun denied that "there now exists, or ever has existed, a wealthy and civilized community in which one portion did not live on the labor of another." In a small republic, this inequality would manifest itself in the conflict between capital and labor, with the ultimate establishment of an oligarchy. In an extensive republic, the inevitable inequality "would tend more in a geographical direction" and result even more swiftly—thanks to governmental favoritism—in a "moneyed oligarchy." It is not necessary to repeat here the argument that sees in slavery a "positive good" and a more humane resolution of the conflict between capital and labor than that prevailing in most countries. It suffices to say that in the slave plantation and in the states where the plantation was the predominant mode of economic organization, Calhoun saw a harmony, union, and stability that other portions, "less fortunately constituted," could not hope to attain. More significantly, Calhoun saw in the slaveholding states—"the conservative portion of the country"—a valuable, indeed indispensable, guarantor of a political and economic equilibrium. They provided what the North lacked: a "central point of union" immune to "the agitation and conflicts growing out of the divisions of wealth and poverty." Such is the reasoning that Calhoun addressed to the "sober and considerate portions" of Northern citizens, "who have a deep stake in the existing institutions of the country."[46]

That reasoning—in its private no less than in its public pronouncements —was cautious, guarded, and, so far as practical measures are concerned, even elusive.

Looking to the future, I can see no hope of a complete restoration of our system, till the men of wealth and talents in the North, shall become convinced, that their true

---

[45] *Works,* VI, 25–26 (1828).
[46] *Works,* II, 152 (1816), 631–32 (1837); III, 180 (1838), 643–44 (1841); IV, 343–44 (1847), 360–61 (1847), 521 (1849), 533 (1849); V, 207–8 (1836); VI, 64 (1831); *Correspondence,* p. 305 (1831).

interest is to rally on the South & on Southern doctrines. We are the real conservative body, equally opposed to aristocracy and agrarianism. So long as the tendency at the north was towards the former our natural union was with the democracy; but now that the democracy of the north tends to the agrarianism, our natural union is the other way. The misfortune is that the old federal party is like the Bourbons. Time stands still with them.[47]

Some interpreters have had no difficulty in seeing in all this a more or less open appeal for the planters and capitalist manufacturers to collaborate against the lower classes. From the recorded actions and opinions of Calhoun and of those who knew him, one can no more easily *prove* that he worked for such a collaboration than that he did not intend any such alliance. The question remains moot. On another occasion, when speaking of the South's being on the conservative side in the conflict between Northern labor and capital, he went on to add: "against the aggression of one or the other side." He censured Daniel Webster for attaching his affections, not to local interests, but to local *class* interests. He condemned the Hamiltonian policy of systematically favoring "the great and powerful classes of society, with the view of binding them, through their interest, to the support of the Government" as "uncongenial and dangerous" to the American system of government. He denied any hostility on his own part to the interests of manufacturers or laborers. He denied that slavery threatened the profits of Northern capitalists or the wages of Northern operatives. Most important of all, he denied that the social cleavage of rich and poor had any significance in the South. "With us the two great divisions of society are not the rich and poor, but white and black; and all the former, the poor as well as the rich, belong to the upper class. . . ."[48] Without appreciating the force of this assertion, one cannot fully understand the *Disquisition's* teaching about class divisions and partisan conflicts.

Calhoun maintained that concurrent majority rule has a "more popular character" than numerical majority rule because it allows for the extension of the right of suffrage—"with safety"—to almost every adult male, "with few ordinary exceptions." Such an extension in a system of simple majoritarianism would entail the predominance of "the more ignorant and dependent portions of the community."

---

[47]Calhoun to Samuel D. Ingham, Apr. 3, 1836, MS letter in John C. Calhoun Collection, South Caroliniana Library, Columbia, South Carolina. See also *Correspondence*, pp. 655–56 (1845).

[48]*Works*, III, 180 (1838), 287 (1838), 392–93 (1839); IV, 183–84 (1842), 196 (1842), 385–86 (1847), 505 (1848). Consider also John Quincy Adams' judgment (Oct. 1, 1831), recorded in Tocqueville's notebook: "Slavery has altered the whole state of society in the South. There the whites form a class to themselves which has all the ideas, all the passions, all the prejudices of an aristocracy, but do not be mistaken, *nowhere is equality between the whites so complete as in the South.* Here we have great equality before the law, but it simply does not affect our ways of life. There are upper classes and working classes. Every white man in the South is an equally privileged being whose destiny it is to make the Negroes work without working himself." Alexis de Tocqueville, *Journey to America*, trans. George Lawrence (New Haven, 1962), p. 61. Italics supplied.

For, as the community becomes populous, wealthy, refined, and highly civilized, the difference between the rich and the poor will become more strongly marked; and the number of the ignorant and dependent greater in proportion to the rest of the community. With the increase of this difference, the tendency to conflict between them will become stronger; and, as the poor and dependent become more numerous in proportion, there will be, in governments of the numerical majority, no want of leaders among the wealthy and ambitious, to excite and direct them in their efforts to obtain the control.

The case is different in governments of the concurrent majority. There, mere numbers have not the absolute control; and the wealthy and intelligent being identified in interest with the poor and ignorant of their respective portions or interests of the community, become their leaders and protectors. And hence, as the latter would have neither hope nor inducement to rally the former in order to obtain the control, the right of suffrage, under such a government, may be safely enlarged to the extent stated, without incurring the hazard to which such enlargement would expose governments of the numerical majority.[49]

Hitherto we have understood Calhoun to say that the principal division to which his political science must address itself is that of tax-consumers and tax-payers, or that of the ins and the outs. Here, however, there is a suggestion that the problem posed by the natural majority, the poor, still is the fundamental problem. This may be taken as a tacit questioning of the efficacy of Publius' remedy for the evil effects of majority factionalism. Of the greatest significance for understanding Calhoun's thought is the quiet, almost casual, assertion of an identity of interest—in the concurrent majority system—of the wealthy and intelligent with the poor and ignorant. How is this deepest social cleavage bridged? What interest or interests can so overwhelm the fear and envy of class conflict?

That there are such preponderant interests common to a particular portion or group is the very cornerstone of Calhoun's system. Otherwise he would not have been able to assume that numerical majorities will not be oppressive or tyrannical *within* any given portion or group. But what would prevent any local numerical majority from going through the same kind of changing alliances as Calhoun observed with despair in the national government? We well may wonder at the ease with which Calhoun believed a group could define itself and identify its particular interest, considering his own difficulties in defining the whole of which those groups are a part and in identifying the community's general interest. I can think of no present interest so overwhelming as to unify—without some injustice—a majority of the politically relevant individuals of one portion vis-à-vis all the other portions of the country. I can think of only one interest that could harmonize individual interests within a portion to the extent that Calhoun foresaw. And that interest is slavery.

If this is so, how did Calhoun expect *national* harmony to be secured by

[49] *Works*, I, 45–46.

the concurrent majority system in a community that included nonslave portions and economic class divisions? His answer, I believe, is suggested by the conservative role he saw for the South. The slaveholding portion would use its veto power to prevent the rich *or* the poor (perhaps especially the latter) from imposing their class interest upon the country. When labor seeks to level wealth, the South would oppose it; when capital seeks fiscal and commercial policies oppressive to labor and agrarians, the South would oppose it. For Calhoun, not the least of slavery's salutary effects was its making the South the balance of the American political system.

III

In the last analysis, the general applicability of Calhoun's system is open to serious question, thereby exposing him to the charge of "closet ingenuity." The least that can be said is that his difficulties are not peculiarly his own. If these difficulties leave his political theory in an unsatisfactory condition, they may, nonetheless, indicate the measure of Calhoun's current significance as a political scientist. Calhoun was one of the first to construct a science of politics on partially articulated principles that we fairly can identify as belonging to today's behavioral political science.[50] Having built his theoretical teaching upon these principles or premises, he rigorously adhered to them well beyond the point at which his practical knowledge of political life cried "halt."

Yet halt he did, and the silent and unmarked substitution of other principles or premises in his argument makes the understanding, as well as the assessment, of Calhoun's teaching a slippery road indeed. His discussion of interest, for example, lacks nothing of modern sophistication. Constitution, institutional arrangements, the forms of legislation, the appearance of equitable generality that marks governmental actions—all were stripped away by Calhoun to reveal the harsher stuff of politics. With a deft hand he traced the course of the many and varicolored threads of interest as they arise out of geography, size, civilization, production, wealth, and office, and go on to color and give texture to political life as a whole. But he did not stop at this; he went on to maintain in effect that self-interest forms the warp and woof of every significant political act. It is only late in his argument—too late—that Senator Calhoun reminded himself of what he had known since young manhood: that "our Union cannot safely stand on the cold calculations of interest alone."[51] The threads of interest are too thin to bear the heaviest burdens, too short to

---

[50]For a detailed discussion of these premises, see Leo Weinstein, "The Group Approach: Arthur F. Bentley," *Essays on the Scientific Study of Politics*, ed. Herbert J. Storing (New York, 1962), pp. 151–224.

[51]*Works*, II, 42 (1812).

reach the highest goals, of political life. Interest was not a sufficient bond of political life because, for Calhoun, those burdens and goals were not imaginary "spooks."

Again, Calhoun's discussion of groups or portions is a remarkable anticipation of the contemporary teaching. Both in his theoretical writing and in his speeches in the Senate, Calhoun showed a keen understanding of the physics or mechanics of group politics. This perhaps is not noteworthy in a man of long political experience. What is surprising is the extent to which Calhoun's discussion of the portions proceeds in virtual disregard of that of which they are parts. If he shunned the word "nation," it was not solely by virtue of his nullifier's creed. The groups or portions have a kind of tangible relevance, easily detectable in their marchings and countermarchings across the political landscape. If there was a whole or entity, what could it be if not the sum of all these discrete groupings? It is almost as though the larger community, which others called the nation or the country, had become a piece of painted scenery for Calhoun, lacking depth and significance, and gradually to be forgotten as the spectators are absorbed in the action downstage. It is almost as though some hostile intruder must burst upon the stage, tearing down the backdrop or putting a torch to it, for it to be recalled to mind. And yet, there is something in Calhoun's view that refuses to be satisfied with such a conception of the larger political community. An admiration of foreign grandeur, a pride of native achievements and promise—feelings that he would not or could not repress— peep through the elaborate argument, disturbing its logical symmetry before it reaches its last necessary deduction.

Or consider, finally, Calhoun's lengthy discussion of concurrent majority rule, in which a process of government becomes in itself the common good. Given a whole that is the arithmetical sum of its parts, given parts that are engrossed in the single-minded pursuit of their self-interest, narrowly conceived, it is hardly cause for amazement that the highest common denominator —the *only* common denominator—is an agreement to persist with the game. Hardly anyone thinks it needful or worth his while to justify the game, and if someone does try to do so, he retreats willy-nilly to a kind of argument and language that the serious players find quaint at best. Calhoun's theory carries him far in this direction, though it is the position that he least satisfactorily explained, defended, or qualified. On the one hand, Calhoun's system moves from irreducible self-interest to enlarged patriotism by way of a dread of stalemate and anarchy. On the other hand, Calhoun considered that man's nature (both its low and high elements, its need for both preservation and perfection), made concurrent majority rule necessary and possible.

The *Disquisition on Government* might be considered as a prescriptive set of "rules of the game," but Calhoun's defense of those rules makes use of standards that fall outside the terms of the game. At the same time, his conception of the common good or public interest as a governmental process earns for him the reward due one who anticipated by several generations this development in political science. Calhoun was some kind of precursor or pioneer of a behavioral science of politics. Greater precision eludes us as long as the line separating his reluctance from his confusion is so indistinct.

This much, however, may safely be said: the modern understanding of parties and group politics shares much more with Calhoun than with the man whom it customarily claims as its intellectual forebear. Not the Madison of *The Federalist,* No. 10, but Calhoun, saw parties as machines or instruments for capturing and monopolizing governmental power and privilege. Not Madison, but Calhoun, had the clearer and fuller understanding of the multifarious and shifting alliances that constitute the political behavior of groups. Similarly, it is Calhoun, more than Madison, who would talk about group interests while stumbling over, or ignoring, the identification of the common good.

Yet if one looks at Calhoun's system as a whole and contrasts it with Publius', it does not look altogether mean. Like Publius, he built upon selfishness and made the pursuit of self-interest the mainspring of civil society. But in criticizing Publius' solution, Calhoun proceeded to develop a system that he believed would induce the generality of men to think about the common good (however vaguely perceived), albeit for selfish reasons. Publius thought he knew what "the permanent and aggregate interests of the community" were, but believed that the system he had devised could dispense safely with much deep or widespread thinking about them. Calhoun was less willing to rely on either the ancient devices or the modern political discoveries to which Publius resorted. He was not satisfied that the habits of a commercial people in a land of great extent and diversity would suffice of themselves to secure and preserve the common good. Something more—the kind of character he expected the concurrent majority system to elicit—was required to lead men to embrace broader goals than their immediate self-interest. Calhoun believed that there always would be a need for thoughtful patriots. He still could envy the "pride and elevation of sentiment" with which the ancients proclaimed: *"I am a Roman citizen."* [52]

In conclusion: Calhoun's new science of politics tries to wed to the narrow premises of a behavioral social science that barely looks beyond the fact of self-interest, the ends held in esteem by a man "of enlarged philosophical

[52] *Works,* I, 105.

views, and of ardent patriotism."[53] His attempt and his failure confirm, in my eyes, Gallatin's judgment of him as "a smart fellow, one of the first amongst second-rate men."[54]

SELECTED SUGGESTED READINGS

The Works of John C. Calhoun. Edited by Richard K. Crallé. 6 vols. Columbia, South Carolina: A. S. Johnston, 1851 and New York: D. Appleton, 1853–1857.

See the following selections from the *Works:*
A Disquisition on Government, Works, I, 1–107.
"The South Carolina Exposition," December, 1828, *Works,* VI, 1–59.
"The Fort Hill Address," July 26, 1831, *Works,* VI, 59–94.
"Speech on the Reception of Abolition Petitions," February 6, 1837, *Works,* II, 625–33.
"Speech on the Veto Power," February 28, 1842, *Works,* IV, 74–100.
"Speech on the Oregon Bill," June 27, 1848, *Works,* IV, 479–512.

Calhoun: Basic Documents. Edited by John M. Anderson. State College, Pennsylvania: Bald Eagle Press, 1952. This readily available volume contains the *Disquisition,* "Speech on the Veto Power," "Speech on the Oregon Bill," and other speeches.

[53] *Memoirs of John Quincy Adams,* ed. Charles Francis Adams (Philadelphia, 1874–1877), V, 361 (Oct. 15, 1821).
[54] Henry Adams, *The Life of Albert Gallatin* (Philadelphia, 1879), p. 599.

★ ABRAHAM LINCOLN   *Harry V. Jaffa*

I

The Lincoln-Douglas debates are justly regarded as the greatest in American history. Whatever their intrinsic merits, the magnitude of their consequences, for good or evil, is incalculable. By opposing Douglas for the senatorship in the Illinois campaign of 1848, Lincoln prevented the Little Giant from capturing the leadership of the Republican party, at a moment when Douglas was being looked on with the greatest favor by the eastern leaders of the party. At one and the same time, Lincoln forced Douglas into warfare with the Republicans, thereby leaving open for himself the leadership of the party, and forced Douglas to take ground that brought about a new and more disastrous split in the Democratic party, a split which resulted in the election of a Republican —and minority—president in 1860. Thus did Lincoln forge a great link in the chain of events that led to secession and civil war.

Popular tradition has surrounded the debates with the aura which, in retrospect at least, always attends a clash of champions. It has ascribed to the debates a level of dialectic and rhetoric befitting such a match. As to the intensity of the campaign, and the emotions it stirred in the principals and followers on both sides, there can be no question. But the merits of the debates cannot be judged merely by popular tradition—particularly when it is remembered that that tradition is today largely the tradition of the descendants of Lincoln's camp. This tradition has pictured Douglas as a brilliant but unscrupulous "doughface," a "northern man with southern principles," whose high-flying career was finally brought to earth by Lincoln's supreme political logic.

But this view of the debates is not regarded highly today by historians. ". . . on their merits," says the late Albert J. Beveridge, one of the most prominent of Lincoln's biographers of the last generation, "the debates deserve little notice." This opinion is followed by the late James G. Randall, long the recognized dean of present-day Lincoln scholars, as well as by George Fort Milton, the leading biographer, and a fierce partisan, of Douglas, who writes:

SOURCE: Harry V. Jaffa, "Expediency and Morality in The Lincoln-Douglas Debates," *The Anchor Review*, No. 2 (1957), 177–204. (Originally delivered as a public lecture at St. John's College, Annapolis, Md., November 30, 1951.)

"Judged as debates, they do not measure up to their reputation. On neither side did the dialectic compare with that in the debates between Webster, Hayne, and Calhoun." More important, however, the belief which is at the root of the debates' fame has been debunked by modern historiography: the belief that Lincoln had opposed Douglas on a great issue, and for the sake of a great cause. This view is best expressed in the following judgment of Professor Randall:

It is surprising how little attention has been given to the actual content of the debates. The canvass had been conducted in dead earnest, yet it has always been easier to relate its picturesque features than to analyze its substance. It was symptomatic of the times that the debates were not concerned with a representative coverage of national questions, but almost entirely with slavery, and with only a limited and comparatively unimportant aspect of that subject. . . .

Swinging up and down and back and forth across Illinois, making the welkin ring and setting the prairies on fire, Lincoln and Douglas debated—what? That is the surprising thing. With all the problems that might have been put before the people as proper matter for their consideration in choosing a senator—choice of government servants, immigration, the tariff, international policy, promotion of education, westward extension of railroads, the opening of new lands for homesteads, protection against greedy exploitation of those lands . . . encouragement to settlers, and the bettering of agriculture, (etc.) . . . instead of a representative coverage of the problems of mid-century America, the debaters gave virtually all their attention to slavery in the territories. More specifically, they were concentrating on the question whether federal prohibition of slavery in western territories, having been dropped after full discussion in 1850, should be revived as if it were the only means of dealing with the highly improbable chance that human bondage would ever take root in such a place as Kansas, Nebraska, or New Mexico. It is indeed a surprising thing to suppose that the negligible amount of human bondage in Kansas, or the alleged inability of the people of that nascent state to decide the matter for themselves, constituted the only American question of sufficient importance to occupy nearly all the attention of senatorial candidates in one of the most famous forensic episodes of the century.

II

Behind the debates were series of famous compromises, once familiar to every American schoolboy.

(1) First, of course, were the compromises concerning slavery in the Constitution. A generation later came the Missouri Compromise. The Missouri Compromise (1820) was, very briefly, the arrangement whereby Missouri was admitted to the Union as a slave state, Maine as a free state, and it was affirmed that, in all the remainder of the territory acquired from France (the Louisiana Purchase), north of the latitude 30°30' (the southern boundary of Missouri), slavery should be forever unlawful. Through the operation of the Compromise, the Union came to consist by 1849 of fifteen slave states and fifteen free states.

(2) This equilibrium was threatened by the application for admission as a free state, in 1849, of California. After a great political upheaval, the Compromise of 1850 was adopted. Under its terms, California was admitted as a free state; but the Utah and New Mexico territories, comprising the present states of New Mexico, Arizona, Nevada, Utah, Colorado, and part of Wyoming, were given territorial organization, with the provision that, when they applied for admission as states, they might come in with either free or slave constitutions, as the inhabitants of the territories might themselves decide at the time. At the same time, the slave trade (but not slavery) was abolished in the District of Columbia, and the South was given a new, and brutally harsh, fugitive slave law, which so endangered the free Negroes of the North that a series of personal liberty laws, which in turn greatly exasperated the South in the ensuing decade, were passed throughout the free states. The South, in allowing the balance of free and slave states to be tipped against it, was thus allowed the prospect of several new slave states, to be formed out of the Utah and New Mexico Territories. The great antislavery moderates who put through the Compromise regarded this, however, as a forlorn hope. These territories were, they thought, highly unsuited to any economic development which would make slavery profitable. Moreover, of the greatest moment, from the point of view of Lincoln's opposition to Douglas, was the fact that, as all this territory had been acquired from Mexico, slavery had been excluded from it—until then —by Mexican law.

Lincoln—following Clay—insisted that Mexican law continued to apply in the absence of specific repeal. Now there were never, in the vast territories of Utah and New Mexico, more than fifty-one slaves. But Lincoln nevertheless laid great stress upon the claim that Mexican law made slavery in those territories illegal. For he insisted that, when the people of a *territory* should come to decide whether, in becoming a state, they wished to have a free or slave constitution, their decision should not be influenced by the *actual presence* of the institution among them. Because of the incredible difficulty presented by the race question, no people, Lincoln felt, who lived among a large body of Negro slaves, would ever willingly adopt a free constitution; just as free whites in America, he thought, acquainted with the advantages of a free labor system, would ever seek to introduce Negroes among themselves. However, the fact remained that the two territories did contain what proved to be a potential of five new slave states—a potential which the North could regard with some complacency as long as the Missouri Compromise remained inviolate, for the remaining Louisiana Territory also contained an equal potential of five new free states (Kansas, Nebraska, the two Dakotas, and Minnesota).

III

Douglas sought a formula which, while guaranteeing the exclusion of slavery from the territories, and hence from the new states, would remove the slavery issue as a bone of national contention. Douglas thought he had discovered that formula in the doctrine of popular sovereignty: according to this doctrine Congress should attempt neither to legislate slavery into, nor out of, any prospective state: but the inhabitants of any territory, while living under a territorial government, should decide that question for themselves; and when they adopted a constitution, with a view to applying for admission as a state, should decide the question for the new state. In the view of Douglas' present-day defenders, this would have guaranteed the victory of freedom, for nowhere in the remaining territories of the continental United States was there any place where slavery could profitably be planted. At the same time, popular sovereignty, by conceding to the South an equal right with the North to make either free or slave states out of any federal territory, would grant the South everything it could reasonably expect. Webster and Clay—the latter the adored leader of Lincoln himself—had defended the provision of the Compromise of 1850 that allowed slavery, in principle, to enter Utah and New Mexico, on the ground that natural causes would nonetheless have kept slavery out.

Now Douglas, following Clay and Webster, had supported popular sovereignty in 1850, as applied to Utah and New Mexico. But in 1854, by proposing the application of popular sovereignty to the Nebraska Territory, which was part of the Louisiana Purchase, Douglas was compelled, at first by implication, but finally by express statement, to repeal the Missouri Compromise. For the Missouri Compromise had "forever" prohibited slavery in the Louisiana Purchase, north of 30°30'. Clearly, Douglas here conceded something to the Southern "ultras." Douglas' present-day defenders insist that he had made a mere paper concession. Douglas himself, at the time, claimed to have been converted to the view that the Missouri Compromise was unconstitutional—and that fairness to the South was his sole motive.

IV

Paper concession or not, it was the signal for one of the greatest political upheavals in this country's history. From the opposition to Douglas' Kansas-Nebraska Bill the Republican party was born: indeed it was for sometime, and in many places, known simply as the anti-Nebraska party. The election of 1856 was the first that the new Republican party fought on a national scale. Its candidate, Frémont, received 1.3 million popular votes, and 114 electoral votes, compared with Buchanan's 1.8 million and 174. The Whig candidate, Fillmore, in the last election seriously contested by his party, received nearly 900 thousand popular votes, but only 8 electoral votes. The ominous and dangerous fact that emerged from this election was that Frémont received not a single electoral, and scarcely a single popular, vote in any slave state. And the moribundity of the Whig party held forth the prospect that, in the future, of the two predominant parties in the nation, one at least would draw all its strength from one geographical section. To avert this result, implicit with catastrophe, Douglas did indeed bend all his strength. He did it, first of all, by making every effort to prevent the fate of the Whig party from overtaking the Democracy. He would say nothing that would prevent any southerner from feeling that his constitutional rights were as sacred to the Democratic party as those of any northern Democrat. Secondly, he would be no party to any move, by any southern ultra, to force slavery upon any territory in which the bona fide inhabitants did not want it. He would, in short, resist equally the demands of abolitionists and slavery fanatics.

One of the charges most frequently repeated, and most damaging to Douglas' reputation in later years, was that he thought moral considerations had no place in politics. The keystone of this charge was Douglas' attitude towards slavery. This, of course, was Lincoln's reiterated assertion, "That Judge Douglas 'don't care' whether slavery is voted up or voted down." The absurdity of Douglas' position was said to appear in this: that he held to the doctrine of popular sovereignty as a great moral principle: the principle that the people had the *right* to decide their own domestic institutions—and, as Douglas incessantly repeated—he would live, fight, and if need be die in the defense of that right—and yet he denied that, in the matter of slavery, there was any principle of right which ought to guide the people's choice. Lincoln, of course, instantly exposed this anomaly, when he asked whether the Douglas Democrats would vote to admit Utah as a state, if the Mormons applied for admission with a constitution sanctioning polygamy (for no one doubted that laws concerning the family were exclusively matters of state jurisdiction).

But the defenders of Douglas rightly insist that Lincoln's consistency and Douglas' inconsistency are not the measure of their difference on this question of morality: Douglas (it is alleged) was as much convinced of the immorality of slavery as Lincoln, but *he could not say so in public.* And this was because, as Lincoln himself emphatically acknowledged, no man could command the confidence of the South who did not confess that slavery was positively good. Douglas did not, in fact, go so far—nor did he ever develop deep roots of political strength in the South; but, as a party leader, he long retained at least the prospect of securing the acquiescence to his leadership of the main body of the party in the South. This influence would have been destroyed the moment he condemned slavery on moral grounds. This was, after all, not different from Lincoln's attitude toward the Know-Nothings; i.e., private condemnation, public silence. Douglas' silence on the morality of slavery—or, rather, his supposed indifference to the morality of the slavery issue—as represented by his famous assertion that he did not care if it were voted up or down, may then in fact have been an act of prudence of the highest kind, because it preserved that influence which alone could have saved the Democratic party as a national party—and the chance of preserving the Union without war. From this point of view, Douglas' suppression of his feelings concerning the morality of slavery would be a higher act of virtue than Lincoln's gratification of his feelings on the subject.

Finally, to appreciate the strength of Douglas' case, one must recall that, just prior to the campaign for the senatorship in 1858, Douglas had been the leader of a tremendous fight to vindicate his Popular Sovereignty, in its application to Kansas. The pro-slavery settlers, who were always a minority of the bona fide inhabitants, had framed a fraudulent constitution sanctioning slavery, and had applied for admission to the Union. President Buchanan, bending under the lash of the slavocracy, tried to railroad through the bill admitting Kansas. Douglas, seeing Popular Sovereignty made a mockery, and his good faith called into question, led the successful fight against the Lecompton Constitution (as it was called). In this fight he commanded the support of a minority of Democrats, and the bulk of his supporters were the solid phalanx of Republicans. His stand brought Douglas great popularity among northern free-soilers and made him, in the view of Horace Greeley—and possibly even Seward (who was virtually the titular leader of the Republicans in the nation), a likely candidate for the Republican presidential nomination in 1860. As such, he would undoubtedly have carried a large Democratic minority with him— as he did in the Lecompton battle.

If this interpretation is to govern our judgment of the two men, we can hardly deny that Lincoln's action, in opposing Douglas in 1858, was a wanton destruction of a substantial opportunity—perhaps the only one—to prevent the Civil War. For with Douglas as president, the South would almost certainly not have seceded.

V

Now no appreciation of the issue that divided the men is possible, unless one overriding fact is grasped—and that is the magnitude and incredible difficulty of the race question. In 1858, no responsible man, in any part of the country, thought that, in their actual condition, moral and intellectual, the great bulk of the black people were fit for civic responsibilities of any kind. No one thought that any large-scale emancipation could fail to have tragic and disastrous consequences for both black and white. The obvious answer suggests itself—why did no one try to gain acceptance for a policy of gradual emancipation of the educated and morally qualified, thus setting a goal for the backward that would give all something to work for? The answer is given by two further facts: first, the unstable character of slavery as an economic institution; and second, the size of the Negro population.

Slavery by 1858 had run through a double cycle. Until the invention of the cotton gin, it was dying from lack of areas in which slaves could profitably be used. Then it became the staff of the booming Cotton Kingdom. Later, it became the bane of the old cotton lands, and the driving force behind the search for ever new lands to exploit. The way of life which came to be the most admired—although not the most widely shared—in the South, became that which depended on the use of large numbers of slaves. Large parts of the older South, e.g., South Carolina and Virginia, although no longer using slaves very profitably at home, were tied to the newer, more profitable slave lands, both by social ideals and by the fact that they exported slaves to the new lands. And anything that threatened the continued expansion of slavery threatened the profits of the dominant class throughout the South.

But independent of profits, slavery seemed to the entire South an essential institution. For, to come to the second great fact: throughout the states that came to comprise the Confederacy, 40 per cent of the population was Negro —and through large areas of the South, the colored population equaled, and in some places greatly exceeded, the white. If men could not employ slaves profitably, they would eventually have no alternative but to emancipate them. The prospect of a free Negro population that might equal—perhaps even greatly outnumber—the white population, was a prospect that no politician, North or South, would, or, perhaps, could, have faced. And this it was that put such force in the drive for the expansion of the slave lands.

VI

The most widely accepted current interpretation of Lincoln's policy between 1854 and 1860 looks upon it as essentially a supremely shrewd grasp at the main chance—a weighing of the diverse and volatile political forces of his time in such manner as to hit upon the one combination that would boost him and his party to power. The repeal of the Missouri Compromise was the *raison d'être* of the Republican party. It was the one issue that united otherwise diverse and, as Lincoln himself said, even hostile interests. And it was the one issue on which Lincoln and Douglas disagreed, and to which, to Professor Randall's unhappiness, they confined all their attention. Professor Randall thinks that the issue of slavery in the territories was not a practical question. If it was not, then Lincoln certainly stands indicted of grave irresponsibility—for, merely for party purposes, he kept alive the only question that gave existence to the Republican party—the one question that could keep alive a wholly sectional party—the one question that could split the Democratic party, elect a sectional president, and precipitate civil war.

The prevailing, though largely implicit, defense of Lincoln made today, is this: that he had a perfect right, as a professional politician, to keep alive any issue that might bring him to power. Such a defense of Lincoln implies that ambition for political honors cannot be judged by any higher principle. Ambition, it is implied, should of course be controlled by virtue. But there is no criterion of virtue beyond the conditions for contesting honors provided by the laws. But this apology will not do, for at least one reason: Lincoln himself rejected it. The problem of ambition, it so happened, was one that he had given thought to throughout his life. Indeed, the problem of controlling ambition was, in his view, the supreme political problem. This Lincoln had stated early in life, and he recurred to it at crucial moments in his career—including the campaign with Douglas. To judge a man one must begin—although one need not end—by measuring him by his own standards. Let us then digress from the issue of Lincoln versus Douglas long enough to understand Lincoln's conception of the problem of ambition.

The fullest statement of his views on this matter are contained in an address delivered before the Young Men's Lyceum of Springfield, in 1838, twenty years before the debates. The subject of the address, "The Perpetuation of Our Political Institutions," so expressive of the task to which his hand was one day to be set, is here explicitly said by Lincoln to be the most difficult task of statesmanship. The reason that it is so, according to Lincoln, may be found in the relation of ambition to honor. The highest honors are paid to the founders of political institutions. Especially great honor is paid to those who found political institutions of a novel character—institutions that hold forth the promise of a good never achieved before, politically, by man. Such institutions, said Lincoln, were founded by the men of the generation of the Revolution —Washington, Jefferson, Madison, Hamilton, the Founding Fathers of our national political life. "Their ambition aspired to display before an admiring world a practical demonstration of the truth of a proposition, which had hitherto been considered at best no better than problematical; namely, *the capability of a people to govern themselves.* If they succeeded, they were to be immortalized: their names were to be transferred to counties and cities, and rivers and mountains; and to be revered and sung, and toasted through all time. If they failed, they were to be called knaves and fools, and fanatics. . . . They succeeded. The experiment is successful; and [they] have won their deathless names in making it so." Lincoln thus echoes Hamilton, in *The Federalist,* who had said that "love of fame is the ruling passion of the noblest minds." But, according to Lincoln, this passion was a force for good in the revolutionary generation precisely because the greatest fame was then to be gained by a great constructive enterprise. Passion supported reason in the Founding Fathers, and their actual virtue was thus due, in no small measure, to opportunities for which they themselves were not in any special sense responsible. But what of succeeding generations?

But the game is caught; and I believe it is true, that with the catching, end the pleasures of the chase. This field of glory is harvested, and the crop is already appropriated. But new reapers will arise, and *they*, too, will seek a field. It is to deny, what the history of the world tells us is true, to suppose that men of ambition and talents will not continue to spring up amongst us. And, when they do, they will as naturally seek the gratification of their ruling passion as others have so done before them. The question, then, is, can that gratification be found in supporting and maintaining an edifice that has been erected by others? Most certainly it cannot. Many great and good men sufficiently qualified for any task they should undertake may ever be found, whose ambition would aspire to nothing beyond a seat in Congress, a gubernatorial or a presidential chair; *but such belong not to the family of the lion, or the tribe of the eagle.* What! think you these places would satisfy an Alexander, a Caesar, or a Napoleon? Never! Towering genius disdains a beaten path . . . It seeks *no distinction* in adding story to story, upon the monuments of fame, erected in the memory of others. . . . It thirsts and burns for distinction; and, if possible, it will have it, whether at the expense of emancipating slaves, or enslaving freemen. Is it unreasonable then to expect that some man possessed of the loftiest genius, coupled with ambition sufficient to push it to its utmost stretch, will at some time spring up among us? And when such a one does, it will require the people to be united with each other, attached to the government and laws, and generally intelligent in order to successfully frustrate his designs. Distinction will be his paramount object, and although he would as willingly, perhaps more so, acquire it by doing good as harm; yet, that opportunity being past, and nothing left to be done in the way of building up, he would set boldly to the task of pulling down.

This remarkable passage draws together many of the deepest strands of Lincoln's political thought and, despite a certain flamboyancy in the rhetoric, which shows the deference of a young man to the popular oratorical style of his day, contains Lincoln's considered and permanent reflections on the paramount problems of statesmanship. First, one must be struck by the assertion that, although the American experiment in government is specifically said to be the demonstration of the truth of the proposition that "the people" can govern themselves, the demonstration is also said to be the work of a small group of heroes—who gain from the political process a good (immortal fame) not to be gained by any others; although, paradoxically, the "others" are the intended beneficiaries of the work of the heroes. But still more paradoxical is the division of mankind into men of heroic mold and men of non-heroic mold —the former being described as belonging to "the family of the lion, or the tribe of the eagle." It is clear that, in Lincoln's view, the Founding Fathers belonged to this class.

But Lincoln implies that there is a higher and more difficult task for statesmanship than that of Washington: it is the task of checking the ambition of the lions and eagles who find no outlet for their thirst for fame in the comparatively prosaic work of maintaining institutions received from other lions and eagles. It was therefore no mere expression of his feelings, however deep, that prompted Lincoln to say, in his farewell to Springfield, in February 1861, that he left "with a task before me greater than that which rested upon Washington." But only one who himself belongs to this superior class or, rather, one who possesses a superiority which transcends that of this class, can control it. And such a one may meet his supreme antagonist either within his own bosom or within that of another. Thus, with respect to Lincoln's theory of democracy: the people can govern themselves if superior men establish them in possession of a good government and good laws. They can continue in possession of their government and laws *if,* as Lincoln explicitly says, they remain strongly attached to them *and,* as he no less forcefully implies, the destructive propensities of future superior men are foreseen and frustrated by even more superior men. In this we may see both the implicit and explicit paradoxes of the Gettysburg Address: "Our fathers" brought forth the nation dedicated to the proposition that all men are created equal. But "our fathers" were not ordinary men. The existence and survival of government of, by, and for the people, the ordinary men, is possible only because of the Washingtons and Jeffersons of the first generation, and because of Lincoln, fourscore and seven years after.

This discussion is strongly suggestive of that passage in the Third Book of Aristotle's *Politics* in which it is said that laws are only for equals, that really superior men can never be subjected to legislation fit for any average. For to make laws for such men, Aristotle said, would be like the folly of the hares in the fable of Antisthenes, who, in the assembly of the beasts, made speeches demanding that all should have equality: to which the lions replied, "Where are your claws and teeth?" Lincoln agrees with Aristotle that laws, of themselves, will never maintain themselves in the face of the claws and teeth of the supermen who thirst for the highest distinction. But Lincoln implies that the true statesman, who perceives the inadequacy of even the best laws to control the inequality among men, and who nonetheless sets himself the task of preserving such laws, performs the highest act of justice.

But what then is the motive of the more than superior man, who forestalls the superior men in their search for a field for honor? Lincoln's true statesman is like Aristotle's magnanimous man who, though claiming the highest honors when they fall due to him, nonetheless holds honor in contempt as ultimately unworthy of perfect virtue. Like Aristotle, therefore, Lincoln holds that the man of perfect virtue, the man who deserves the highest honor, must always be prepared to give up even honor, in obedience to the dictates of virtue.

From this analysis we may understand the task that Lincoln believed was set for the true statesman in his own lifetime, and the standard by which he thought this work was to be measured. That Lincoln never lost sight of the standard set forth in his speech "On the Perpetuation of Our Political Institutions" is shown by the conclusion of his last speech in the campaign against Douglas in 1858:

Ambition has been ascribed to me. God knows how sincerely I prayed from the first that this field of ambition might not be opened. I claim no insensibility to political honors; but today could the Missouri Restriction be restored, and the whole slavery question replaced on the ground of "toleration" by *necessity* where it exists, with unyielding hostility to the spread of it, on principle, I would, in consideration, gladly agree that Judge Douglas should never be *out*, and I never *in*, an office, so long as we both, or either, live.

Lincoln would not, then, have justified his opposition to Douglas on any grounds other than the supreme necessity of restoring the Missouri Compromise. But was there such a supreme necessity?

VII

Lincoln firmly believed that the spread of slavery had to be halted by a principle that treated slavery as a wrong *everywhere*. In this Lincoln may seem doctrinaire or opportunistic, as he seems to Douglas' defenders. Yet no one was, in general, more prone than Lincoln to follow that dictate of prudence, by which one attempts always to remove evils without shocking the prejudices that support them—allowing time and circumstances rather to wear down the prejudices. No one was more intolerant of mere "pernicious abstractions" that set people by the ears for no practical ends. But Douglas' doctrine of letting the people of a territory decide whether or not they wanted slavery involved the specific repeal of the Missouri Compromise, a compromise that, in the minds and hearts of a great majority of the North, canonized a great national principle: the principle that, wherever the national territory had not already been infected with the virus of slavery, it should not be permitted to enter. This principle was merely a corollary of that supreme axiom of our national existence: "That all men are created equal." To Lincoln, the repeal of the Missouri Compromise involved the repudiation of the Declaration of Independence.

What the Declaration of Independence meant to Lincoln is difficult for us, who are no longer accustomed to live among sacred things, to appreciate. It must suffice for the present to say that for Lincoln it embodied the principle of distributive justice: that for the sake of which our Union and our laws existed and were instituted. The key to Lincoln's policy must be found, above all, in the relation of this principle to the Constitution and the Union.

"Our government," Lincoln said over and over, "rests upon public opinion. Whoever can change public opinion can change the government practically just so much." What Lincoln understood by public opinion, however, was not what Dr. Gallup tries to measure. Over and again, in the debates against Douglas, Lincoln said: ". . . he who molds public sentiment goes deeper than he who enacts statutes and pronounces decisions. He makes statutes or decisions possible or impossible to execute." But public opinion is not, primarily, opinion about individual statutes or decisions: "Public opinion, on any subject, always has a 'central idea' from which all its minor thoughts radiate." The central idea at the founding of our government, from which all minor thoughts radiated, was "the equality of all men." The repudiation of this "central idea" meant to Lincoln not merely the possible opening of the Nebraska Territory to slavery, but the changing of the entire basis of our national existence. In Aristotelian terms, it meant the substitution of a new end—a different conception of the ultimate political good—for the original one. The following is perhaps Lincoln's classic statement of what our central national political idea meant. It is from his speech on the Dred Scott decision:

Chief Justice Taney, in his opinion in the Dred Scott case, admits that the language of the Declaration is broad enough to include the whole human family, but he and Judge Douglas argue that the authors of that instrument did not intend to include Negroes, by the fact that they did not at once actually place them on an equality with the whites. Now this grave argument comes to just nothing at all, by the other fact, that they did not at once, *or ever afterwards,* actually place all white people on an equality with one another. And this is the staple argument of both the Chief Justice and the Senator, for doing this obvious violence to the plain, unmistakable language of the Declaration. I think the authors of that notable instrument intended to include *all* men, but they did not intend to declare all men are equal *in all respects.* They did not mean to say all were equal in color, size, intellect, moral developments, or social capacity. They defined with tolerable distinctness, in what respects they did consider all men created equal—equal in "certain inalienable rights, among which are life, liberty, and the pursuit of happiness." This they said, and this they meant. They did not mean to assert the obvious untruth, that all were then actually enjoying that equality, nor yet that they were able to confer it immediately upon them. In fact they had no power to confer such a boon. They meant simply to declare the *right,* so that the enforcement of it might follow as fast as circumstances should permit. They meant to set up a standard maxim for free society, which could be familiar to all, and revered by all; constantly looked to, constantly labored for, and even though never perfectly attained, constantly approximated, and thereby constantly spreading and deepening its influence, and augmenting the happiness and value of life to all people of all colors everywhere.

"A standard maxim," "familiar to all," "revered by all," "constantly looked to": it is impossible not to recognize the similarity of expression to that of the greatest of all lawgivers:

And these words, which I command thee this day, shall be in thine heart:
And thou shalt teach them diligently unto thy children, and shalt talk of them when

thou sittest in thine house, and when thou walkest by the way, and when thou liest down, and when thou risest up.

It was impossible to place the slavery question on the footing Douglas wished to put it without repudiating the Declaration of Independence—or, which came to the same thing, without caricaturing it into Douglas' interpretation: so that "all men are created equal" was said to mean that "all British subjects on this continent were equal to British subjects born and residing in Great Britain." For whatever private expressions of repugnance to slavery Douglas' biographers may dig up, the fact remains that all his public expressions were calculated to gain acceptance of the proposition that slavery was a matter of moral indifference. This, to Lincoln, meant inscribing new words in the heart of America, in place of the old ones.

Douglas stumped up and down the country, asserting his humanity by saying that "we ought to extend to the Negro race, and to all other dependent races, all the privileges, and all the immunities which they can exercise consistently with the safety of society . . ." From this Lincoln would not have dissented. But, in answer to the question, what are those rights and privileges? Douglas answered: "Each state, and each territory, must decide that for itself: We of Illinois have decided for ourselves. We tried slavery, kept it up for twelve years *and, finding that it was not profitable,* we abolished it *for that reason.*" Thus, as Lincoln repeatedly charged—not the safety of society, but the profitability of slavery—was to be made the measure of the Negro's rights. Whether or not Lincoln was just in ascribing a positive zeal for slavery to Douglas, he was undoubtedly right in implying that there was no practical difference between a position of alleged neutrality and one of positive zeal. The following is from Lincoln's Peoria speech:

This declared indifference, but, as I must think, covert real zeal for the spread of slavery, I can not but hate. I hate it because of the monstrous injustice of slavery itself. I hate it because it deprives our republican example of its just influence in the world—enables the enemies of free institutions, with plausibility, to taunt us as hypocrites—causes the real friends of freedom to doubt our sincerity, and especially because it forces so many really good men amongst ourselves into an open war with the very principles of civil liberty—criticizing the Declaration of Independence, and insisting that there is no right principle of action but self-interest.

According to Lincoln, the unique value of the American Union lay in its incorporating a moral principle: change the principle by virtue of which the Union constitutes a moral association of a certain kind, and you have dissolved the Union. Lincoln did, at one time, say that he would consent even to the extension of slavery, rather than see the Union dissolved, just as he would consent to any great evil in order to avoid a greater one. What he meant, however, was that he would consent to practical compromises, such as those of 1820 and 1850, which did not imply more than a readjustment of the *modus vivendi.* But the compromise Douglas offered the southern radicals in 1854 was not one in which a lesser evil was accepted, but one in which what had heretofore been regarded as evil was now acknowledged not to be an evil at all. If such an acknowledgment was once made, there would be no grounds for resisting the evil in the future. As Lincoln correctly predicted, such an appetite as that which Douglas appeased grows by what it feeds upon. Before the Repeal of the Missouri Compromise all the southern leaders had asked for was acknowledgment of their rightful claims in the national territory. Soon thereafter, they were demanding congressional protection for slavery in that territory. And, as Lincoln forcefully pointed out, if there was no moral difference between taking slaves and hogs to Kansas, if both were equally property, there was no moral reason why both should not be bought on the cheapest market—and as slaves might be bought cheapest on the coast of Africa, he was certain that demands for revival of the slave trade would also soon be made. Once the premises were firmly fixed, it was only a question of time until the public mind could be brought to accept all the consequences. The only point at which resistance to all these consequences could be made, Lincoln believed, was at the point which established their premises. This was Douglas' Nebraska Bill.

Lincoln's attitude toward this whole problem is, again, suggestive of one of the central themes of Aristotle's *Politics.* Aristotle asks, by virtue of what is it that the identity of a *polis* is established? It is not because men inhabit a certain place, Aristotle says, because a wall could be built around the Peloponnesus—but that would not make those so embraced fellow citizens. Similarly, it is not any particular group of citizens; for the citizens who comprise a city are always changing, like the water in a river. A *polis,* Aristotle says, is a partnership or association, a partnership in a *politeia.* And the *politeia* is the form of the *polis,* as the soul is the form of the body. Therefore the *polis* is no longer the same when the *politeia* changes, any more than a chorus is the same when the persons who have comprised a tragic chorus now constitute a comic chorus. I have had to use the Greek word *politeia,* because it is usually translated *constitution,* as in the expression *American Constitution.* But the Constitution is a set of laws, albeit fundamental laws. However, the *politeia* is not the laws, but is rather the animating principle of the laws, by virtue of which the laws are laws of a certain kind. Consequently, Aristotle says, "the laws should be laid down, and all people do lay them down, to suit the *politeiai* and not the *politeiai* to suit the laws." This relationship is beautifully expressed in a fragmentary writing of Lincoln's in which he draws an analogy based on a verse in the Book of Proverbs: "A word fitly spoken is like apples of gold in pictures of silver":

Without the Constitution and the Union, we could not have attained the result; but even these are not the cause of our great prosperity. There is something back of these, entwining itself more closely about the human heart. That something is the principle of "Liberty to all"—the principle that clears the path for all—gives hope to all—and, by consequence, enterprise and industry to all. The expression of that principle, in our Declaration of Independence, was most happy, and fortunate . . . The assertion of that principle, at that time, was the word "fitly spoken," which has proved an "apple of gold" to us. The Union, and the Constitution, are the pictures of silver, subsequently framed around it. The picture was made, not to conceal, or destroy the apple; but to adorn and preserve it. The picture was made for the apple—not the apple for the picture.

To preserve that apple of gold Lincoln joined battle with Douglas.

VIII

I said before, in presenting Douglas' case, that all, or nearly all, eminent present-day historians are agreed that slavery had reached its natural limits of expansion in 1858, and that therefore Douglas' popular sovereignty formula would have operated to make the remaining territory of the continental United States into free states. I should feel greater diffidence than I actually do in opposing the great array of authorities with whom I now join issue, were it not for the fact that all of those with whom I am acquainted seem to me to share certain common unexamined premises.

To show how unjustified is the assurance that slavery would not have spread, let me first present a passage which contains Lincoln's chief explicit arguments against the notion that popular sovereignty could prevent the expansion of slavery:

How has the planting of slavery in new countries always been effected? It has now been decided that slavery cannot be kept out of our new territories by any legal means. In what do our new territories differ in this respect from the old Colonies when slavery was first planted within them? It was planted, as Mr. Clay once declared, and as history proves true, by industrious men in spite of the wishes of the people; the mother government refusing to prohibit it, and withholding from the people of the Colonies the authority to prohibit it for themselves. Mr. Clay says this was one of the great and just causes of complaint against Great Britain by the Colonies, and the best apology we can now make for having the institution amongst us. In that precise condition, our Nebraskan politicians have at last succeeded in placing our own new territories. . . .

In line with the argument of this passage, Lincoln frequently called attention to the configuration of slavery on the map. You can see that large parts of Missouri, Kentucky, Virginia, Maryland, and Delaware, which contained slavery (in some parts a great deal of slavery), were of the same latitude as, and not conspicuously different in soil and climate from, large parts of Illinois, Indiana, and Ohio. Only a legal prohibition, the Ordinance of 1787, Lincoln said, had kept slavery from the latter. And Lincoln did not hesitate to labor the point that the southern part of Nebraska, i.e., the present state of Kansas, was in a latitude, and of a soil and climate, not conspicuously different from Missouri. As a point of information, I add that the heaviest concentration of slaves, from 25 to 37 per cent of the population, was in the block of counties that extended east from Kansas City, across the center of the state of Missouri. The southern part of the state, except the southeast corner, was almost entirely free of slaves.

Professor Randall speaks of the "negligible amount of slavery" in Kansas in 1858. But a sufficient, if not a necessary, reason why there was a negligible amount of slavery in Kansas in 1858 was because northern free-soilers were literally in arms in their determination to keep slavery out of Kansas—and the Republican party was a great and active political vehicle for supporting this determination. Slaveowners would not go to Kansas with their peculiar property at the risk of great personal financial loss. But if the public mind in the North could have been brought to regard Negro slaves as merely a species of property, and there had been no further hostility on the part of Northerners to slaveowners entering Kansas, how do we know that slavery might not then have been planted there?

A good deal has been said and written about the "natural limits of slavery expansion." Douglas himself repeated over and over again that where soil, climate, and economic conditions did not conspire to make slavery profitable, it would never go. But what, precisely, is the criterion of profitability? The institution of slavery was, as I have said, both uneconomic and dynamic. The race problem attached the South to its peculiar institution with a ferocity which could never be measured in dollars and cents. And the very unprofitability of slavery made the necessity to find new profitable lands for slavery ever more urgent. It is idle to say that this vicious circle could have been broken by "natural" economic forces. Even if a compromise had been reached in 1858 by which slavery was in fact given up in *all* the territories of the continental United States, but in which compromise the moral right of slavery was unquestioned—do we know that this would not have turned the pressure of the southern leaders towards foreign conquest and enslavement? Was not the Mexican War largely motivated by this? And was not Douglas himself in favor of the purchase, or conquest, of Cuba—as a large new slave property?

One more point with respect to the thesis of a "natural" limit to slavery expansion: It is a point which Lincoln makes implicitly, yet emphatically. In a passage which is repeated in many of his speeches, he says that:

Brooks of South Carolina once declared that when this Constitution was framed, its framers did not look to the institution existing until this day. When he said this, I think he stated a fact that is fully borne out by the history of the times. But he also said they were better and wiser men than the men of these days; yet the men of these days had experience which they had not, and by the invention of the cotton gin it became a necessity in this country that slavery should be perpetual. I now say that, willingly or unwillingly, purposely or without purpose, Judge Douglas has been the most prominent instrument in changing the position of the institution of slavery—which the fathers of the government expected to come to an end ere this—and putting it upon Brooks's cotton gin basis—placing it where he openly confesses he has no desire there shall ever be an end of it.

"Brooks's cotton gin basis"—what does this really mean? Lincoln does not draw the full and most weighty inferences—inferences which would not have been rhetorically effective. The institution of slavery, said Brooks, in agreement with Lincoln (and I think no one seriously disputes this), was thought by the Founding Fathers to be in the course of extinction. The Founding Fathers were wise men—but men less wise know something which the Fathers' wisdom could not encompass—the "necessity" for slavery which was born with the cotton gin. In other words, the invention of the cotton gin revolutionized the institution of slavery. The "natural" limits to slavery in 1790 were totally destroyed before the year 1791 was out. There are then no natural limits to slavery, except what is relative to certain highly "artificial" circumstances.

Lincoln, of course, never criticized the Founding Fathers, yet he implicitly finds fault with a too great optimism on their part that circumstances would solve the slavery problem. Whatever excuse there may have been for them, he thought that there could be no excuse for anyone in his day, with the experience of the cotton gin, to rely on such circumstances. Prudence is in large part an adaptation of principle to circumstance. Perhaps it is more a consideration of circumstances than of principles. Yet it is a part of prudence —perhaps the highest part—to foresee the impossibility of foreseeing future circumstance. The only guarantee that slavery would not become national in the future, Lincoln felt, was in enshrining the moral conviction that slavery was wrong in the heart of all policy dealing with it. Only in this way could unforeseen and unforeseeable contingencies be provided for. To anyone who thinks that experience has shown that no future inventions would have again revolutionized slavery, as the cotton gin did, I would ask, How does he know what course the struggle between capital and labor would have taken had chattel slavery been at hand as a real alternative? Who knows that, particularly in such fields as mining, ranch farming, and many branches of manufacturing, slavery might not have proved "profitable"?

The thesis is widely accepted that slave labor could never have competed with free labor. But historians write with a backward glance at the masses of free labor that actually came to our shores in the latter part of the nineteenth century. But do we know that the spread of slavery, by one means or another, would not have prevented this immigration? There is a tacit premise that an industrial society could only develop upon the basis of free labor. That that was actually the way it developed in America in the latter half of the nineteenth and twentieth centuries is true. But does not the experience of national social-ism and communism show that this is by no means necessarily the case? If the South could have been wedded to an uneconomic labor system because of the race question, do we know that similar factors might not have fastened it upon an industrial North? Could a demonstration that the introduction of the American Constitution would vastly increase productivity in the Soviet Union induce the men in the Kremlin to relax their grip on power? I do not suggest any of these questions as indicating probabilities, although I think they do indicate possibilities. The range of the possibilities is, however, so great, that some of them may have been quite probable. That they do not seem probable to us today only indicates, I think, how well Lincoln did his work. For these possibilities became impossibilities because, but only because, Lincoln fought his great fight in 1858 primarily on the basis of moral principle.

IX

There is one thing more that must be emphasized in order to understand why Lincoln believed such a fight was so essential in 1858. Lincoln's concern with world freedom has appeared in many of the passages cited here. And, of course, no one who has heard or read the Gettysburg Address can ever forget it. Lincoln did, indeed, believe that our Union was the "last, best hope of earth" that men might live under free institutions. Whether the political order Lincoln believed to be the best, and freest, was, or is, the best and freest possible, need not be disputed for present purposes. Few, however (outside the Iron Curtain) would doubt that the future of mankind's freedom did then, as it does now, rest largely with this Union. Lincoln never felt that any price was too high to pay to preserve the Union. He might have doubted this had the welfare of Americans alone been at stake. But to Lincoln the ultimate responsi-bility of American statesmanship was always, not to Americans, but to the world. Standing in Independence Hall, Philadelphia, in 1861, on his way to take office, Lincoln made it clear that he would make no concession, even to save what men might call the Union, that involved a repudiation of the Decla-ration of Independence. For, Lincoln implied, the Declaration of Independ-ence, although proclaiming the *rights* of humanity as the just basis of every political order, laid upon the first nation dedicated to the justice it proclaimed a *duty* that took precedence of every right. In his words at that time, the Declaration of Independence "gave liberty not alone to the people of this country, but hope to all the world, for all future time. It was that which gave promise that in due time the weights would be lifted from the shoulders of all men, and that all should have an equal chance."

SELECTED SUGGESTED READINGS

The Collected Works of Abraham Lincoln. Edited by Roy P. Basler. 9 vols. New Brunswick: Rutgers University Press, 1953.

See the following selections from the *Collected Works:*
"Speech at Peoria, Illinois," October 16, 1854, *Collected Works*, II, 247–83.
"Speech at Springfield, Illinois," June 26, 1857, *Collected Works*, II, 398–410.
"A House Divided: Speech delivered at Springfield, Illinois," June 16, 1858, *Collected Works*, II, 461–69.
"Address at Cooper Institute, New York," February 27, 1860, *Collected Works*, III, 522–50.
"First Inaugural Address," March 4, 1861, *Collected Works*, IV, 262–71.
"Emancipation Proclamation," January 1, 1863, *Collected Works*, VI, 28–30.
"To Erastus Corning and Others," June 12, 1863, *Collected Works*, VI, 260–69.
"To James C. Conkling," August 26, 1863, *Collected Works*, VI, 406–10.
"Gettysburg Address," November 19, 1863, *Collected Works*, VII, 17–23.
"Second Inaugural Address," March 4, 1865, *Collected Works*, VIII, 332–33.

Created Equal? The Complete Lincoln-Douglas Debates of 1858. Edited by Paul M. Angle. Chicago: University of Chicago Press, 1958.

In the Name of the People: Speeches and Writings of Lincoln and Douglas in the Ohio Campaign of 1859. Edited by Harry V. Jaffa and Robert W. Johanssen. Columbus: Ohio State University Press, 1959.

★ FREDERICK DOUGLASS *Herbert J. Storing*

One of the major themes of American statesmanship and political thought is the indelible impression made upon the American polity by the institution of slavery. Few men understood that institution so well as Frederick Douglass. Few men labored so wisely and effectively to destroy it. Few men saw so deeply into its implications. Douglass never abandoned the perspective of the black American. He was always and deliberately a partisan, in the sense that he adopted the stance and the duties of one who speaks for only a part (though in this case a uniquely important part) of the political whole. Yet few men deserve so fully the rank of American statesman.

Douglass began his public career when, not three years after his escape from slavery and while leading the hard life of a common laborer in New Bedford, Massachusetts, he accepted an invitation to speak a few words at an 1841 anti-slavery convention on his experiences as a slave. He spoke so well that he was invited by the Massachusetts Anti-Slavery Sociey to become one of its agents, telling of his experiences throughout the eastern states. But it was not enough for him to follow the advice of his white abolitionist friends: "Give us the facts," they said, "we will take care of the philosophy." Douglass' mind was always working; he could not talk about slavery without thinking about it. "It did not entirely satisfy me to *narrate* wrongs—I felt like *denouncing* them."[1]

Inevitably doubts were expressed whether a man who reasoned so well and in such fine and eloquent language could ever have been a slave. Partly in response to these doubts Douglass wrote the first of his several autobiographical works, *A Narrative of the Life of Frederick Douglass, An American Slave*, published in 1845.[2] The facts were established—at considerable risk to Douglass, for his whereabouts thereby became known in Maryland—but the small volume is a good deal more than a narrative. It is, in fact, an excellent treatise, in narrative form, on the inner workings and principles of the institution of American slavery. Like Harriet Beecher Stowe, who drew on his volume, Douglass showed how the best in slavery is implicated in the worst and pulled

[1]Frederick Douglass, *Life and Times of Frederick Douglass, the Complete Autobiography* (New York, 1962), p. 217. Hereafter cited as *Life and Times*.
[2]Frederick Douglass, *A Narrative of the Life of Frederick Douglass, An American Slave* (Garden City, New York, 1963).

down to it. He described how his kind and tender-hearted Baltimore mistress, who first taught him to read, painfully learned "that I sustained to her the relation of a mere chattel, and that for her to treat me as a human being was not only wrong, but dangerously so"; and he described the evil effects upon her of the lesson. He described the slave-breaker, Covey, who could rent slaves cheaply because of his reputation for restoring them to their masters chastened and despirited. But at what a cost! Covey lurked around his own plantation, spying on the slaves, sometimes crawling on his hands and knees to surprise them—utterly degrading himself in the exercise of his miserable mastership. Though Douglass spent his rare moments of rest with Covey "in a sort of beast-like stupor," the natural human desire for liberty continued to burn fitfully. It burst into flame when, unjustly attacked by Covey, Douglass successfully defended himself in a two-hour struggle. From that time on he ceased being a slave in fact, though he might remain a slave in form; for he determined that in the future no one should succeed in beating him without succeeding in killing him.

Covey represented the depths of slavery; and Douglass' condition improved thereafter, but the improvements only made the slave less contented with his bonds. Hired by his master to a fair and kind man who treated him well, Douglass responded by making an unsuccessful attempt to escape. Instead of selling him south, his master permitted him to return to Baltimore where he was hired out and later permitted to hire his own time. Yet the experience only flaunted the robbery of slavery before Douglass' eyes and made him more anxious to escape. The more slavery adopted the characteristics of freedom, the more intolerable it became. Douglass experienced the contradiction of the house divided against itself, and he understood it fully:

I have observed this in my experience of slavery,—that whenever my condition was improved, instead of its increasing my contentment, it only increased my desire to be free, and set me to thinking of plans to gain my freedom. I have found that, to make a contented slave, it is necessary to make a thoughtless one. It is necessary to darken his moral and mental vision, and, as far as possible, to annihilate the power of reason. He must be able to detect no inconsistencies in slavery; he must be made to feel that slavery is right; and he can be brought to that only when he ceases to be a man.[3]

MORAL REFORM AND POLITICAL ACTION

During his first years as a public man Douglass was a devoted disciple of William Lloyd Garrison, fully accepting his argument that the Constitution was a pro-slavery document and his doctrine of non-voting. "With him, I held it to be the first duty of the non-slaveholding states to dissolve the union with

---

[3]Douglass, *A Narrative*, p. 98. See *Life and Times*, p. 150.

the slaveholding states, and hence my cry, like his, was 'No union with slave-holders'."[4] Douglass liked "radical measures," whether by the abolitionists or the slaveholders. "I like to gaze upon these two contending armies, for I believe it will hasten the dissolution of the present unholy Union, which has been justly stigmatized as 'a covenant with death, an agreement with hell.' "[5] He held the Constitution to be "radically and essentially slave-holding." "For my part I had rather that my right hand should wither by my side than cast a ballot under the Constitution of the United States."[6]

Douglass carried these views with him when he moved to Rochester, New York, and established his own abolitionist newspaper. "Slavery will be attacked in its stronghold—the compromises of the Constitution, and the cry of disunion shall be more fearlessly proclaimed, till slavery be abolished, the Union dissolved, or the sun of this guilty nation must go down in blood."[7] The Constitution and government of the United States are "a most foul and bloody conspiracy" against the rights of the slaves. "Down with both, for it is not fit that either should exist!"[8] The oath to support the Constitution "requires that which is morally impossible."[9] As for the Free Soilers, who attempted to justify their support of the Constitution as a way of promoting beneficial measures, "they have our sympathies, but not our judgment." Douglass rejected their "theory of human government, which makes it necessary to do evil, that good may come." A Constitution at war with itself cannot be lived up to, and therefore "the platform for us to occupy, is outside that piece of parchment."[10]

As he exercised his always strong and independent judgment, Douglass became increasingly doubtful of the Garrisonian position, and in 1851 he announced his break with it.[11] He adhered to the opinion that the basic problem was a moral one and that the abolition of slavery depended upon a moral regeneration. But he concluded that the Garrisonians had no adequate answer to the question of how this was to be done. Moreover, he came to see that the Garrisonian position was not only politically but morally defective. For all their righteousness, the Garrisonians needed to learn morality in the politics of a free (though imperfect) republic. "As a mere expression of abhorrence of slavery," the Garrisonian sentiment of no union with slaveholders was a good one; "but it expresses no intelligible principle of action, and throws no light

[4] *Life and Times*, p. 260.
[5] Philip S. Foner, ed. *The Life and Writings of Frederick Douglass*, (New York, 1950), I, 269–70. Hereafter cited as *Life and Writings*.
[6] *Life and Writings*, I, 274–5.
[7] *Life and Writings*, I, 347.
[8] *Life and Writings*, I, 379.
[9] *Life and Writings*, II, 117.
[10] *Life and Writings*, II, 119.
[11] *Life and Times*, pp. 260–61.

on the pathway of duty. Defined, as its authors define it, it leads to false doctrines, and mischievous results."[12] It amounted, in fact, to an abandonment of the great idea with which the anti-slavery movement began: "It started to free the slave. It ends by leaving the slave to free himself."[13]

Douglass adopted the position of the political abolitionists that slavery was "a system of lawless violence; that it *never was lawful, and never can be made so. . . .*"[14] He was "sick and tired of arguing on the slaveholders' side of this question,"[15] and he came to the conclusion that the slaveholders were not only wrong about slavery but were also wrong about the Constitution. He adopted the view "that the Constitution, construed in the light of well established rules of legal interpretation, might be made consistent in its details with the noble purposes avowed in its preamble; and that hereafter we should insist upon the application of such rules to that instrument, and demand that it be wielded in behalf of emancipation."[16] Douglass came to understand the design of the Framers of the Constitution who tried, while making necessary provision for the existing institution of slavery, to leave no principle in the Constitution that would sanction slavery and no word that would defile the constitution of a free people. Once he penetrated this design, Douglass seized the opportunity it provided. The black could now speak fully the language of the law, the language of defense of the Constitution. He could now call upon the country to return, not only to the fundamental political principles of the republic as expressed in the Declaration of Independence, but to its fundamental legal principles as expressed in the Constitution.

Under his new persuasion Douglass held that "it is the first duty of every American citizen, whose conscience permits him so to do, to use his *political* as well as his *moral* power for its overthrow."[17] "Men should not, under the guidance of a false philosophy, be led to fling from them such powerful instrumentalities against Slavery as the Constitution and the ballot."[18] Thus Douglass embarked upon a course of political activity that sought to maintain the moral purity and therefore the moral power of Abolition, while at the same time finding ways of making it politically effective. Defending his support of the Free Soil candidate in 1852, Douglass stated the following rule of political action.

It is evident that all reforms have their beginning with ideas, and that for a time they have to rely solely on the tongue and pen for progress, until they gain a sufficient

[12] *Life and Writings,* II, 351.
[13] *Life and Writings,* II, 350.
[14] *Life and Writings,* II, 156.
[15] *Life and Writings,* II, 149.
[16] *Life and Writings,* II, 155.
[17] *Life and Writings,* II, 156.
[18] *Life and Writings,* II, 177.

number of adherents to make themselves felt at the ballot-box. . . . We ask no man to lose sight of any of his aims and objects. We only ask that they may be allowed to serve out their natural probation. Our rule of political action is this: the voter ought to see to it that his vote shall secure the highest good possible, at the same time that it does no harm. [19]

With his tongue and pen Douglass continued to fight for uncompromising abolition; but when the time came to go to the polls he focussed on the good that he could do in the immediate future rather than on the good he was aiming for in the long run.

The mission of the political abolitionists of this country is to abolish slavery. The means to accomplish this great end is, first, to disseminate anti-slavery sentiment; and, secondly, to combine that sentiment and render it a political force which shall, for a time, operate as a check on violent measures for supporting slavery; and, finally, overthrow the great evil of slavery itself. [20]

Douglass' problems well illustrate the apparent dilemma of the reformer in politics. In 1856, for example, writing on "What is My Duty as an Anti-Slavery Voter?" Douglass argued that "the purity of the cause is the success of the cause." While he might participate in politics, "the first duty of the Reformer is to be right. If right, he may go forward; but if wrong, or partly wrong, he is as an house divided against itself, and will fall." Since the Republican Party did "not occupy this high Anti-Slavery ground, (and what is worse, does not mean to occupy it)," Douglass urged his readers to vote for the presidential candidate of the Radical Abolitionists, even at the risk of throwing the election to the Democrats and losing Kansas to slavery. "We deliberately prefer the loss of Kansas to the loss of our Anti-Slavery integrity." [21] Yet four months later, in August, 1856, Douglass abandoned the Abolitionist candidate, Gerrit Smith, and announced his support of Republicans John Fremont and William Dayton. The purity of the cause was subordinate, even for the partisan reformer, to a higher morality.

The time has passed for an honest man to attempt any defence of a right to change his opinion as to political methods of opposing Slavery. Anti-Slavery consistency itself, in our view, requires of the Anti-Slavery voter that disposition of his vote and his influence, which, in all the circumstances and likelihoods of the case tend most to the triumph of Free Principles in the Councils and Government of the nation. It is not to be consistent to pursue a course politically this year, merely because that course seemed the best last year, or at any previous time. Right Anti-Slavery action is that which deals the severest deadliest blow upon Slavery that can be given at that particular time. Such action is always consistent, however different may be the forms through which it expresses itself. [22]

[19] *Life and Writings*, II, 213–14.
[20] *Life and Writings*, II, 220.
[21] *Life and Writings*, II, 391–94.
[22] *Life and Writings*, II, 397.

On this basis, Douglass later supported Abraham Lincoln, although often with grave doubts and usually with impatience and exasperation. His criticisms of Lincoln, especially during the years prior to the Emancipation Proclamation, were often cutting and even harsh. He found Lincoln's first Inaugural Address a "double-tongued document"; he accused him of being destitute of anti-slavery principle; he contended that he was "active, decided, and brave" for the support of slavery, "and passive, cowardly, and treacherous to the very cause of liberty to which he owes his election"; he questioned his honesty.[23] He found the Emancipation Proclamation itself disappointing, making a burden of what should have been a joy, touching neither justice nor mercy.[24] "Abraham Lincoln, President of the United States, Commander-in-Chief of the army and navy, in his own peculiar, cautious, forbearing and hesitating way, slow, but we hope sure, has, while the loyal heart was near breaking with despair, proclaimed and declared" the Emancipation Proclamation.[25]

As circumstances drew the black leader and the white statesman closer together, Douglass grew in his understanding of Lincoln. This is not to say that their relations were ever smooth or that Douglass saw matters as Lincoln saw them. Regarding the use by the Union of black troops, for example, they were constantly at odds. After months of urging that black troops should be used and long negotiations about how they would be used, Douglass reluctantly agreed to support a system that was in some respects unfair to black troops, because he thought that the cause of black freedom was served by cooperation even on such terms.

Douglass met in Lincoln true statesmanship and came to understand his own and his people's place in relation to it. While Charles Sumner was "to me and to my oppressed race . . . higher than the highest, better than the best of all our statesmen," Lincoln was simply "the greatest statesman that ever presided over the destinies of this Republic."[26] Douglass gave expression to this understanding in 1876 on the occasion of the unveiling of the Freedman's Monument in Washington, D.C.[27] Lincoln was not, he said, "in the fullest sense of the word, either our man or our model. In his interests, in his associations, in his habits of thought, and in his prejudices, he was a white man." He came to office on the principle of opposition to the extension of slavery, but he was prepared to defend and perpetuate slavery where it existed, and his whole policy was motivated by "his patriotic devotion to the interests of his own race." Yet, "while Abraham Lincoln saved for you a country, he delivered

[23] *Life and Writings,* III, 72, 186, 268, 127, 267.
[24] *Life and Writings,* III, 309.
[25] *Life and Writings,* III, 273.
[26] *Life and Writings,* IV, 239, 368.
[27] *Life and Writings,* IV, 309ff.

us from a bondage, according to Jefferson, one hour of which was worse than ages of the oppression your fathers rose in rebellion to oppose." Lincoln's very prejudices were an element of his success in preparing the American people for the great conflict and bringing them safely through it. "Viewed from the genuine abolition ground, Mr. Lincoln seemed tardy, cold, dull, and indifferent; but measuring him by the sentiment of his country, a sentiment he was bound as a statesman to consult, he was swift, zealous, radical, and determined."

The blacks believed in Lincoln, despite acts and words that tried the faith and taxed the understanding.

When he tarried long in the mountain; when he strangely told us that we were the cause of the war; when he still more strangely told us that we were to leave the land in which we were born; when he refused to employ our arms in defence of the Union; when, after accepting our service as colored soldiers, he refused to retaliate our murder and torture as colored prisoners; when he told us he would save the Union if he could with slavery; when he revoked the Proclamation of Emancipation of General Freemont; when he refused to remove the popular commander of the Army of the Potomac, in the days of its inaction and defeat, who was more zealous in his efforts to protect slavery than to suppress rebellion; when we saw all this, and more, we were at times grieved, stunned, and greatly bewildered; but our hearts believed while they ached and bled.

Nor was this merely a blind, unreasoning faith. "Despite the mist and haze that surrounded him; despite the tumult, the hurry, and confusion of the hour, we were able to take a comprehensive view of Abraham Lincoln. . . ." Douglass never abandoned his point of view as a black spokesman and leader, but he did come to understand the deeper harmony of black and white of which Lincoln was the guardian.

It mattered little to us what language he might employ on special occasions; it mattered little to us, when we fully knew him, whether he was swift or slow in his movements; it was enough for us that Abraham Lincoln was at the head of a great movement, and was in living and earnest sympathy with that movement, which, in the nature of things, must go on until slavery should be utterly and forever abolished in the United States.[28]

"WHAT COUNTRY HAVE I?"

In England between 1845 and 1847, where he had fled to prevent recapture and to preach Abolitionism, Douglass often explained that he was "an outcast from the society of my childhood, and an outlaw in the land of my birth." "That men should be patriotic is to me perfectly natural; and as a philosophical fact, I am able to give it an *intellectual* recognition. But no further can I go."[29]

[28] *Life and Writings,* IV, 314.
[29] *Life and Writings,* I, 126.

I have no love for America, as such; I have no patriotism. I have no country. What country have I? The institutions of this country do not know me, do not recognize me as a man. . . . I have not, I cannot have, any love for this country, as such, or for its Constitution. I desire to see its overthrow as speedily as possible, and its Constitution shivered in a thousand fragments, rather than this foul curse should continue to remain as now.[30]

When Douglass abandoned Garrisonianism he no longer saw the black as, strictly speaking, an "outlaw," because he now held that slavery was not lawful under the Constitution. The black was still an "outcast," because he was in fact held a slave; but he had a moral and a legal claim to the protection of "his" country. This is the theme of one of Douglass' major pre-war statements, an oration given in Rochester, New York, in 1852, on "The Meaning of July Fourth for the Negro."

Fellow-citizens, pardon me, allow me to ask, why am I called upon to speak here to-day? What have I, or those I represent, to do with your national independence? Are the great principles of political freedom and of natural justice, embodied in that Declaration of Independence extended to us? . . .

Would to God, both for your sakes and ours, that an affirmative answer could be truthfully returned to these questions. . . .

. . . This Fourth July is *yours* not *mine.* You may rejoice, I must mourn. To drag a man in fetters into the grand illuminated temple of liberty, and call upon him to join you in joyous anthems, were inhuman mockery and sacrilegious irony. Do you mean, citizens, to mock me, by asking me to speak to-day?[31]

In return for mockery, Douglass gave his audience the whip of America's self-betrayal. Looking at the day from the slave's point of view, he declared that the character and conduct of the nation had never looked blacker. "America is false to the past, false to the present, and solemnly binds herself to be false to the future." To those who said that the Abolitionists denounce when they ought to persuade, Douglass asked, what is it that needs argument? That the slave is a man? That a man is entitled to liberty? That slavery is wrong? That slavery is not divine? Words are valuable now only as they move to action.

At a time like this, scorching irony, not convincing argument, is needed. O! had I the ability, and could reach the nation's ear, I would to-day pour out a fiery stream of biting ridicule, blasting reproach, withering sarcasm, and stern rebuke. For it is not light that is needed, but fire; it is not the gentle shower, but thunder. We need the storm, the whirlwind, and the earthquake. The feeling of the nation must be quickened; the conscience of the nation must be roused; the propriety of the nation must be startled; the hypocrisy of the nation must be exposed; and its crimes against God and man must be proclaimed and denounced.[32]

---

[30] *Life and Writings,* I, 236.
[31] *Life and Writings,* II, 188–89.
[32] *Life and Writings,* II, 192.

And so Douglass flayed his fellow-citizens:

Fellow-citizens, I will not enlarge further on your national inconsistencies. The existence of slavery in this country brands your republicanism as a sham, your humanity as a base pretense, and your Christianity as a lie. It destroys your moral power abroad: it corrupts your politicians at home. It saps the foundation of religion; it makes your name a hissing and a bye-word to a mocking earth. It is the antagonistic force in your government, the only thing that seriously disturbs and endangers your *Union.* It fetters your progress; it is the enemy of improvement; the deadly foe of education; it fosters pride; it breeds insolence; it promotes vice; it shelters crime; it is a curse to the earth that supports it; and yet you cling to it as if it were the sheet anchor of all your hopes.[33]

Strong words; yet words directed to "fellow citizens," as Douglass repeatedly addressed his audience. Five years later, however, the Supreme Court in the *Dred Scott* decision, denied Douglass' interpretation of the Constitution, holding that blacks could claim none of the rights and privileges secured by the Constitution to citizens of the United States. In his speech on this decision Douglass was not scorching fellow citizens, (a term he used here only once, and that in the formal salutation) but defending himself against an enemy. The decision was "infamous," "devilish," "the judicial incarnation of wolfishness," "an open, glaring, and scandalous tissue of lies." Douglass appealed against "this hell-black judgment of the Supreme Court, to the court of common sense and common humanity." He declared that "all that is merciful and just, on earth and in Heaven, will execrate and despise this edict of Taney."[34] On most occasions, as Douglass gave ample evidence of understanding, such an unqualified partisan attack on the supreme instrument of lawfulness would be utterly irresponsible and self-defeating. But the Court's decision in *Dred Scott* amounted to an act of outright war against the black, excluding him from participation in the American political community; and the black had to defend himself in like manner, even at the risk of seriously damaging that very political community in which he sought to secure his rightful place. Thus Douglass confessed in his autobiography to a feeling allied to satisfaction at the prospect of a war between North and South. "Standing outside the pale of American humanity, denied citizenship, unable to call the land of my birth my country, and adjudged by the Supreme Court of the United States to have no rights which white men were bound to respect, and longing for the end of the bondage of my people, I was ready for any political upheaval which should bring about a change in the existing condition of things."[35]

It is instructive in this connection to compare Douglass' speech on the *Dred Scott* decision with his speech in 1883 on the *Civil Rights* case, striking down federal legislation prohibiting discrimination against blacks. The war

---

[33] *Life, and Writings,* II, 201.
[34] *Life and Writings,* II, 410–12.
[35] *Life and Times,* p. 329.

was over, for the country and for the black, and the character of the speech was determined by that great fact. This is not to suggest that the *Civil Rights* case was not a serious blow. Douglass saw it as standing in a line that included the forcing of slavery into Kansas, the enactment of the Fugitive Slave Act, the repeal of the Missouri Compromise, and the *Dred Scott* decision. "We have been, as a class, grievously wounded, wounded in the house of our friends," he said at the mass meeting called to protest the *Civil Rights* decision.[36] But although wounded, the blacks were not turned out of their political house, as they had been in *Dred Scott;* and Douglass' rhetoric was governed by that difference. Here there was none of the violence of his attack on the Taney decision. He began by noting that he had taken the trouble to write out his remarks, that they might be "well-chosen, and not liable to be misunderstood, distorted, or misrepresented." He suggested that it may be that "the hour calls more loudly for silence than for speech," and he exhibited an unusual reluctance to enter into the criticism he had to utter. He aimed to achieve a certain kind of silence, while speaking. He contended that the most serious evil in the land, "which threatens to undermine and destroy the foundations of our free institutions," is—not race prejudice or injustice to blacks, as one might have expected, but—"the great and apparently increasing want of respect entertained for those to whom are committed the responsibility and the duty of administering our government." Douglass urged his partisan audience never to forget that "whatever may be the incidental mistakes or misconduct of rulers, government is better than anarchy, and patient reform is better than violent revolution." While not interfering with fair criticism, he would give "the emphasis of a voice from heaven" to the repugnance felt by all good citizens to any disrespect for governors.[37] Coming "a little nearer to the case now before us," he began his criticism, but again interrupted himself to caution that "if any man has come here to-night with his breast heaving with passion, his heart flooded with acrimony, wishing and expecting to hear violent denunciation of the Supreme Court, on account of this decision, he has mistaken the object of this meeting and the character of the men by whom it is called."[38] Douglass then entered into a vigorous criticism, but he did so only after having introduced the subject with the greatest circumspection and concern for maintaining the dignity and authority of the Court and the law for which it spoke. This was now the blacks' Court as well as the whites'. Better to have a Court that does serious harm to blacks than to have none at all.

Indeed, the privilege of having a part in the American political institutions was a precious victory that Douglass had helped to win. This privilege did not,

[36] *Life and Writings,* IV, 392ff.
[37] *Life and Writings,* IV, 394.
[38] *Life and Writings,* IV, 395–96.

as Douglass clearly understood, necessarily accompany emancipation. Emancipation could justly be claimed on the basis of the fundamental principles of the American Declaration of Independence and Constitution, and it could therefore be justly argued that in this respect the black's interest was fundamentally identical with the interest of the rest of the nation. Even in his speech on *Dred Scott,* Douglass concluded, "all I ask of the American people is, that they live up to the Constitution, adopt its principles, imbibe its spirit, and enforce its provisions."[39] But while the black fought to be a free man, he also fought to be a free *American.* And while the best American statesmen had always agreed that American principles demanded freedom for the black, there was much less agreement about whether they demanded freedom for the black *in the United States.* With respect to this question—whether the blacks, once freed, should stay in the United States or go elsewhere—it was not so clear that the good of the black and the good of the country were identical. It is of some interest to note that the first official reception by any president of a group of blacks came in 1862 when Abraham Lincoln invited a committee of blacks to lend their support to a plan for colonizing blacks in Central America.[40]

The colonization issue was, of course, an old one. The first printed notice of Frederick Douglass, indeed, was a report in the Garrisonian *Liberator* of March 29, 1839, that the young ex-slave had addressed an anti-colonization meeting, arguing "that the inordinate and intolerable scheme of the American Colonization Society shall never entice or drive *us* from our native soil."[41] From this time until the very end of his long career Douglass fought the numerous schemes of colonization put forward as solutions to the "Negro problem."[42]

Douglass argued the civilizing effect of a permanent location, which the American blacks were just beginning to experience. "We say to every colored man, *be a man where you are.* . . . You must be a man here, and force your way to intelligence, wealth and respectability. If you can't do that here, you can't do it there. By changing your place, you don't change your character." The argument was not simply directed against restless nomadism, although that is part of it. "We believe that contact with the white race, even under the many unjust and painful restrictions to which we are subjected, does more toward our elevation and improvement, than the mere circumstance of being sepa-

[39] *Life and Writings,* II, 424.
[40] Abraham Lincoln, *The Collected Works of Abraham Lincoln,* ed. Roy P. Basler (New Brunswick, New Jersey, 1953), V, 370–75.
[41] *Life and Writings,* I, 25.
[42] The last two substantive pieces in Foner's *Life and Writings* are a "Lecture on Haiti" (1895, IV, 478) and a long essay on "Why the Negro is Lynched" (1894, IV, 491), both of which contain substantial discussions of the colonization issue.

rated from them could do."[43] Although he despised many who made the argument, Douglass nevertheless saw "that the condition of our race has been improved by their situation as slaves, since it has brought them into contact with a superior people, and afforded them facilities for acquiring knowledge"[44] and he fought to keep the blacks in contact with that superior people—superior, it is hardly necessary to add, not in nature but in fact. Douglass saw that the contact was not of equal advantage to the two sides. Speaking of the profit to himself of association with the son of his former master, he said "the law of compensation holds here as well as elsewhere. While this lad could not associate with ignorance without sharing its shade, he could not give his black playmates his company without giving them his superior intelligence as well."[45]

Whatever the whites might think was best for America, the blacks knew what was best for them; and, according to Douglass, they would fight to stay. "Our minds are made up to live here if we can, or die here if we must; so every attempt to remove us, will be, as it ought to be, labor lost. Here we are, and here we shall remain."[46] The black has stayed despite his great differences from the European, despite "greater hardships, injuries and insults than those to which the Indians have been subjected," and despite cunning schemes to teach his children that this is not his home.

It is idle—worse than idle, ever to think of our expatriation, or removal. . . . *We are here,* and here we are likely to be. To imagine that we shall ever be eradicated is absurd and ridiculous. We can be remodified, changed, and assimilated, but never extinguished. We repeat, therefore, that *we are here;* and that this is *our* country; and the question for the philosophers and statesmen of the land ought to be, what principles should dictate the policy of the action toward us?[47]

Douglass did argue that there was no ineradicable prejudice against blacks and that the proper response to prejudice is to root it out rather than to pander to it. He argued that the South had a positive need for the blacks' labor. He argued on the basis of human brotherhood, and he sometimes suggested that greater intercommunication of the races was historically necessary and morally desirable. But he never formed these various suggestions into a comprehensive argument that colonization would be, like slavery, as bad for the country as for the black. Douglass' argument here might be paraphrased as follows. "I think that the United States has a duty to keep her black step-children; I think that she will be enriched by so doing, and that the problems involved in it can be solved. However, the cost to the country of retaining the

---

[43] *Life and Writings,* II, 173.
[44] *Life and Writings,* II, 173.
[45] *Life and Times,* p. 44.
[46] *Life and Writings,* I, 351.
[47] *Life and Writings,* I, 417.

freedman and its possible damage to the fabric of American political life are not questions that it is my duty to ponder deeply. The black is willing—must be willing—to see the American polity pay almost any price, run almost any risk, to admit him. For him it is a matter, not, it is true, of life or death or freedom or slavery, but of that for the sake of which life and freedom are sought; and he will resist any attempt, however reasonable to others, to loosen his grip on the white man's civilization."

The colonization issue was the last great battle in the black's paradoxical war with America to become part of America, and it was in principle his most difficult battle, more difficult than Emancipation, on the one side, or the securing of civil and political rights, on the other. The black's victory in this struggle was commemorated in Douglass' oration at the unveiling of the Freedman's Monument in 1876, from which we have already quoted.[48] This speech contains one of the most profound statements ever made of the relations between the American blacks and the American polity. Douglass described, in stately terms, the setting in the capital of the nation and the audience drawn from all the segments of the government, present to give witness to the blacks' entry into the American community through their praise of America's greatest statesman. He did not succumb to the temptation of shallow praise; he did not claim Lincoln for the blacks; he felt no need to blur the truth. "We fully comprehend the relation of Abraham Lincoln both to ourselves and to the whole people of the United States." Lincoln was a white man, an American of the Americans.

He was preeminently the white man's President, entirely devoted to the welfare of white men. He was ready and willing at any time during the first years of his administration to deny, postpone, and sacrifice the rights of humanity in the colored people to promote the welfare of the white people of this country. In all his education and feeling he was an American of the Americans. . . . The race to which we belong were not the special objects of his consideration. . . . We are at best only his step-children; children by adoption, children by forces of circumstances and necessity.

But the circumstances were such that Lincoln could not promote the welfare of whites without promoting the welfare of blacks, for both rested on the same principle, individual freedom; and their destinies were too entwined ever to be separated. The Freedmen's Monument stood for the blacks' praise of Lincoln but also for their *title* to praise him—step-children, indeed, but, for better or worse, his and the country's children. "Fellow-citizens, I end, as I began, with congratulations. We have done a good work for our race today. In doing honor to the memory of our friend and liberator, we have been doing highest honors to ourselves and those who come after us; we have been fastening ourselves to a name and fame imperishable and immortal. . . ."

[48] *Life and Writings*, IV, 309ff.

WHAT SHALL WE DO WITH THE BLACK?

If, then, the blacks were to stay in the United States, the question was asked, what shall we do with them? Douglass answered, "do nothing with them; mind your business, and let them mind theirs. Your *doing* with them is their greatest misfortune." The question implies "that slavery is the natural order of human relations, and that liberty is an experiment." But the reverse is true, and consequently human duties are mostly negative. "If men were born in need of crutches, instead of having legs, the fact would be otherwise. We should then be in need of help, and would require outside aid; but according to the wiser and better arrangement of nature, our duty is done better by not hindering than by helping our fellow-men; or, in other words, the best way to help them is just to let them help themselves."[49] While not wishing to check any benevolent concern, Douglass suggested pointedly, "Let the American people, who have thus far only kept the colored race staggering between partial philanthropy and cruel force, be induced to try what virtue there is in justice." The black's misfortune is precisely that "he is everywhere treated as an exception to all the general rules which should operate in the relations of other men."[50] "[I]f the Negro cannot stand on his own legs, let him fall. . . . All I ask is, give him a chance to stand on his own legs! Let him alone!"[51]

Let the Negro alone. This was the touchstone; obviously it was not exhaustive. Douglass was well aware that the black did need crutches, for his limbs were stiff from the shackles of slavery. "Time, education, and training will restore him to natural proportions, for, though bruised and blasted, he is yet a man."[52] Douglass knew the debt owed the black, but he did not harp on it. He knew, and in various ways presented, the black's need for generous help as well as his demand for justice; but there was never any question about the priority of the black's demand to be allowed to stand or fall as he is capable of standing or falling.

The demand to be let alone is, however, not so negative as it might sound, due to the scope and character of the whites' "doing" for the blacks in the past. Douglass demanded "the most perfect civil and political equality, and . . . all the rights, privileges and immunities enjoyed by any other members of the body politic." "Save the Negro and you save the nation, destroy the Negro and you destroy the nation, and to save both you must have but one great law

[49] *Life and Writings*, III, 188–90.
[50] *Life and Writings*, III, 190.
[51] *Life and Writings*, IV, 164.
[52] *Life and Writings*, IV, 435.

of Liberty, Equality and Fraternity for all Americans without respect to color."[53]

The two main objectives of Douglass' campaign to have the blacks "left alone," in this fundamental sense of being subject only to the one great law for all Americans, were the right to vote and freedom from color prejudice. The former need not detain us here. Blacks wanted the vote, as Douglass repeatedly explained, because it was their right, because it was a means of education, because its denial was "to brand us with the stigma of inferiority," because it was a means of self defense in a hostile South, and because it was an instrument for maintaining Federal authority in the South.[54]

Douglass' concern with prejudice against the black requires more attention. From the beginning he saw this prejudice as arising from and contributing to the black's enslavement, his proposed expatriation, and his actual degradation. "This prejudice must be removed; and the way for abolitionists and colored persons to remove it, is to act as though it did not exist, and to associate with their fellow creatures irrespective of all complexional differences." Douglass marked out this path for himself and pursued it "at all hazards."[55] He spoke and acted against any form of public discrimination whatsoever against blacks. On trains and ships, in hotels and restaurants, in meetings and other public places, he resisted the conventional expressions of race prejudice. He described what might in modern parlance be called a "stroll-in," when he passed the time waiting for a steamer in New York City walking with two white ladies and had to beat off the attentions of several ruffians as a result. He engaged in such behavior, he said, "with no purpose to inflame the public mind; not to provoke the popular violence; not to make a display of my contempt for public opinion; but simply as a matter of course, and because it was right to do so."[56] Douglass certainly had that love of sheer combat that is necessary to the good politician—"I glory in the fight as well as in the victory"[57]—but he rarely did something that was right unless he thought it was also politic. This was certainly true of his persistent testing and challenging of coventions of race discrimination.

"The question is not can there be social equality?" for that does not exist anywhere. The question is rather, "Can the white and colored people of this country be blended into a common nationality, and enjoy together, in the same country, under the same flag, the inestimable blessings of life, liberty and the pursuit of happiness, as neighborly citizens of a common country?" This

[53] *Life and Writings,* III, 348–49.
[54] *Life and Writings,* IV, 159–60.
[55] *Life and Writings,* I, 387.
[56] *Life and Writings,* II, 126.
[57] *Life and Writings,* I, 137.

is not simply a matter of public behavior. It is true that Douglass argued that "men who travel should leave their prejudices at home,"[58] but fundamentally Douglass believed that men should not *have* any color prejudice that needs to be left at home. For blacks and whites to live together as fellow-citizens, color prejudice must be eradicated. In an essay in 1866 on "The Future of the Colored Race" Douglass stated as his "strongest conviction" that the black would neither be expatriated nor exterminated, nor forever remain a separate and distinct race, "but that he will be absorbed, assimilated, and will only appear finally . . . in the features of a blended race."[59] He emphasized that this would not happen quickly or by any forced process or "out of any theory of the wisdom of such blending of the two races." He did not, he said, advocate intermarriage between the two races; neither did he deprecate it. But seeing this as the only condition finally in which the Negro could survive and flourish in the United States, he naturally advocated a course of action that would prepare for it.

Douglass often displayed the concern with the psychological effects of segregation with which we are today so familiar. Thus an aspect of his campaign to get blacks into the army during the Civil War was the effect that this would have on the blacks' own self-regard, both directly and indirectly through an enhanced regard in the eyes of others. He had a similar concern in other areas, such as voting, but the psychological consideration was never the only reason for Douglass' policy and seldom a major one.

Such considerations were of more than usual importance in the education of the young. Douglass indignantly described how he withdrew his 9-year-old daughter from a private school when it was proposed to teach her separately, "as allowing her to remain there in such circumstances, could only serve to degrade her in her own eyes, and those of the other scholars attending the school."[60] More than twenty years later he urged passage of a bill providing for mixed schools in the District of Columbia "in order that the mad current of prejudice against the Negro may be checked; and also that the baleful influence upon the children of the colored race of being taught by separation from the whites that the whites are superior to them may be destroyed." "Educate the poor white children and the colored children together; let them grow up to know that color makes no difference as to the rights of a man; that both the black man and the white man are at home; that the country is as much the country of one as of the other, and that both together must make it a valuable country." "We want mixed schools not because our colored schools are inferior to white schools—not because colored instructors are inferior to

[58]*Life and Writings*, II, 450.
[59]*Life and Writings*, IV, 195.
[60]*Life and Writings*, I, 372.

white instructors, but because we want to do away with a system that exalts one class and debases another."[61]

There is, then, a connection between the views of Douglass and those of today's integrationists with regard to race prejudice and segregation. But the main lesson lies in the differences. First, although all such segregation carries an implication of black inferiority in the opinion of the white segregators, not all segregation is equally harmful merely on that account. The harm is great in the case of black children, Douglass thought, but it is small as more mature blacks are the objects of segregation. Unlike Martin Luther King, Jr., Douglass did not see segregation as doing any harm *to himself.*[62] Describing harassment by a Syracuse mob in 1861, Douglass said that the aim was to humble and mortify him. "Just as if a man could feel himself insulted by the kick of a jackass, or the barking of a bull-dog. It is, to be sure, neither pleasant to be kicked nor to be barked at, but no man need to think less of himself on account of either."[63] At the same time that he fought to prevent the damage that segregation can do to the self respect of black children and to child-like adults, Douglass held himself forward as an example of the man who has risen above that kind of harm.

Douglass fought prejudice and all its manifestations fundamentally not because of its psychological effect, but because of the objective harm to which prejudice leads. He did express the belief that "the tendency of the age is unification, not isolation; not to clans and classes, but to human brotherhood"; but he did not rest his political case on it. Indeed he expressed this belief in the context of the deep and firm moral and political hold the black has upon *this* country.[64] Douglass' political concern was to free the black from very clear and objective oppression, provide him with the platform of equal opportunity, and show him how to use his opportunity to live a decent, independent, civilized life.

Having despised us, it is not strange that Americans should seek to render us despicable; . . . having denounced us as indolent, it is not strange that they should cripple our enterprise; having assumed our inferiority, it would be extraordinary if they sought to surround us with circumstances which would serve to make us direct contradictions to their assumption.[65]

What concerned Douglass was not fundamentally the whites' despising, denouncing, or assuming, but their rendering despicable, their crippling of enterprise, their imposition of degrading circumstances. The black's fight

---

[61] *Life and Writings,* IV, 288–89.
[62] Martin Luther King, Jr., *Stride Toward Freedom* (New York, 1958), pp. 20–21.
[63] *Life and Writings,* III, 182.
[64] *Life and Writings,* IV, 412.
[65] *Life and Writings,* II, 268.

against prejudice was not, in Douglass' view, fundamentally a fight for "integration"; it was a fight to establish the outworks of his claim to be left alone. "The spirit which would deny a man shelter in a public house, needs but little change to deny him shelter, even in his own house."[66] Douglass was concerned mainly with the shelter, not the spirit.

Consistently with this view, Douglass linked almost every one of his criticisms of social and other forms of segregation with observations on the black's duty to exert himself. "It is too true, that as a People, our aspirations have not been sufficiently elevated; and it is also equally true, that we have been and still are the victims of an ostracism as relentless as the grave. . . ." Yet, "our elevation as a race, is almost wholly dependent upon our own exertions."[67] "He who would be free must strike the first blow," Douglass repeated again and again. But this is not enough—at least in Douglass' opinion. Not all restrictions on freedom are imposed by others. Not all prejudice has its source simply in the mind of the bigot. While striking off his shackles, the black also had to take a responsibility for the good use of his freed limbs and mind.

WHAT SHALL THE BLACK MAN DO WITH HIMSELF?

Douglass was acutely aware of the extremely limited means for self-improvement available to the blacks. Speaking of southern blacks in 1886, he said, "They are asked to make bricks without straw. Their hands are tied, and they are asked to work. They are forced to be poor, and laughed at for their destitution."[68] Nevertheless every major part of Douglass' argument— whether dealing with Abolition, black troops, the vote, color prejudice, or anything else—was accompanied by stern calls to the black man to exert himself.

We have but to toil and trust, throw away whiskey and tobacco, improve the opportunities that we have, put away all extravagance, learn to live within our means, lay up our earnings, educate our children, live industrious and virtuous lives, establish a character for sobriety, punctuality, and general uprightness, and we shall raise up powerful friends who shall stand by us in our struggle for an equal chance in the race of life. The white people of this country are asleep, but not dead.[69]

Again and again, Douglass asked, as he did, for example, in his newspaper in 1848, "What is the use of standing a man on his feet, if, when we let him go, his head is again brought to the pavement?" No matter how much we beg and pray our white friends for assistance, he said, and no matter how gener-

[66] *Life and Writings*, IV, 295.
[67] *Life and Writings*, II, 373, 360.
[68] *Life and Writings*, IV, 436.
[69] *Life and Wrtings*, IV, 441.

ously they provide it, "unless we, the colored people of America, shall set about the work of our own regeneration and improvement, we are doomed to drag on in our present miserable and degraded condition for ages."

What we, the colored people, want is *character*, and this nobody can give us. It is a thing we must get for ourselves. We must labor for it. It is gained by toil—hard toil. Neither the sympathy nor the generosity of our friends can give it to us. . . . It is attainable; but we must attain it, and attain it each for himself. I cannot for you, and you cannot for me. . . . We must get character for ourselves, as a people. A change in our political condition would do very little for us without this. . . . Industry, sobriety, honesty, combined with intelligence and a due self-respect, find them where you will, among black and white, must be *looked up to*—can never be *looked down upon*. In their presence, prejudice is abashed, confused and mortified.[70]

Here, as usual, Douglass speaks of what he clearly regards as good in itself, regeneration and character, as means to the end of removing prejudice. Douglass' argument is, "Be a man and you will, in time, be treated as a man." In a comprehensive view, as Douglass saw, the end is to be a man. While we urge that Congress and the country perform their duties toward the black,

we must never forget that any race worth living will live, and whether Congress heeds our request in these and other particulars or not, we must demonstrate our capacity to live by living. We must acquire property and educate the hands and hearts and heads of our children whether we are helped or not. Races that fail to do these things die politically and socially, and are only fit to die.[71]

Nevertheless from the point of view of the black, hampered and oppressed by the effects of prejudice, the immediate end is to be treated like a man, to which being one is a means. Douglass' statements typically contain the more comprehensive view but focus on the more particular one. The following is one further example, taken from dozens, written in 1883.

[A]fter all, our destiny is largely in our own hands. If we find, we shall have to seek. If we succeed in the race of life, it must be by our own energies, and our own exertions. Others may clear the road, but we must go forward, or be left behind in the race of life.

If we remain poor and dependent, the riches of other men will not avail us. If we are ignorant, the intelligence of other men will do but little for us. If we are foolish, the wisdom of other men will not guide us. If we are wasteful of time and money, the economy of other men will make our destitution the more disgraceful and hurtful. If we are vicious and lawless, the virtues and good behavior of others will not save us from our vices and our crimes.

We are now free, and though we have many of the consequences of our past condition to contend against, by union, effort, co-operation, and by a wise policy in the direction and the employment of our mental, moral, industrial and political powers, it

[70] *Life and Writings,* I, 316–18.
[71] *Life and Writings,* IV, 388.

my soul, that we can blot out the handwriting of popular prejudice,
stumbling-blocks left in our way by slavery, rise to an honorable place in
tion of our fellow-citizens of all classes, and make a comfortable way for
in the world.[72]

CLUSION

In Frederick Douglass we find a deep understanding of the dependence of the
partial good, the good of blacks, on the good of the whole American community. It is well that there are leaders who take upon themselves the duty of
promoting the good of the part, but that duty includes a recognition of and
participation in a higher statesmanship. A Douglass knows the horizons of a
Lincoln, although he does not himself need often to climb so high and scan
so widely. The partisan and the statesman have ultimately the same end, but
they begin from different points. They meet, in our system of government,
in the political arena, where the parts take (at least implicitly) some responsibility for the whole, while they make demands on the whole—as Douglass did
when he supported Fremont for the presidency in 1858 and when he criticized
and defended the Supreme Court in 1883.

Douglass argued that the black's greatest struggle was the struggle to
become a part of the American political community and that the reason for
that struggle was his creditable desire to keep his grip on the civilization that
the white man possessed. Douglass was not assailed by refined doubts about
"identity" or about the meaning of "civilization." For the time being, at any
rate, the matter seemed clear enough. Speaking in 1868 at the inauguration of
the Douglass Institute in Baltimore, Douglass elaborated on the grounds and
the structure of civilization:

Now, what are those elemental and original powers of civilization about which men
speak and write so earnestly, and which white men claim for themselves and deny to
the Negro? I answer that they are simply consciousness of wants and ability to gratify
them. Here the whole machinery of civilization, whether moral, intellectual or physical, is set in motion.

. . .

We who have been long debarred the privileges of culture may assemble and have
our souls thrilled with heavenly music, lifted to the skies on the wings of poetry and
song. Here we can assemble and have our minds enlightened upon the whole circle
of social, moral, political and educational duties. Here we can come and learn true
politeness and refinements. Here the loftiest and best eloquence which the country has
produced, whether of Anglo-Saxon or of African descent, shall flow as a river, enrich-
ing, ennobling, strengthening and purifying all who will lave in its waters. Here may
come all who have a new and unpopular truth to unfold and enforce, against which old
and respectable bars and bolts are iron gates. [73]

[72] *Life and Writings*, IV, 366–67.
[73] *Life and Writings*, IV, 181–82.

Douglass saw, moreover, that if the object is to share in this civilization the means of securing that share must be designed so as to do no damage, or as little as possible, to that civilization.

Above all Douglass taught that the black, like every man, must walk the road of opportunity himself. As the black makes good use of the opportunities he has, more opportunities will open up; as he gives less reason for prejudice, prejudice will decline.

Without pretending to have exerted ourselves as we ought, in view of an intelligent understanding of our interest, to avert from us the unfavorable opinions and unfriendly action of the American people, we feel that the imputations cast upon us, for our want of intelligence, morality and exalted character, may be mainly accounted for by the injustice we have received at your hands. What stone has been left unturned to degrade us? What hand has refused to fan the flame of popular prejudice against us? What American artist has not caricatured us? What wit has not laughed at us in our wretchedness? What songster has not made merry over our depressed spirits? What press has not ridiculed and condemned us? What pulpit has withheld from our devoted heads its angry lightning, or its sanctiminious hate? Few, few, very few; and that we have borne up with it all—that we have tried to be wise, though denounced by all to be fools—that we have tried to be upright, when all around us have esteemed us knaves—that we have striven to be gentlemen, although all around us have been teaching us its impossibility—that we have remained here, when all our neighbors have advised us to leave, proves that we possess qualities of head and heart, such as cannot but be commended by impartial men.[74]

It is said that in 1895 a young man asked Frederick Douglass' advice about what the young black just starting out should do. "The patriarch lifted his head and replied, 'Agitate! Agitate! Agitate!' " Four years later the same youth asked the same question of Booker T. Washington, "who answered, 'Work! Work! Work! Be patient and win by superior service.' "[75] The contrast is full of significance, but for the present it is sufficient to reiterate that this agitator laid a striking amount of emphasis upon work. Some tell you to go to Africa or Canada or to go to school, Douglass told his readers in 1853. "We tell you to go to work; and to work you must go or die. Men are not valued in this country, or in any country, for what they *are;* they are valued for what they can *do.* It is vain that we talk about being men, if we do not do the work of men."[76]

"Agitate!" but at the same time, "Work!" Work because that is a good form of agitation, and work because the opportunity to work is what you are agitating *for.* External obstacles are not, after all, decisive. Obviously that is no reason placidly to accept them. Douglass in fact spent most of his energy and most of his words in trying to remove them. But while he was concerned,

---

[74] *Life and Writings,* II, 266–67.
[75] Philip S. Foner, "Frederick Douglass," *Life and Writings,* IV, 149.
[76] *Life and Writings,* II, 224.

partly by chance and partly by deliberate choice, mainly with helping to provide the conditions of the good life for the black, Douglass did not lose sight of the fact that possession of the opportunity to live well is not living well. Concluding his autobiography, Douglass described what he had tried to teach:

... that knowledge can be obtained under difficulties—that poverty may give place to competency—that obscurity is not an absolute bar to distinction, and that a way is open to welfare and happiness to all who will resolutely and wisely pursue that way—that neither slavery, stripes, imprisonment, nor proscription need extinguish self-respect, crush manly ambition, or paralyze effort—that no power outside of himself can prevent a man from sustaining an honorable character and a useful relation to his day and generation—that neither institutions nor friends can make a race to stand unless it has strength in its own legs—that there is no power in the world which can be relied upon to help the weak against the strong or the simple against the wise—that races, like individuals, must stand or fall by their own merits. . . .[77]

SELECTED SUGGESTED READINGS

Life and Times of Frederick Douglass, The Complete Autobiography. New York: Collier Books, 1962.

The Life and Writings of Frederick Douglass. Edited by Philip Foner. 4 vols. New York: International Publishers, 1950.
See especially the following selections:
"What are the Colored People Doing for Themselves," 1848, *Life and Writings*, I, 314–20.
"The Destiny of Colored Americans," 1849, *Life and Writings*, I, 416–18.
"The Meaning of the Fourth for the Negro," 1852, *Life and Writings*, I, 181–204.
"Oration in Memory of Abraham Lincoln," 1876, *Life and Writings*, IV, 309–19.

What Country Have I? Political Writings by Black Americans. Edited by Herbert J. Storing. New York: St. Martins Press, 1970. The above selections are also printed in this volume (pp. 27-56).

[77] *Life and Times*, pp. 479.

★ OLIVER WENDELL HOLMES, JR. *Walter Berns*

I

It is not customary to regard judges as statesmen, but the unique powers of the Supreme Court of the United States make it easier for an American judge to gain this distinction. In a very real sense the task of expounding the Constitution converts the Supreme Court justice into a lawgiver, because to expound the meaning of the powers granted, the limits imposed, and the relations established by this document is to give the nation the law by which it lives. Nor is this merely law in the narrow sense of the term. On the contrary, in the course of its regular work the Court has the opportunity to give the nation the principles by which it governs itself, which is to say, the principles by which it lives. An English friend of Oliver Wendell Holmes understood this when he said that the "Supreme Court of the United States is not merely a tribunal where the controversies of men are resolved; it is also a legislature in which the life of the nation is given form and color." [1]

It is sometimes said that the Court follows the election returns, and there is some truth to this; but in a larger sense the relationship is reversed, and what the Court says to the nation is likely to be of more importance than what the nation says to the Court. The Court speaks mainly through its decisions, and legal decisions embody principles. In the case of constitutional decisions these are principles that are supposed to guide the conduct of public affairs. The Court also speaks in its opinions, and these opinions can affect public affairs by affecting public sentiment. "With public sentiment, nothing can fail; without it nothing can succeed," Abraham Lincoln said; and the democratic statesman must heed the sentiment expressed by the public in an election. But Lincoln knew that the public did not generate a sentiment on public questions independent of the words and deeds of political leaders, so he went on to add that "he who moulds public sentiment, goes deeper than he who enacts statutes or pronounces decisions [because he] makes statutes and decisions possible or impossible to be executed." [2] Opinions in important constitutional cases may play as significant a role in the molding of public sentiment as do the decisions making the law. Professor Edmond Cahn had this in mind when he

---

[1] Harold J. Laski, "Mr. Justice Holmes," *Mr. Justice Holmes* ed. Felix Frankfurter (New York, 1931), p. 138.
[2] Speech at Ottawa, Illinois, August 21, 1858, *Created Equal? The Complete Lincoln-Douglas Debates of 1858*, ed. Paul M. Angle (Chicago, 1958), p. 128.

said of one member of the current Court, Justice Hugo Black, that he is not only "one of the few authentically great judges in the history of the American bench," but also a member of a "certain select company of heroes [Thomas Jefferson, James Madison, John Marshall and Abraham Lincoln] who, at various crises in the destiny of our land, have created, nurtured, and preserved the essence of the American ideal."[3] Perhaps some students of the contemporary political situation would regard this praise of Black as extravagant, doubting that any jurist, however great, can justly be put in the exalted company of those who found and preserve great nations. But Lincoln's greatness consisted as much in his words as in his deeds, and anyone who knows, with Lincoln, that, generally speaking, laws depend on opinion, or sentiment, and that opinion is formed by words, knows the role of rhetoric in statesmanship. A seat on the bench, even the supreme bench, is not the equivalent of a presidential platform at Gettysburg when the president is Lincoln, but a great jurist's words do not fall on deaf ears; they are heard and studied by men outside the courtroom, by journalists and teachers, as well as by legislators, who themselves speak to the public and thereby sometimes teach it.

Oliver Wendell Holmes was a master of words and is commonly reckoned to be one of the greatest of our Supreme Court justices. He was born in 1841 and had already achieved a fair measure of fame by the time he took his place on the Supreme Court in 1902. The son of a famous father, he graduated from Harvard with the class of 1861 and served with distinction in the Twentieth Regiment, Massachusetts Volunteers during the Civil War, being three times wounded. He returned to Harvard for his legal education, established his reputation as a legal scholar with the publication in 1881 of *The Common Law* and his reputation as a judge by his long service—almost twenty years —on the Supreme Judicial Court of Massachusetts. President Theodore Roosevelt appointed him to the Supreme Court of the United States in 1902, from which he retired in 1932 at the age of 91 after almost thirty years' service. It was here that he acquired his reputation as one of America's greatest statesmen.

Men noted for their sobriety have praised him in the most extravagant of terms.

No judge of the Supreme Court has done more to establish it in the consciousness of the people. Mr. Justice Holmes is built into the structure of our national life and has written himself into the slender volume of the literature of all times. [4]

So wrote Felix Frankfurter, himself a celebrated jurist and professor of law. Benjamin Cardozo, who took Holmes' place on the Supreme Court on his

[3]Edmond Cahn, "Justice Black and First Amendment 'Absolutes': A Public Interview," *New York University Law Review*, xxxvii (June 1962), p. 549.

[4]Felix Frankfurter, *Mr. Justice Holmes and the Supreme Court*, 2nd ed. (Cambridge, 1961), p. 112.

retirement, said this of him: "He is today for all students of the law and for all students of human society the philosopher and the seer, the greatest of our age in the domain of jurisprudence, and one of the greatest of the ages."[5] "He has been a great judge because he has never ceased to be a philosopher," said Harold Laski.[6]

It is significant that unlike others who have gained fame as judges, Holmes is so frequently praised for his theoretical understanding as well as for his practical work on the Court. John Marshall was a great American judge, and to the extent that he is remembered at all in other places, it is solely for his services to his own country. Holmes, unlike Marshall and the others, occupied a place in a larger world. An American patriot surely—to the end of his life he recounted episodes from his wartime experiences at Ball's Bluff and Antietam—nevertheless he sometimes expressed a preference for England, or at least for certain qualities of English life and society.[7] Most judges would draw their friends from the political world; Holmes drew his from the world of ideas: Harold Laski, William James, Leslie Stephen, Sir Frederick Pollock, Henry and Brooks Adams. Marshall lived in American law, Holmes in Law; Marshall was concerned with men, and perforce, American men, Holmes reflected on Man. Brandeis studied the condition of workers in the textile industry and was a reformer; Holmes reflected on the place of man in the universe and was disdainful of reformers and, indeed, of the very possibility of reform. In short, Holmes was—or was said to be—a philosopher, and his work on the Supreme Court reflects this detachment from the affairs of the world around him. He was, as a more recent and more critical commentator so aptly puts it, "The Judge as Spectator."[8] According to Felix Frankfurter, this detachment was the source of the special quality he brought to his work on the Court.

> Though he did not bring to the Court the training of a lawyer accustomed to great affairs, his work is yet in the school of statesmanship. Where others are guided through experience of life, he is led by the divination of the philosopher and the imagination of the poet. He is, indeed, philosopher become king. [9]

Despite such praise of Holmes, and the reputation of the men who bestowed

---

[5]Benjamin N. Cardozo, "Mr. Justice Holmes," *Mr. Justice Holmes*, ed. Frankfurter p. 5.

[6]Laski, "Mr. Justice Holmes," *Mr. Justice Holmes*, ed. Frankfurter, p. 148.

[7]"[Notices of my appointment to the Supreme Court] are so favorable that they make my appointment a popular success but they have the flabbiness of American ignorance. I had to get an appreciation for my book in England before they dared say anything here except in one or two quarters." Holmes to Pollock, Sept. 23, 1902, *Holmes-Pollock Letters*, ed. Mark deWolfe Howe (Cambridge, 1941), I, 106.

[8]Yosal Rogat, "The Judge as Spectator," *University of Chicago Law Review*, XXXI (Winter 1964), p. 213.

[9]Felix Frankfurter, "Mr. Justice Holmes and the Constitution," *Mr. Justice Holmes*, ed. Frankfurter, p. 54.

it, it is the thesis of this chapter that no man who ever sat on the Supreme Court was less inclined and so poorly equipped to be a statesman or to teach, as a philosopher is supposed to teach, what a people needs to know in order to govern itself well.

II

The American government was constituted in order to secure the rights that all men, by nature, possess equally, and to do this with, and only with, the consent of the governed. So declares the Declaration of Independence. The two criteria of good government are complementary but, unfortunately, not necessarily compatible, as we know from our own history where it has so frequently been impossible to get the consent of the governed to policies designed to secure the rights of all. We sometimes forget that so many of our political failures as a nation have been due precisely to the fact that we are a democracy, a regime in which political power is held by the people.

The possibility of democratic misrule was not overlooked by the authors of the Constitution. Indeed, it is a principal theme of *The Federalist* that while the people will rule by right, they will misrule by inclination unless directed by instruction or, more emphatically, checked by carefully contrived institutions. One such institution is judicial review, by means of which the courts enforce the limits placed directly on governments and indirectly on the people. They will rule, but the courts—and primarily the Supreme Court—exist to prevent their ruling in such a manner as to deprive anyone of his "life, liberty, or property, without due process of law"; or to deny "the equal protection of the laws"; or to refer to another area in which the Court was active during Holmes' tenure, to abridge the freedom of speech. Thus, it has fallen to the courts to frame the remedies required to secure the rights.

To do this the courts must, of course, first define the rights, and as Sir William Blackstone makes clear in his *Commentaries on the Laws of England*, [10] however easy it might be to define a natural right, the rights to be secured by civil society, while derived from or based on natural rights, must be modified, or, strictly speaking, civilized. This is especially true of the right to acquire and use property.

Allowing for the variety of ways in which it manifested itself in litigation, the issue with which the Supreme Court was chiefly concerned during Holmes' tenure was the extent to which the Constitution permitted the national and state governments to regulate the business affairs of a modern

[10]Sir William Blackstone, *Commentaries on the Laws of England* 1778 ed., II, 3, 8–9, and *passim*.

industrial nation. Both were forbidden to deprive any person of liberty and property without due process of law, but it was no simple matter to expound the meaning of these deceptively simple words. The doctrine underlying one view of them, usually designated *laissez-faire*, derived ultimately from the political theory of John Locke and the political-economic theory of Adam Smith, according to which—to state it succinctly—the wealth of nations increases to the extent to which the avarice of men is not inhibited by moral and, what is more to the point here, legal restraints. Men were therefore to be let alone to pursue their own interests and the good of all would be served. But as it turned out, the self-interest of those who owned property—especially the new commercial or industrial property—would lead them to exploit children, to pay low wages, to require long hours of labor and pledges not to join labor unions; it would lead them to set high rates for their services and high prices for their goods. It was this behavior by the capitalists that was followed by the demands for regulation by the socialists or other reformers, and the issue was then drawn.

Holmes was not opposed to capitalism, but he became something of a hero to labor and to those who fostered what many at the time called socialist legislation because his views on the Constitution, and on the manner of its proper interpretation, led him frequently to dissent from decisions favored by capitalists. A famous example is his dissent in the New York Bakery case, *Lochner* v. *New York*.

In a statute typical of those coming out of the reform movement of the time, the state of New York had limited hours of employment in bakeries to sixty hours a week and ten hours a day. A bare majority of the Court invalidated the statute as a violation of the Fourteenth Amendment insofar as it deprived employer and employee alike of their liberty—and more precisely, their liberty to contract with respect to hours of employment.[11] Eight members of the Court acknowledged the priority of the rule of liberty to contract, which meant that in most cases the liberty to enter into contracts, whether for the buying and selling of labor or for the buying and selling of insurance,[12] could not be regulated by Congress or the states. The same eight members of the Court also acknowledged exceptions to this general rule, because they knew that no civil and constitutional right could be absolute. Utah, for example, was permitted to limit hours of employment in mines and smelters to eight hours a day, because of the character of the conditions of such labor, which were understood to be unhealthy and hazardous.[13] The issue to be judged was whether employment in bakeries was hazardous or detrimental to the health

[11]*Lochner* v. *New York*, 198 U. S. 45 (1905).
[12]*Allgeyer* v. *Louisiana*, 165 U. S. 578 (1897).
[13]*Holden* v. *Hardy*, 169 U. S. 366 (1898).

of those who contracted to work in them. On this issue the eight justices were divided, 5–3, the majority holding that it was not. Justice John Harlan, who wrote the dissenting opinion for the three, argued, one would have thought persuasively, that the conditions in bakeries led to a high incidence of respiratory diseases, among other things; but his effort did not persuade the five led by Justice Rufus Peckham.

Holmes was alone in his dissent. In what was to become one of his most famous opinions, he objected to the Court's disposition of the case and, as well, to the manner in which it framed the issue. For dissent the case did not turn on its particular facts; the conditions in bakeries were irrelevant. Indeed, the Constitution was silent on the economic issue:

This case is decided upon an economic theory which a large part of the country does not entertain. If it were a question whether I agreed with that theory, I should desire to study it further and long before making up my mind. But I do not conceive that to be my duty, because I strongly believe that my agreement or disagreement has nothing to do with the right of the majority to embody their opinions in law....[A] constitution is not intended to embody a particular economic theory, whether of paternalism and the organic relation of the citizen to the State or of *laissez faire.* It is made for people of fundamentally differering views. . . .[14]

Here, as in so many cases to follow during his tenure, Holmes' constitutional views happened to correspond to the political views held by reformers and those who later on were to become New Deal Democrats, and he gained their esteem as a result. A few examples will suffice. Three years after the Bakery case he dissented when the Court struck down national legislation providing for the arbitration of labor-management disputes in the railroad industry and outlawing "yellow dog" contracts, that is, contracts by which workers, as a condition of employment, agree not to join a union.[15] In 1918 he voted with the minority to uphold the right of Congress, under its power to regulate commerce among the states, to forbid the interstate shipment of goods produced by child labor. "The question," he insisted, was merely "whether the exercise of its otherwise constitutional power by Congress can be pronounced unconstitutional because of its possible reaction upon the conduct of the States. . . . I should have thought that the most conspicuous decisions of this court had made it clear that the power to regulate commerce . . . could not be cut down or qualified by the fact that it might interfere with the carrying out of the domestic policy of any State. . . ."[16] In 1923 the Court had a case involving a congressional minimum wage law for women employed in the District of Columbia. A divided Court saw it as another deprivation of the liberty to contract and therefore a violation of the Fifth Amendment's due process clause. Speaking for the majority, Justice Sutherland argued that to

[14]*Lochner* v. *New York,* at pp. 75–6. Dissenting opinion.
[15]*Adair* v. *United States, 208 U. S. 161 (1908).*
[16]*Hammer* v. *Dagenhart, 247 U. S. 251, 278 (1918).* Dissenting opinion.

"sustain the individual freedom of action contemplated by the Constitution, is not to strike down the common good but to exalt it; for surely the good of society as a whole cannot be better served than by the preservation against arbitrary restraint of the liberties of its constituent members."[17] The Chief Justice, William Howard Taft, dissenting for himself and one other member of the Court, insisted that women constituted a special case, thus making the kind of distinction from a general rule that Harlan had made in *Lochner.* Again Holmes, in a separate dissent, would have none of this. The way he read the Constitution there was nothing in it to prevent Congress from setting minimum wages for everyone, men as well as women. Finally, to cite one last example, he wrote a powerful dissent when the Court refused to allow New York to regulate the resale price of theatre tickets.

I think the proper course is to recognize that a state legislature can do whatever it sees fit to do unless it is restrained by some express provision in the Constitution. . . . The truth seems to me to be that, subject to compensation when compensation is due, the legislature may forbid or restrict any business when it has a sufficient force of public opinion behind it.[18]

Whatever form the regulatory legislation took, Holmes was almost sure to vote to uphold it, and to do so in memorable language. ("To quote from Mr. Justice Holmes' opinions," Frankfurter wrote, "is to string pearls.")[19] Nor was he always in dissent. One of his most enduring opinions was written for a unanimous Court in a case upholding an indictment under the Sherman Anti-Trust Act. Just a few years earlier the Court had drawn an arbitrary distinction between manufacturing and commerce, holding the refining of sugar to be the former and therefore not subject to regulation by the national government under its power to regulate interstate commerce.[20] In an opinion that harks back to Marshall's great opinion in *Gibbons* v. *Ogden,* Holmes disposed of the distinction with a figure of speech that focused attention on the enterprise as a whole—here the vast meat packing business—rather than on a particular aspect of it taking place in a stockyard located within one state.

When cattle are sent for sale from a place in one State, with the expectation that they will end their transit, after purchase, in another, and when in effect they do so, with only the interruption necessary to find a purchaser at the stock yards, and when this is a typical, constantly recurring course, the current thus existing is a current of commerce among the States, and the purchase of the cattle is a part and incident of such commerce.[21]

---

[17]*Adkins* v. *Children's Hospital,* 216 U. S. 525, 561 (1923).
[18]*Tyson Bros.* v. *Banton,* 273 U. S. 418, 446 (1927). Dissenting opinion.
[19]Frankfurter, "Mr. Justice Holmes and the Constitution," *Mr. Justice Holmes,* ed. Frankfurter, p. 85.
[20]*United States* v. *E. C. Knight Co.,* 156 U. S. 1 (1895).
[21]*Swift and Co.* v. *United States,* 196 U. S. 375, 398–9 (1905).

The consequences of this decision were felt not only by the meat packers, who had been accused of conspiring to fix prices in the buying and selling of cattle and meat; the decision also provided the constitutional basis for the exercise of the vast powers needed by a modern industrial state.

In the short run, however, Holmes was usually in the minority in these business regulation cases, and it was not until after he had retired (and Franklin Roosevelt had made a political issue of the Court's handling of them) that the cases in which he had dissented were themselves overruled. Yet his position has never been fully accepted by the Court. He saw the Constitution as granting almost plenary regulatory powers to Congress (and as not denying such powers to the states), and these powers could be used by capitalist and socialist alike. Except that it required compensation for a public taking of property,[22] the Constitution was economically neutral, "made for people of fundamentally differing views."[23] The powers it granted could be used wisely or foolishly—as a judge he did not care how they were used—by those who managed to gain political power. He especially deprecated "the use of the Fourteenth Amendment beyond the absolute compulsion of its words to prevent the making of social experiments that an important part of the community desires . . . even though the experiments may seem futile or even noxious to me and to those whose judgment I most respect."[24] Because the Constitution was almost completely silent on the subject, there was no role the Court could properly play in the governing of this important aspect of the national life. Strangely enough for a man reputed to be a philosopher-king, he exercised no rule in this area and had nothing whatever to teach his "subjects." He thought their efforts to reform foolish, and others may have regarded them as destructive of great constitutional principles, but that was no business of his. From public affairs he was not only remarkably detached, but he was almost wholly indifferent to the efforts of his contemporaries to build a better world. Indeed, he saw "no reason for attributing to man a significance different in kind from that which belongs to a baboon or to a grain of sand."[25]

III

It is interesting to reflect on what his reputation might have been had his tenure extended into the period after World War II when judicial restraint ceased to be popular among those who constitute the Court's critical audience.

---

[22]See his opinion for the Court in *Pennsylvania Coal Co.* v. *Mahon,* 260 U. S. 393 (1922).
[23]*Lochner* v. *New York,* at p. 76.
[24]*Truax* v. *Corrigan,* 257 U. S. 312, 344 (1921).
[25]Holmes to Pollock, August 30, 1929, *Holmes-Pollock Letters,* II, 252.

In the eyes of this audience it was one thing to allow the dominant forces of the community to express in law their opinions of business corporations, but it was something else to allow the same forces to embody in law their opinions of other human beings, and especially, other classes of human beings. Such laws were frequently discriminatory and, as such, violations of constitutional principles—for example, the constitutional guarantee of the equal protection of the laws. They rarely were to Holmes. Considering his reputation, it is astonishing to read his opinions in cases such as *Bailey* v. *Alabama, Patsone* v. *Pennsylvania,* and above all *Buck* v. *Bell.*

Bailey was a case challenging the notorious system by which state power was utilized to force poor Negroes into a condition of peonage. The system is well described in the *Encyclopaedia of the Social Sciences:*

> [A] source of widespread peonage in the south was the custom of making yearly contracts with Negro farm laborers or tenants. Advances were usually made to them so that they could be held for the contracted period and coerced into renewal. . . . In addition statutes provided that to draw advances on "false pretenses" was a criminal offense. The courts interpreted every attempt to leave the plantation as an offense under the statute. The penalty was frequently a fine, which the complaining employer paid, so that the Negro was again in his power.[26]

Bailey signed a one-year contract and received an advance on his wages of one dollar and twenty-five cents a month, or fifteen dollars in all. He quit almost immediately and did not refund the fifteen dollars. The Alabama statute under which he was then convicted made the refusal to perform the labor, or to return the money advanced, *prima facie* evidence of an intent to defraud. In effect, given the facts of what Bailey had done, the jury was required to find fraud, thus to convict of crime, without any evidence of Bailey's purposes or state of mind when he entered into the contract. Chief Justice Hughes, writing for the majority of the Court, said that this arrangement violated the Thirteenth Amendment's provision against involuntary servitude. Holmes, despite his well-known admonition to "think things not words,"[27] dissented, treating the whole matter as if it were a simple breach of contract. If a fine may be imposed for a breach of contract, he argued, then there was no reason why "imprisonment may [not] be imposed in case of failure to pay it."[28] So far as he was willing to look—which was not very far—it was a "perfectly fair and proper contract," and he saw "no reason why the State should not throw its weight on the side of performance."[29] Thus, it was left to the "conservative" Hughes to disclose the enormity only slightly concealed in this system of

[26]*The Encyclopaedia of the Social Sciences,* 1934 ed., Vol. 12, 71.

[27]Oliver Wendell Holmes, "Law in Science—Science in Law," *Collected Legal Papers* (New York, 1921), p. 238.

[28]*Bailey* v. *Alabama,* 219 U. S. 219, 246–7 (1911).

[29]*Bailey* v. *Alabama,* at p. 247.

which the statute itself was only a part, albeit a necessary part, and to declare it a violation of the national Constitution. Holmes, however, true to his principle of deference to legislative authority, which meant here a readiness to accept the legislature's presumption of the intent with which persons such as Bailey entered into these contracts, was unwilling to participate in such an analysis. So far as he was concerned, there was nothing in the Constitution to prevent the dominant forces in Alabama from imposing involuntary servitude on a helpless part of the population, so long as the statute on its face did not declare this to be the intention. This is not the kind of judging that makes heroes in our day, or ought to make heroes in any day, but it was the kind of judging that was all too typical of Holmes. [30]

A Pennsylvania statute made it unlawful for any alien to kill any wild bird or animal and, "to that end," made it unlawful for any alien to own or possess a shotgun or rifle. Patsone, a resident alien, was convicted of owning a shotgun, and was subjected to a fine of twenty-five dollars and a forfeiture of the gun. In addition to a due process argument, he maintained that the statute, directed as it was solely to aliens, denied him the equal protection of the laws. The case turned on the legitimacy of the classification made by the statute, and this could be determined only in the light of the legislative purpose, assuming that purpose itself to be legitimate. More concretely, assuming that purpose was indeed to preserve the state's wild life (and not to disarm riotous working men), was there any evidence to show that aliens were a greater threat to wild life than were citizens? Holmes, who wrote the majority opinion, argued that the Constitution did not require such evidence. Since a state may classify with reference to the evil it seeks to prevent, the question, according to Holmes, was whether the Court could say that Pennsylvania was unwarranted "in assuming as its premise for the law . . . that aliens were the peculiar source of the evil. . . ." What evidence was the state required to produce in support of this dubious premise? He said it was enough that the Court "had no such knowledge of local conditions" that would allow it to say that the legislature was "manifestly wrong" in its determination.[31] As Yosal Rogat has pointed out, this test of constitutionality is no test at all, especially as applied to the facts of the *Patsone* case. So applied, it "seems to leave no limits at all on the classifications a legislature may make without violating the equal protection

---

[30]His unwillingness to probe beneath the surface of this statute was consistent as well with his account of the development of the common law and especially his discussion of fraud and intent in chapter 4 of his book, *The Common Law*, where he argues that here as elsewhere the law attempts to substitute external standards for "moral standards." He meant by this that the law seeks to avoid the problem of looking into the defendant's state of mind at the time the act was committed by working out an external standard of what would be fraudulent, for example, in the case of the prudent man, and requires every man to avoid that at his peril. See also Yosal Rogat, "Mr. Justice Holmes: A Dissenting Opinion," *Stanford Law Review*, XV, (December 1962, March 1963), 276–7.

[31]*Patsone* v. *Pennsylvania*, 232 U. S. 138, 144–5 (1914).

clause,"[32] Whence would come the evidence to prove that the "popular speech" of Pennsylvanians was "manifestly wrong" in asserting a tendency on the part of aliens to kill wild life, a tendency not shared by citizens or, for that matter, overcome when the aliens become naturalized? Pennsylvania asserted an interest in preserving wild life, and, Holmes said, since that was a lawful object, "the means adopted for making it effective also might be adopted."[33] Stated otherwise, since the *alleged* end was lawful, the means were lawful, and the Constitution does not require the Court to determine whether the alleged end was the real end, or whether the means adopted were reasonably related to that end.

It was fashionable at that time to praise judicial restraint, because the Court too often acted as if it were a superlegislature with the authority to act as a censor of almost all legislation; but Holmes' answer to the question of the limits of legislative power amounts to judicial abdication. He was not judging; he was refusing to judge; he was willing to accept at face value the legislature's statement of its purpose, and to do this determined the outcome of the case.[34] It would have determined the outcome in *Yick Wo* v. *Hopkins*[35] too, where the statute paraded as a safety measure but was actually a means of discriminating against Chinese laundrymen, if the Court had probed no more deeply than was Holmes' custom. Consider a case coming after he had retired, *Takahashi* v. *Fish and Game Commission,* where the facts were very similar to those in *Patsone.* A California law forbade commercial fishing licenses to aliens who were ineligible for citizenship. Although one of the two dissenters, Justice Reed, made as much as he could out of Holmes' *Patsone* opinion, the Court refused to allow the statute to pass as a conservation measure, striking it down for what it was: an act palpably discriminating against a relatively powerless group of state residents.[36]

But *Bailey* and *Patsone* pale into insignificance when compared with *Buck* v. *Bell,* which could be regarded as one of the most infamous decisions ever

[32]Rogat, "Mr. Justice Holmes: A Dissenting Opinion," *Stanford Law Review,* XV, 42.

[33]*Patsone* v.*Pennsylvania,* at p. 143.

[34]See also Holmes' dissent in *Keller* v. *United States,* 213 U. S. 138, 149–51 (1909), where he went so far as to allow Congress to make an irrebuttable presumption respecting the purposes of anyone who hired an alien woman for purposes of prostitution within three years of her entry into the country. His argument ran as follows: Congress may assume that a woman who becomes a prostitute within three years of her entry into the country came as a prostitute or with the intent of becoming one, and such a woman is deportable on the ground that her entry was fraudulent; Congress may also punish anyone who cooperated in such fraudulent entry, or in her unlawful stay in the country; and Congress may presume that anyone who hires her is cooperating in her unlawful stay, and this presumption is not open to rebuttal. In effect, Keller, an American citizen, was presumed to have brought the woman into the country for purposes of prostitution, even though, as Justice Brewer pointed out in his majority opinion, the facts showed incontrovertibly that he had absolutely nothing to do with her entry into the country.

[35]*Yick Wo* v. *Hopkins,* 118 U. S. 356 (1886).

[36]*Takahashi* v. *Fish and Game Commission,* 334 U. S. 410 (1948).

handed down by the Court, and probably would be were it not associated with Holmes' great name. His opinion for the majority here displays characteristics that had become familiar by that time: it was brief, epigrammatic, and contemptuous. It was in this spirit that the Constitution was held not to stand in the way of a fascist-like compulsory sterilization program.[37] The program was based on the presumption that feeble-mindedness was simply a recessive unit particle transmitted from generation to generation according to the law discovered by Mendel working with his pea plants. To rid the state of Virginia of mentally defective persons, it was, presumably, only necessary to prevent the carriers of recessive genes from procreating, and this the state proposed to do by performing compulsory surgical operations on the inmates of state institutions. This is "social experimentation" beyond the ordinary—at least in the United States where it has not been customary to permit state officials to tamper with human life; and one would have thought the Court would look long and hard at the legislative facts. For example, even assuming that feeble-mindedness is analogous to a dwarf pea-plant, it would not be asking too much of men whose job it is to preserve constitutional principles to ask the obvious question: how effective will be a program of sterilizing only the known defectives in state institutions? Or, how is it proposed to identify the carriers of recessive genes? That is to say, in a family of four children one of whom is found to be mentally defective (a "dwarf "), it would be necessary to sterilize three: the known defective and the two others who, according to Mendel's law, carry genes 50 per cent recessive but who, like the fourth child, appear to be normal. By sterilizing only the likes of Carrie Buck, the known defective, it has been estimated that sixty-eight generations would be required to effect a ten per cent decrease in the number of mentally defective—even assuming the validity of Mendel's thesis. But who are the carriers of cells 50 per cent recessive? No one could know. Nevertheless, Virginia was permitted, by a vote of 8–1, to embark on its program. No one questioned the state's presumptions—even though the case had all the earmarks of a friendly suit. (Carrie Buck did not care what was done to her, had no relatives to protect her interests, and her court-appointed attorney was actually a close friend of Bell, the superintendent of the institution). No one on the Court insisted that the record appeared to be obviously defective, even though while the state called "expert" witnesses to testify on behalf of the statute, there was no record of anyone testifying against it. Justice Butler dissented, but without opinion. Thus Holmes' words were the only ones written in the case. If the grounds for sterilization exist, he said, and he made no effort to find out whether they

---

[37]See Walter Berns, "*Buck* v. *Bell*: Due Process of Law?" *Western Political Quarterly, VI* (December 1953), 762–75.

did, "they justify the result."[38] Not only did he feel nothing outrageous about a state program of compulsory surgical operations, but that there was nothing special about it. "The principle that sustains compulsory vaccination is broad enough to cover cutting the Fallopian tubes. . . ." No smallpox in the one case and no children in the other, but no matter: Carrie Buck was feeble-minded, and her mother was feeble-minded, and her illegitimate child was thought to be at least subnormal. "Three generations of imbeciles are enough," Holmes said disdainfully. As for Carrie Buck's claim that she was denied equal protection because the law applied only to those in state institutions, Holmes dismissed it as the "usual last resort of constitutional arguments. . . ."

The truth is that in *Buck* v. *Bell* Holmes was not merely exercising judicial restraint, or refusing to substitute his judgment as to the wisdom or reasonableness of the statute for the judgment made by the legislature. This was a case that engaged his passions. Whereas he never tired of saying no good would come from the economic regulations or, as he put it more than once, "by tinkering with the institutions of property," he believed in taking "life in hand," eliminating the unfit, and "trying to build a race." That, he said, "would be [his] starting point for an ideal for the law."[39] As Yosal Rogat has said, the high spirits he displayed in his opinion in *Buck* v. *Bell* were "not due to bad taste alone."[40]

These illustrations may serve to remind us that a case can be made for the approach to constitutional interpretation adopted by those colleagues he so frequently opposed. Peckham, for example, may be criticized for the manner in which he judged the facts in the New York Bakery case, but not for a lack of respect for constitutional rights. He may have been wrong concerning the health conditions in bakeries, but he was not wrong to insist that the framing of a remedy to secure a constitutional right requires the Court to exercise an independent judgment concerning the facts alleged in the statutes. In his words, "the mere assertion that the subject relates . . . to the public health [safety, or welfare] does not necessarily render the enactment valid."[41] *Bailey, Patsone,* and *Buck* v. *Bell* are sufficient to prove that.

Surely it is easier to accept the legislature's statement of a statute's purpose and the presumptions underlying it; and it is simpler to say there are no limits to legislative power, because to say there are limits requires the judge to define them. That requires judgment, and it is easier to allow the Constitution to speak for itself. Hence, as Holmes said in *Tyson* v. *Banton,* unless restrained

---

[38]*Buck* v. *Bell,* 274 U. S. 200, 207 (1927).

[39]"Ideals and Doubts," *Collected Legal Papers,* p. 306; Holmes to John C. H. Wu, July 21, 1925, in Max Lerner, *The Mind and Faith of Justice Holmes* (New York, 1943), p. 428.

[40]Rogat, "Mr. Justice Holmes: A Dissenting Opinion," *Stanford Law Review,* XV, 28.

[41]*Lochner* v. *New York,* at p. 57.

by some express provision in the Constitution, "a state legislature can do whatever it sees fit to do."[42] But the Constitution does not speak for itself, and the provisions in the Constitution are never (or, at least, only very rarely) expressly violated, for the simple reason that a challenged statute does not come to the Court labeled "bill of attainder," "deprivation of liberty without due process," or "denial of equal protection." It comes labeled a health measure, an innocuous fire prevention law, or conservation law. May Congress, for example, enact a law to protect migratory birds? Surely, because the treaty with the Canadians had to be enforced. But are there no limits to the treaty-making power? Holmes found no expressly stated limits, and delighted his admirers by going on to declare that the particular treaty in question was not forbidden either by any "invisible radiation from the general terms of the Tenth Amendment."[43] Memorable words, these. Words almost as famous as "three generations of imbeciles are enough." Words quoted many times during the struggle over the so-called Bricker amendment some thirty years later when an attempt was made to amend the Constitution in order to specify the limits of the treaty power that Holmes refused to specify. And what help did anyone engaged in this struggle receive from Holmes' famous opinion? None at all. He admitted there were limits, but added that "they must be ascertained in a different way."[44] What way, he did not deign even to adumbrate.

What, then, were the Holmesian principles that John Dewey predicted would one day be "accepted commonplaces"?[45] What did this philosopher-king teach his countrymen? In the area of the Court's principal business during his tenure, he taught judicial restraint, and he did so in a manner that exalted the legislative authority by depreciating constitutional authority. It was not that he trusted the legislature, or the people electing it; on the contrary, he had no respect whatever for them. He was simply of the opinion that what others regarded as constitutional questions were in fact merely political questions to be decided with finality in the political process. The majority, or the stronger, were to rule and would receive no instruction from him concerning the manner of their rule because, in this area, the Constitution did not care. His colleagues disagreed, men such as Peckham obviously, for it was they who were responsible for developing the doctrine of liberty of contract that constituted so formidable an obstacle to the political will of the majority or of the stronger; but Harlan and Taft too, for it was they who worked out the exceptions to liberty of contract, exceptions that permitted regulation when employ-

[42] *Tyson Bros.* v. *Banton*, at p. 446. Dissenting opinion.
[43] *Missouri* v. *Holland*, 252 U. S. 416, 434 (1920).
[44] *Missouri* v. *Holland*, at p. 433.
[45] John Dewey, "Justice Holmes and the Liberal Mind," *Mr. Justice Holmes*, ed. Frankfurter, p. 54.

ment was unhealthy, or hazardous, or when women were involved, or when the business was "affected with a public interest."[46] To them, even in cases where he voted with them, he left the task of defining the constitutional limits to this law-making power, which is to say, in this area of constitutional law he left to others the task of judging.[47]

Indeed, as Professor Robert K. Faulkner has shown so convincingly, Holmes did not particularly admire judging. In his mind it was less interesting, and as Faulkner puts it, less admirable,[48] than, to use Holmes' own words, "transforming thought." His keenest interest was excited not, he said, "by what are called great questions and great cases, but by little decisions which the common run of selectors would pass by because they did not deal with the Constitution . . . yet which have in them the germ of some wider theory, and therefore of some profound interstitial change in the very tissue of law."[49] Thus, he preferred to trace the common law with Pollock, his English friend, than to discuss a constitutional question with Brandeis, his colleague and friend on the Court. Constitutional questions are very practical questions; they deal with the governing of men. In addition to being legal, they are prudential questions, for their proper answers require a balance to be struck between word and deed, the Constitution and political power, the constitutional principles and the political exigencies. Marshall, as Holmes readily admitted, excelled at this, which is to say, he excelled at judging; and among the qualities that permitted him to excel was his attachment to the Constitution and to the principles of justice it embodied. Holmes lacked this attachment and lacked, as a result, any passionate concern for the civil rights to be defended in constitutional cases.

This is admitted by his friends insofar as property rights were concerned, but they would insist that he was the greatest of all champions of First Amendment rights. It is to this subject that we must now turn.

IV

Holmes certainly did not begin as a libertarian in the modern sense of that term. In 1893 he dissented when a majority of his brethren on the Massachusetts court held it was not a libel for a newspaper to report the arrest on a drunkenness charge of one H. P. Hanson when the man actually arrested had been an A.P.H. Hanson. Unfortunately for the newspaper there was a man

[46]See *Wolfe Co.* v. *Industrial Court,* 262 U. S. 522, 535–6 (1923).
[47]"Nowhere in any of the cases we have considered did Holmes help in framing a remedy to secure a constitutional right." Rogat, "Mr. Justice Holmes: A Dissenting Opinion," *Stanford Law Review,* XV, 305.
[48]*The Jurisprudence of John Marshall* (Princeton, New Jersey, 1968), p. 234.
[49]"John Marshall," *Collected Legal Papers,* p. 269.

named H.P. Hanson who otherwise corresponded to the description published, and he sued. Holmes would have awarded him judgment because, to state it in the terms of the old common law rule Holmes would have adopted, whenever or whatever a man publishes, he publishes at his peril, regardless of his intent. "The only ground, then, on which the matters alleged of and concerning that subject can be found not to be alleged of and concerning the plaintiff, is that the defendant did not intend them to apply to him"[50] and Holmes was unwilling to consider intent, denying that the common law required a showing of malice, and insisting that a man should be held absolutely liable for the natural consequences of his act. Thus, in fashioning a rule, he would have looked to the common law of torts and not to a free government's need of a free and vigorous press. In so doing he took obvious delight in displaying his historical learning, and he did the same thing, but this time while speaking for the Court, when in 1909 the Supreme Court of the United States decided a similar case.[51]

No doubt there is something to be said for a rule of law that protects a man from even innocently published libels, and it did not take *N.Y. Times* v. *Sullivan*[52] to show us the constitutional problems of applying the old rule of absolute tort liability to defamation. It must also be conceded that at the time these two cases were decided libel was thought not to involve constitutional questions of free speech and press.[53] Nevertheless, it is significant, but not at all strange, that Holmes did not bother to wonder whether a rule fashioned by Lord Mansfield in 1774 to be applied in a constitutional monarchy was appropriate in 1893 or 1909 to a constitutional democracy. Other judges had done so. James Kent, following the brief submitted by Alexander Hamilton, who was counsel for the defendant newspaper publisher, had long before recognized the need for adapting the old common law of defamation to make it more suitable to republican government,[54] so there was no lack of respectable precedent for what Holmes refused to do. But public law questions, because they involved reflections on what *ought* to be the principles by which a people govern themselves, interested Holmes far less than thought about the law as such, the law independent of its effects on the people subject to it.[55]

---

[50]*Hanson* v. *Globe Newspaper Co.*, 159 Mass. 293, 301 (1893).

[51]*Peck* v. *Tribune Co.*, 214 U.S. 185 (1909).

[52]*N.Y. Times* v. *Sullivan*, 376 U.S. 254 (1964).

[53]Holmes wrote the majority opinion in *Patterson* v. *Colorado*, 205 U.S. 454 (1907), in which it was held that contempt is a matter of local law (the case involved the libeling of a state judge). He left undecided the question of whether the Fourteenth Amendment incorporated the speech and press provisions of the First. Furthermore, he added, the main purpose of these speech and press provisions was to prevent only previous restraints upon publications and not to prevent subsequent punishment of words that "may be deemed contrary to the public welfare." This, he said citing Blackstone, was the common law of criminal libel. *Patterson* v. *Colorado*, at p. 462.

[54]*People* v. *Croswell*, 3 John's Cases (N.Y.) 337 (1804).

It was of course World War I and its aftermath that first required the Supreme Court to expound the meaning of the constitutional rights of free speech and press. With minor exceptions, questions that had been decided finally in the state courts now came to the Supreme Court, and did so for two reasons. In the first place, Congress, essentially for the first time since 1798, began to legislate in a manner involving the First Amendment; and, secondly, because it was held soon after the war that the Fourteenth Amendment contained prohibitions similar to those found in the First Amendment. That is to say, the Constitution was now held to protect speech and press from state abridgement. Holmes played an active role in the deciding of these cases. Indeed, he wrote the opinion for a unanimous Court in the first of them, *Schenck* v. *United States.*[56]

Despite the acclaim he won from libertarians for his famous opinion in that case, it requires no extensive analysis to show that the law he expounded deserves no special place in the hall of libertarian fame. Schenck went to jail, and a week later so did Debs and Frohwerk;[57] and so would every speaker whose words constituted a clear and present danger of bringing about some evil that Congress has a right to prevent. It was, Holmes said, "a question of proximity and degree," which meant a question of how close the words spoken came to effecting the end sought—here the obstruction of the recruitment service. It was assumed without discussion that this was an evil that Congress had a right to prevent. But is the constitutional right to speak freely limited merely to innocuous or ineffective speech, speech that does not threaten what Congress wants to preserve or promote? Holmes ignored this question altogether in *Schenck*, yet an exposition of the constitutional right to free speech surely requires facing it.

Holmes did face it for the first time at the end of that same term when the Court had another Espionage Act case in *Abrams* v. *United States.* This time he was in the minority, and for it he wrote one of the most famous of all dissenting opinions.[58] Here he was not content to allow Congress to define the prohibited end while leaving to the courts only the question of how closely the speech came to effecting that end. Here he attempted to explain to a hostile public why it was important to allow men to express themselves freely, even if what was said was hateful to the dominant opinion. To allow opposition by speech, he suggested at the beginning of his analysis, may be thought to imply one of three things: "that you think the speech impotent . . . or that you do

[55]See pp. 181 of this text.
[56]*Schenck* v. *United States,* 249 U.S. 47 (1919).
[57]*Debs* v. *United States,* 249 U.S. 211 (1919); *Frohwerk* v. *United States,* 249 U.S. 204 (1919).
[58]"I think that dissent will influence American thinking in a fashion to which only your work in *Lochner* and the *Adair* case have rivalry." Laski to Holmes, April 2, 1920. *Holmes-Laski Letters,* ed. Mark deWolfe Howe (London, 1953), I, 257.

not care wholeheartedly for the result, or that you doubt either your power or your premises."[59] Since he had already referred to Abrams' words as "poor and puny anonymities" and to the leaflet distributed as "silly," a leaflet incapable of causing any injury to any legitimate public interest, it might appear that he adopted the first of these as the ground for his opinion. This would have been wholly in accord with his opinion in *Schenck:* "poor and puny anonymities" present no clear and present danger, and, therefore, Congress may not, because it need not, suppress them. But Holmes did not leave it at this. "To allow opposition by speech" only "seems" to imply one of these three premises, and in what follows Holmes makes clear that his reason for supporting Abrams rests on an entirely different basis, a basis that he found implied in the First Amendment:

> But when men have realized that time has upset many fighting faiths, they may come to believe . . . that the ultimate good desired is better reached by free trade in ideas —that the best test of truth is the power of the thought to get itself accepted in the competition of the market, and that truth is the only ground upon which their wishes safely can be carried out. That at any rate is the theory of our Constitution.[60]

Free speech is good because it provides the conditions out of which the truth emerges, and truth is the only ground, or the only safe ground, on which legislation can rest. This is the theory of the First Amendment. This is why it allows opposing speech. It is an experiment, but so is all of life, and so long as it is "part of our system," there can be no suppression of even loathsome opinions "unless they so imminently threaten immediate interference with the lawful and pressing purposes of the law that an immediate check is required to save the country."[61] Except in such rare cases, all opinions must be permitted by the law because, as he said in still another famous dissent, "if there is any principle of the Constitution that more imperatively calls for attachment than any other it is the principle of free thought—not free thought for those who agree with us but freedom for the thought that we hate."[62] We may hate a particular doctrine—the dominant forces of the community may hate it—but we may not suppress it because we need not fear it unless it is the truth, and in that case we ought not to fear it. If it is true it will win in the free competition of the market, and the Founding Fathers, by commanding Congress to make no law abridging the freedom of speech, commanded us not to fear the truth but rather to live by it. So reads Holmes' exposition in the *Abrams* case.

Such an exposition of why free speech is good may appear to have very

---

[59]*Abrams* v. *United States,* 250 U.S. 616, 630 (1919). Dissenting opinion.
[60]*Abrams* v. *United States,* at p. 630.
[61]*Abrams* v. *United States,* at p. 630.
[62]*United States* v. *Schwimmer,* 279 U.S. 644, 654–5 (1929). Dissenting opinion.

respectable antecedents,[63] but it coexists uneasily with some of Holmes' other statements concerning the Constitution as well as with his philosophical position. The Constitution, he said in the Bakery case,[64] "is made for people of fundamentally differing views," and now he interpreted the First Amendment in a manner designed to give the expression of these differing views the protection they need against the dominant opinion. Yet in *Gitlow* v. *New York*, where once again he dissented, this time in favor of the right "of an anarchist (so-called) to talk drool in favor of the proletarian dictatorship,"[65] he wrote a statement that is simply incompatible with his *Abrams* position: "If in the long run the beliefs expressed in proletarian dictatorship are destined to be accepted by the dominant forces of the community, the only meaning of free speech is that they should be given their chance and have their way."[66] This is not an expression of confidence in the power of truth to win in the competition of the market; this is a statement expressing indifference as to which doctrine wins in the competition of the market. It reminds us of one of the seemingly rejected premises in *Abrams*, namely, that "you" allow opposition by speech because "you do not care whole-heartedly for the result." This is to say that the Constitution is politically neutral. But if this is so, if the Constitution is really "made for people of fundamentally differing [political] views"—republican, monarchist, fascist, or communist—then it is emphatically not true that "the only meaning of free speech is that they should be given their chance and have their way." It is not true because if the Constitution does not care which doctrine emerges victorious from the competition of the free market, free speech has no meaning whatever. Why, in such a case, is free speech good? To that question Holmes now had no answer.

He was not here the advocate of judicial restraint, but the purpose for which the judiciary would now intervene was essentially no different from the reason why, in the economic cases, it would refuse to intervene. The Constitution is silent on the large questions of the economic system and on the manner in which the dominant forces in the community use their power to regulate it, whether wisely or foolishly, and the Court may not intervene. The Constitution is equally silent on the larger question of the nature of the polity, or as to whether the doctrine that wins public support is wise or foolish, and here the Court will intervene but only to prevent Congress from doing so. It

[63]"Let [truth] and falsehood grapple; who ever knew truth put to the worse, in a free and open encounter?" John Milton, *Areopagitica* (toward the end).
"Liberty, as a principle, has no application to any state of things anterior to the time when mankind have become capable of being improved by free and equal discussion . . . (a period long since reached in all nations with whom we need here concern ourselves). . . ." John Stuart Mill, *On Liberty* (Introductory).
[64]See pp. 171–72 of this text.
[65]Holmes to Pollock, June 18, 1925, *Holmes-Pollock Letters*, II, 163.
[66]*Gitlow* v. *New York*, 268 U.S. 652, 673 (1925). Dissenting opinion.

amounts to the same thing: in expounding the law of the Constitution the Court has nothing to teach those who manage to gain political power. If anything can be said to constitute the opposite of statesmanship, this is surely it. Holmes would not deny it. He readily admitted it when he said, brutally but truly, "that if my fellow citizens want to go to Hell I will help them. It's my job."[67]

V

Holmes' indifference to constitutional law was expressed implicitly in his speech to the Harvard Law School Association of New York: "I do not think the United States would come to an end if we lost our power to declare an Act of Congress void."[68] It depends on what is meant by the United States. If one means a number of people occupying a certain defined part of the Western Hemisphere, Holmes is probably correct, for then the United States remains the United States whether constituted as it is or as a dictatorship of the proletariat or of a so-called master race. But if one means a republic dedicated to the proposition that all men are created equal in the sense that all men equally possess the rights to life, liberty, and the pursuit of happiness, then Holmes' declaration becomes exceedingly dubious. For this republic now depends, and has depended since at least the days of John Marshall, on the acknowledgement by the people of the United States of three related political propositions: that the majority is capable of misusing the power it enjoys by right, that the Constitution provides the criteria by which the proper use and the misuse of this power are distinguished, and that the Supreme Court is entrusted to enforce these criteria against the majority or whomever it is that manages to exercise political power. It is not simply a case of invalidating legislation that offends constitutional principle; on the majority of occasions when the Court does not invalidate, it nevertheless plays a significant role in maintaining in the public mind an awareness of the distinction between legitimate and illegitimate government and legislation. The Court, precisely because it has the power to invalidate, is, in the words of Professor Charles L. Black, Jr., "the legitimator of the government." In a very real sense, he writes, "the Government of the United States is based on the opinions of the Supreme Court."[69] Holmes' Court could not perform this function because his Court, more than that of any other judge to sit on it, would deny itself the power that Marshall first asserted and that has been an institution of American govern-

[67]Holmes to Laski, March 4, 1920, *Holmes-Laski Letters*, I, 249.
[68]*Collected Legal Papers*, pp. 295–6. He continued: "I do think that the Union would be imperiled if we could not make that declaration as to the laws of the several States."
[69]Charles L. Black, Jr., *The People and the Court* (New York, 1960), p. 52.

ment ever since. The power to validate and legitimate rests, of course, on the power to invalidate, and "if it ever so much as became known . . . that the Court would not seriously ponder the questions of constitutionality presented to it and declare the challenged statute unconstitutional if it believed it to be so, then its usefulness as a legitimatizing institution would be gone."[70]

Holmes was a man of the law, but the Supreme Court of the United States is not simply, and in one sense not even primarily, a court of law; and this explains his failure as a justice. The Supreme Court is primarily a court of constitutional law in the sense that its power to enforce constitutional principle gives it a role—in one sense the decisive role—in the governing of Americans. But Holmes, who managed to ignore official Washington even while living in it and who took pride in the fact of not reading newspapers, had no interest in government. He said that the law "draws all the juices of life [from] considerations of what is expedient for the community concerned,"[71] but no judge in the history of the Supreme Court made less of an effort to learn what was expedient for the United States, or what the Constitution regarded as expedient for the United States. And contrary to the Holmesian iconographers, no man with anything approaching his length of service on the Court, contributed so little in the development of the constitutional law that defines the rights, privileges and immunities of Americans even as it imposes limits on the government.

The cause of his failure in this respect is not hard to find. The Constitution occupied no special place in his thoughts,[72] because the idea of natural principles of justice which the Founders understood to be embodied in the Constitution was wholly alien to his thought. Professor Faulkner has gone so far as to say that what "Marshall had raised, Holmes sought to destroy. The natural constitution behind the written constitution, characteristic of Marshall's jurisprudence and the object of the court's solicitude, was to give way to the will of society and the competitive conditions for its appearance."[73] He was disdainful of the idea of natural rights and of natural law. He saw "no meaning in the rights of man except what the crowd will fight for,"[74] or in the consequences of their breach;[75] or, as he said in still another place, "a right is only the hypostasis of a prophecy."[76] And to say that the "crowd" will fight for something it designates as a right is to say nothing of its existence otherwise:

---

[70]Black, *The People and the Court*, p. 53.

[71]Oliver Wendell Holmes, *The Common Law* (Boston, 1881), p. 35.

[72]He never wrote a significant article or delivered a significant speech on the Constitution or on any of its provisions.

[73]Faulkner, *The Jurisprudence of John Marshall*, p. 256.

[74]Holmes to Laski, July 28, 1916, *Holmes-Laski Letters*, I, 8.

[75]"The Path of the Law," *Collected Legal Papers*, pp. 168–9.

[76]"Natural Law," *Collected Legal Papers*, p. 313.

"A dog will fight for his bone."[77] Those who believe otherwise are "naive."[78] Holding such views it is not remarkable that Holmes eschewed the role of judicial statesman.

Rather than attempt to influence the development of American political life guided by the principles of the Constitution, Holmes turned to the study of private law and attempted to find the law of its development in something resembling history.

The development of our law has gone on for nearly a thousand years, like the development of a plant, each generation taking the inevitable next step, mind, like matter, simply obeying a law of spontaneous growth.[79]

But the growth is not really spontaneous; it is moved by a basic force which is the will of society, and it is the job of the judge to convert that will into law by enforcing it. Whatever he himself may have thought of society's will, as a judge he saw himself as "the supple tool of power."[80] He would attempt to measure the strength, not the justice, of the competing desires of the litigants in a case,[81] and in all doubtful cases rule in favor of the stronger.[82] He regarded this as his duty because it would be compatible with his view of the best government. The best government is not the one established by the Constitution or otherwise modeled on the Declaration of Independence, but one that allows the "dominant power" to rule, regardless of the manner of its rule:

What proximate test of excellence can be found except correspondence to the actual equilibrium of force in the community—that is, conformity to the wishes of the dominant power? Of course, such conformity may lead to destruction, and it is desirable that the dominant power should be wise. But wise or not, the proximate test of a good government is that the dominant power has its way.[83]

This is an astonishing statement for an American judge to make, and what is perhaps more astonishing is that he gained fame with it, and with others like it. Consider his advice to lawyers: "If you want to know the law and nothing else, you must look at it as a bad man, who cares only for the material consequences which such knowledge enables him to predict. . . ."[84] The truly bad man would be the best lawyer, because he would be the best prophet, and the

---

[77]"Natural Law," *Collected Legal Papers*, p. 314.
[78]"Natural Law," *Collected Legal Papers*, p. 312.
[79]"The Path of the Law," *Collected Legal Papers*, p. 185.
[80]Quoted in Merlo J. Pusey, *Charles Evans Hughes* (New York, 1952), II, 287. The relation between the will of society and the judge is actually somewhat more complicated, but the format of this chapter does not permit its elaboration. The judge in the future may affect "the path of the law," which he may do by availing himself of science, or of a social science, to enable him to know society's will. For an admirable analysis of Holmes' thoughts on this subject, as well as of the emptiness of what it leads to, see Faulkner, *The Jurisprudence of John Marshall*, p. 239 ff.
[81]"Law in Science—Science in Law," *Collected Legal Papers*, p. 231.
[82]"Law in Science—Science in Law," *Collected Legal Papers*, p. 239.
[83]"Montesquieu," *Collected Legal Papers*, p. 258.
[84]"The Path of the Law," *Collected Legal Papers*, p. 171.

"prophecies of what the court will do in fact, and nothing more pretentious are what [Holmes meant] by the law."[85] This advice is, of course, of no use whatever to the judge—and Holmes was a judge when he made the statement —and it is also bad advice for the lawyer, who, precisely because he would be a bad man, is unable to weigh the moral considerations that a judge in fact weighs when he makes a decision. A few pages later, for example, Holmes admonishes judges for failing "to recognize their duty of weighing considerations of social advantage" when deciding a case,[86] but a bad man, to the extent that he is bad, will be the instrument least qualified to weigh such considerations. He will be insensitive to them.[87]

Holmes' greatest admirer admitted that he had no experience in public affairs, but insisted that he was able to be a statesman because he was "led by the divination of the philosopher and the imagination of the poet," and that he therefore was able to be the "philosopher become king."[88] It would be truer to say Holmes was a dilettante who dabbled in philosophical works[89] and who was led by his attraction to theory to make theoretical statements about the law. His writings are characterized by a moral skepticism, a brutal cynicism concerning man and political reform, and a lack of attachment to political things. His work gave rise to what is mislabled legal realism, as well as to the newer "realists," the judicial decision-making school; but it is of no value whatever to anyone who would use the offices of law better to govern, or even

[85]"The Path of Law," *Collected Legal Papers*, p. 173.

[86]"The Path of Law," *Collected Legal Papers*, p. 184.

[87]Holmes' bad man would make a good (Holmesian) lawyer because he could best separate law and morals, which, according to Holmes, is a condition of accurate prediction. But consider an example Holmes provides a few pages later. "Three hundred years ago a parson preached a sermon and told a story out of Fox's Book of Martyrs of a man who had assisted at the torture of one of the saints, and afterward died, suffering conpensatory inward torment. It happened that Fox was wrong. The man was alive and chanced to hear the sermon, and thereupon he sued the parson. Chief Justice Wray instructed the jury that the defendant was not liable, because the story was told innocently, without malice. He took malice in the moral sense, as importing a malevolent motive." *Collected Legal Papers*, p. 176. If Wray was wrong to do this and therefore wrong about the law, the bad man who tried to predict would have been wrong about the decision. If Wray was correct about the law, it shows that, in this area at least, law and morals cannot be separated. Either way, Holmes is giving bad advice.

[88]Frankfurter, "Mr. Justice Holmes and the Constitution," *Mr. Justice Holmes*, ed. Frankfurter, p. 54.

[89]The Holmes-Laski letters are published in two volumes and 1481 pages, yet there is nothing resembling or approaching a serious discussion of a philosophical problem or even of a philosophical work. References to philosophers abound—both Holmes and Laski regarded themselves and each other as philosophers—but what is said is best described as chit-chat. The reader is invited to test this statement by consulting the index entries under Hobbes, of which there are some 79. A typical reference by Holmes reads as follows: John M. Zane "thinks Bentham, Austin, and Hobbes little better than asses" (I, 180). There is one reference to statesmanship. It reads as follows in its entirety: I was not greatly impressed by Dean Acheson's support of Brandeis in the *New Republic*, "except for the admirable politeness with which he expressed his difference. He thought B's view more statesmanlike—which is an effective word but needs caution in using it" (I, 473–4). There is no index entry under justice.

merely to govern, the United States. As Faulkner so well says, an "orientation by moral and political ends is absent from Holmes' jurisprudence,"[90] and it is absent because, although he held government office for fifty years, he had no interest in government.

SELECTED SUGGESTED READINGS

Collected Legal Papers. New York: Harcourt, Brace, 1921.

The Common Law. Boston: Little, Brown, 1963.

Holmes-Laski Letters. Edited by Mark DeWolfe Howe. 2 vols. New York: Atheneum, 1963.

The Holmes-Pollock Letters. Edited by Mark DeWolfe Howe. Cambridge: Harvard University Press, 1961.

The Mind and Faith of Justice Holmes. Edited by Max Lerner. New York: Modern Library, 1943. This volume includes Holmes' leading judicial opinions and some letters and speeches.

[90]Faulkner, *The Jurisprudence of John Marshall,* pp. 264–5.

★ WOODROW WILSON *Harry Clor*

Woodrow Wilson was a scholar and an academic student of government long before he was a politician and a president of the United States. He came to the practice of politics after many years of sustained reflection on its nature and purposes. But Wilson's reflections on politics were never really academic in character; they were not intended to be abstract inquiries. They are more adequately described as preliminary exercises in that leadership of public opinion and constructive statesmanship to which, from the beginning, he passionately devoted his life.

Wilson's first thoughts about public affairs centered on the nature of statesmanship and its vital role in modern and American democracy. His last acts as president of the United States reflect a determined effort to employ his life-long vision of statesmanship in the establishment of political arrangements that would make the world safe for democracy. Between those first thoughts and those last acts there appear a multitude of writings, speeches, policies, and decisions which, because they are not always consistent and sometimes seem paradoxical, confront us with preplexing problems in the interpretation of Woodrow Wilson. Yet, in spite of apparent contradictions or changes of mind, there are certain pervasive themes, attitudes, and ideas which entitle us to speak of a Wilsonian system of political thought—a distinctively Wilsonian view of the common good and the American purpose.

I

In an essay published while he was still a student at Princeton, Wilson noted "a marked and alarming decline in statesmanship" in this country.[1] His first major work, *Congressional Government,* published in 1884, involved a systematic exploration of the reasons for this alarming decline. The Introduction to *Congressional Government* heavily emphasizes the author's intention to observe the dominant facts and trends of American government in the light of an unqualified realism—to "escape from theories and attach himself to facts."[2]

---

[1]Woodrow Wilson, "Cabinet Government in the United States," *A Day of Dedication: The Essential Writings and Speeches of Woodrow Wilson,* ed. Albert Fried (New York, 1965), p. 67.

[2]Woodrow Wilson, *Congressional Government: A Study in American Politics* (Cleveland, 1956), p. 30. Referred to hereafter as *Congressional Government.*

The basic fact, according to Wilson, was that of congressional government; contrary to the official theory of the separation of powers, all the substantial powers of the national government had gravitated to the legislative branch. He did not believe that Congress was organized for effective action; it could not really govern because its functions were divided up and parcelled out among a multiplicity of autonomous committees and committee chairmen. Among "this many-headed leadership . . . there is no thought of acting in concert. . . . It is impossible to discover any unity or method in the disconnected and therefore unsystematic, confused, and desultory action of the House, or any common purpose. . . ."[3]

It is not only because of its incapacity to make coherent, consistent public policy that Wilson deplores the dispersed leadership of Congress. The processes by which this disintegrated legislature conducts the public business are too complicated and too obscure for public understanding. The people cannot understand, and therefore cannot control, such a disorganized representative body. Further, since the real work of Congress is done in the secrecy of committee rooms, the people are denied that indispensible political education that results from vigorous and open discussion of public issues. Throughout *Congressional Government* and elsewhere Wilson insists that the primary purpose of legislative discussion, and indeed the primary function of a representative body, is "the instruction and elevation of public opinion."[4] The public cannot be enlightened by arguments which it does not hear, and it could never be enlightened by the kind of arguments that characterize congressional consideration of issues. The committee system ensures that public policy will be divided up into relatively small fragments to be considered piecemeal by men whose authority and influence rarely extends beyond the narrow subject matter of their committee. And this ensures that the speeches made in committee hearings will be insignificant and, hence, uninstructive. Such debates are not debates:

They are as a rule the pleas of special pleaders, the arguments of advocates. They have about them none of the searching, critical, illuminating character of the higher order of parliamentary debate, in which men are pitted against each other as equals, and urged to sharp contest and masterful strife by the inspiration of political principle and personal ambition, through the rivalry of parties and the competition of policies. They represent a joust between antagonistic interests, not a contest of principles.[5]

Wilson affirms that an intelligent public opinion can be developed only by grand debate over basic political principles conducted by strong party leaders whose fortunes (and those of their parties) will hang on the outcome of the debate. The sustained interest of ordinary citizens will be captured by

[3] *Congressional Government*, p. 59.
[4] *Congressional Government*, p. 72.
[5] *Congressional Government*, p. 72.

such a contest in which the power of a great leader or party is at stake, as it cannot be captured by the uninspiring or unexciting analysis of small details by relatively weak men. It is such reflections as these that led Wilson to an early espousal of "cabinet government" in which the executive power of the state is in the hands of the leaders of the majority party in the legislature, as long as they can retain leadership by defending their policies in the glaring light of critical debate.

Wilson was well aware that such a system would unite those political powers that the Founding Fathers had carefully separated, and would considerably modify the institutional checks and balances that the Founders thought essential for the health of American republicanism. But Wilson was never afraid of the concentration of power as long as it could be held responsible to the public. Indeed, such concentration was regarded as a condition of responsibility:

If there be one principle clearer than another, it is this: . . . *somebody must be trusted,* in order that when things go wrong it may be quite plain who should be punished. . . . *Power and strict accountability for its use are the essential constituents of good government.* [6]

Power—opportunity for the exercise of great influence over men and affairs—is also a condition of high statesmanship. Wilson saw that the potential statesman is an ambitious man; he will not be attracted to the services of government, or induced to energetic exertions in it, by the small rewards available in a system that jealously limits and subdivides authority. Minds and characters of a high order will be attracted and stimulated only by the opportunity to exercise substantial authority and broad discretion in the making of important decisions. Wilson stresses the importance of institutional arrangements—the structural organization of government—for the quality of political life. Great thought and debate require great men; to produce great men it is necessary to organize institutions so that they provide sufficiently for positions of power and dignity.

The essential argument of Wilson's proposals for governmental reform seems to be two-sided: concentrated, concerted leadership is essential for the health of democracy because, by rendering the actions of statesmen conspicuous, it enables the public to scrutinize and control them, *and* such concentration is essential because it promotes the development of commanding statesmen who can enlighten, elevate and guide the public. The proposed reforms appear designed (in equal measure) to render government more representive of the will of the people and to render representatives more effective leaders and educators of the popular will.

Woodrow Wilson was not a devotee of direct or plebiscitarian democracy;

[6] *Congressional Government,* pp. 186–87.

he was not a radical populist. Wilson's influential essay on public administration explicitly recognizes certain limits to the capacities of the public or the average man—certain "preconceived opinions; i.e., prejudices which are not to be reasoned with because they are not the children of reason."[7] In order to define the legitimate sphere of popular competence and limits of popular control in government, the essay seeks to draw a sharp distinction between "politics" and "administration." In the sphere of politics, where policies and goals are determined, the wishes of the people are decisive. But the people must resist the temptation to interfere with "administration" where expert knowledge is required in determining the technical means for the most effective execution of policies. If government is to be wise and efficient, as well as democratic, the skilled administrator must have, to a considerable degree, unhampered discretion in the use of his knowledge. Even in the realm of politics Wilson consistently insisted on a measure of independence for executive officials; they are not to be reduced simply to instruments of legislative assemblies representing popular majorities.

In "The Character of Democracy in the United States," an article published in 1893, Wilson undertook to identify the crucial emerging problems of American life—those upon the solution of which the health of our democracy would depend. The dilemmas of the future, he suggested, will be those arising from the growing diversity and heterogeneity of our population. To avoid the dangers of "disintegration" we will require leadership of a very decisive kind. The multitudes of a vast nation cannot unify themselves, for, as Wilson claimed, no large mass of men can be spontaneously self-directed. The people cannot by themselves formulate and agree upon clear, comprehensive, and consistent judgments on the issues confronting them. Thus, "the size of modern democracy necessitates the exercise of persuasive power by dominant minds in the shaping of popular judgments."[8] It is indisputable that Wilson regarded majority rule and responsiveness of institutions to popular wishes as essential ingredients of political freedom. But to affirm this is to recognize only one side of Wilsonian democracy. For he understood republican institutions and politicians as molders of a public mind, not simply reflectors of popular demands, movements and forces. Such a democracy is both agent and educator of its citizens.

This duality, if it should be called that, is evident in Wilson's reformulated views on the role of the presidency. By the time he came to write *Constitutional Government in the United States* (1908), he had concluded that the presi-

---

[7]Woodrow Wilson, "The Study of Administration" (Indianapolis, n.d.), p. 492.

[8]Woodrow Wilson, "The Character of Democracy in the United States," *An Old Master and Other Political Essays* (New York, 1893), p. 130. This essay is referred to hereafter as "Character of Democracy."

dency, properly utilized, is capable of providing that vigorous leadership which had been so lacking in the decades following the Civil War. The president can make himself the representative of the whole nation as no other politician or group of politicians can. The key to his influence over Congress and his party is his ability to understand and express the underlying sentiments or aspirations of the great mass of ordinary men. Wilson describes the effective president as a spokesman for the fundamental, if half-articulated, purposes of the people: "If he rightly interpret the national thought and boldly insist upon it, he is irresistible." But Wilson also describes the president as the leader who defines national purpose and gives coherent direction to the opinion of the country: "A president whom it trusts can not only lead it, but form it to his own views."[9]

Evidently, Wilson does not distinguish sharply, as does *The Federalist*, between "the interests of the people" (which the executive must serve) and "their inclinations" (which at times the executive must firmly oppose).[10] In Wilsonian thinking about the relation between the people and its leaders, that distinction tends to be somewhat blurred or modified. Finally, it is replaced by a differentiation between the fundamental values and strivings of a people, and the explicit ideas, policies, and programs necessary for their fulfilment. With regard to the former, the true political leader is in tune with his people; he is deeply sensitive to their just aspirations. But these aspirations need articulation in a body of coherent ideas and objectives; they need the clarification and direction that can come only from statesmanship.

It is in this light that one can begin to understand Wilson's frequent affirmation that politics is a necessary and desireable dimension of human life —that man is by nature a political animal. But the Wilsonian view of the nature of politics requires further exploration. That view places much emphasis upon oratory, upon the rhetorical arts of persuasion. Wilson thought it quite appropriate that the leaders of self-governing nations be orators of high quality. And he was convinced that a great speaker is likely to possess the virtues requisite for distinguished political performance—seriousness of purpose, clarity of intellect, insight into the needs of his times, courage, and imagination. With these virtues one can touch the imaginations of common men, give clear voice to their half-conscious longings, and inspire in a diverse multitude the zest for united action. The people are inherently capable of political and social enlightenment, but for such enlightenment they require moral drama provided by political men. Wilson thought little of the newspapers as a source of public instruction and he did not think that formal education is enough. A congress

---

[9]Woodrow Wilson, *Constitutional Government in the United States* (New York, 1961), p. 68. Referred to hereafter as *Constitutional Government*.

[10]*Federalist*, ed. E.M. Earle, (New York, 1937), No. 71 p. 465.

or a president can truly educate because of their authoritative position as representatives of the nation, and because their words are related to important actions that they have the power to take.

But, for Wilson, there is something still more critical than the statesman's dramatization of issues. There is the overriding need for utter candor and complete publicity about all that concerns the affairs of government. The essence of good politics is "public discussion: the methods of leadership open and above board."[11] In every period of his mature life Wilson can be found declaiming against one form or another of secrecy, obscurity, or deception in political matters. Secrecy—political understandings concealed from the public view—inevitably arouses suspicion and undermines that mutual trust which is the foundation of self-government. Wilson affirmed not only that the secret conduct of any public business is an unqualified evil, but also that this evil can be eradicated from the politics of democracy and that its eradication is one of the most important ends of self-governing communities. In the campaign of 1912, the voters were told that "government ought to be all outside and no inside. I, for my part, believe there ought to be no place where anything can be done that everybody does not know about."[12]

No public man has the right to do anything that he does not explain, or that he would not be willing to make known in full to the whole nation. Wilson refuses to allow the defense that there are some occasions in which acts vital for the public interest cannot be explained to everyone, because they would not, in the circumstances, be understood or tolerated. Acts the validity and integrity of which cannot be made clear to the public are justly open to suspicion.

These Wilsonian views rest on the premise that corruption, dishonesty or exploitation cannot survive the light of publicity. And they rest on the premise that effective politics can survive the light of total publicity. Wilson is not among those who wish for the eradication of politics from human affairs. But his conception of political life does involve the elimination of certain qualities that have usually beeen associated with it and that are traditionally thought to be inseparable from it. Wilsonian politics would be purified of those rhetorical deceptions and distortions by which statesmen often seek to conceal differences and satisfy antagonistic interests. It would be purified of the secret meetings in which opposing leaderships reach agreement by compromises that fall short of the demands of their constituents. And it would be purified of all those occasions in which valuable ends are sought by devious or coer-

---

[11]Woodrow Wilson, *The New Freedom* (Englewood Cliffs, New Jersey, 1961), p. 76.
[12] *The New Freedom*, p. 76.

cive means that fall short of the highest moral rectitude.

The Wilsonian politician is not a broker in the business of resolving conflict by distributing the greatest amount of satisfactions to the greatest number of self-interested groups. Wilson does not see democratic institutions primarily as arenas for the struggle of competing factions or as devices for the accomodation of opposing demands by means of piecemeal compromises, but rather primarily as arrangements for grand inquiry into common problems and debate over principles and objectives. Democracy is a massive discussion or dialogue. Wilson's favorite synonym for democratic politics is "common counsel." The best politician is he who resolves conflict by most effectively promoting the common counsel of the citizens and their representatives. This is accomplished not by ignoring or obscuring issues of principle, but by raising them. Politics, to Wilson, is above all a moral, that is, a principled enterprise.

This is not to say that Wilson deliberately adopted a doctrinaire approach to political matters. Indeed, he was most critical of those thinkers or reformers who seek the solution of concrete problems by imposing the demands of some abstract doctrine. The dogmatist was vigorously criticized for ignoring a crucial fact: most political questions are, at bottom, moral questions, and precisely because of this they cannot be resolved without sensitive practical insight into particular circumstances and consequences. The relation between the theoretical and the practical in public affairs is a consideration perpetually arising in Wilson's writings and pronouncements prior to his presidency. And most of these writings and pronouncements appear to involve a deliberate depreciation of theory.[13] Regarding himself as, in many things, a disciple of the British conservative thinker Edmund Burke, Wilson joined Burke in denouncing the philosophy associated with the French Revolution. The American Declaration of Independence was to be treated as preeminently a practical document—a guide and inspiration for our action much more than a theory of government.

Wilson thought little of political philosophy as a generator and foundation of sound popular government. He sometimes differentiated between two types of popular government: the sound Anglo-American form and the defective European form. The former does not rest upon a reasoned philosophy; it is the result of slow and gradual historical development rooted in customs and traditions. The latter is based upon abstract doctrine and the discontents or revolutions generated by doctrine. The attempt of European radicalism to create new forms of polity on the basis of theories about what ought to be is dangerous

---

[13]See particularly "The Study of Politics" and "Character of Democracy," both in *An Old Master and Other Political Essays: Constitutional Government,* chapter 1; and Wilson's essay on Edmund Burke, "The Interpreter of English Liberty," in *Mere Literature and Other Essays* (Boston, 1896).

folly. Political institutions rest upon habits, upon one kind or another of human character, and we can no more create our own form of government than a man can abolish his character and create a new one. Wilson taught that genuine popular government presupposes qualities of character such as "self-reliance, self-knowledge, and self-control."[14] These virtues are developed in free societies; they are habits promoted by the practices of local self-government and common counsel. But they require a long period of growth. If you do not have them, or are not on the way to their acquisition, then, regardless of the demands of political theory, you are not yet ready for full-scale democracy.

Wilson rejected the "speculative" approach to politics because it tends to promote a hazardous experimentalism and consequent instability in human affairs. He also rejected it because it can blind us to the defects in our institutions and stand in the way of necessary changes. It will be remembered that Wilson first appeared in the intellectual world as a reformer determined to take a realistic look at the actual operations of American government. He charged that Americans had been blinded to the real workings of their system by the legal and official theory of the Constitution, including the separation of powers. Part of the difficulty lay with the old political science which, taking its bearings from the forms of the Constitution, concealed from view historical changes at variance with those forms. Wilson worked for the enthronement of a new political science that would be both more empirical and more imaginative than the old. The new study of politics would turn away from legalistic categories and rationalistic reflections, and it would combine careful observation of particular facts with an artistic sensitivity to their larger implications and meanings.[15]

Both the study and the practice of politics require sustained attention to concrete circumstances; both are incapacitated by a rationalistic emphasis upon abstract concepts and principles. But how can we distinguish, without theorizing, between valid and invalid principles? How can we determine, without any philosophy, what are the right or highest ends of political action? Wilson's writings frequently suggest that ultimate standards of right and wrong are self-evident, or, at least, that they do not require the validation of systematic philosophy. He commends the Anglo-American political tradition for its "practical character," its exclusive concern with methods and techniques, "as if principles were taken for granted."[16] The most important questions to be answered by political inquiry are not questions about ultimate ends or first principles, they are questions about *how* to achieve objects that almost all decent men would agree upon. "Many obvious duties of man to man [are]

[14]Wilson, "Character of Democracy," *An Old Master*, p. 117.
[15]See Wilson, "The Study of Politics," *An Old Master*.
[16]*Constitutional Government*, p. 9.

suggested by the universal moral consciousness of the race."[17] Wilson can be said to have held the view that the fundamental standards of justice and duty are discoverable in man's historical *experience* which reveals a common awareness or sense of right. And the most decisive historical experience is the emergence and increasingly prevalence in modern times of self-governing communities with the virtues of initiative, self-discipline, and sociability requisite for their success.

But Woodrow Wilson obviously did not believe that men can do without systematic thought and knowledge about their political problems. He admired Burke for his avoidance of speculative theorizing remote from real problems, not for an avoidance of comprehensive and consistent reflection upon human affairs. "And yet Burke unquestionably had a very definite and determinable system of thought, which was none the less a system for being based upon concrete, and not upon abstract premises."[18] It is in this manner that Wilson understood his own political thought. The political thinker must be useful, and that means focusing upon the pressing issues of one's time. To deal usefully with such issues one must bring to them a broad and coherent understanding or view of things. But this broad and coherent view, to be valid, must be based upon "concrete premises." Wilson sought for such premises in perceptions of political experience, historical movements and, ultimately, in the "moral consciousness of the race." At any rate, whether based upon concrete or abstract premises, he does present us with an articulated conception of the purposes of government and the public interest—a conception that can be related to his public policies and programs.

II

The ideas of Wilson the academician concerning the nature and functions of government are best derived from his most "theoretical" works: *The State*, published in 1890 and one of the first comparative government textbooks ever written, and *Constitutional Government in the United States*, published in 1908. With regard to the origins of the state, Wilson discards the social contract theory which attributes political association to a definite agreement whereby men emerged from a presocial "state of nature." The state was not created or established by human decision; it is as old as human life itself. It follows from this that the ends of government cannot be defined as the preservation of certain natural rights possessed by men prior to political association. Wilson, therefore, does not rely upon a doctrine of natural rights as the foundation for

[17]Woodrow Wilson, *The State: Elements of Historical and Practical Politics* (Boston, 1890), p. 625. Referred to hereafter as *The State*.
[18]Wilson, "The Interpreter of English Liberty," *Mere Literature*, p. 142.

political judgment. Constitutional regimes, however, rest upon a more or less explicit agreement among citizens and governors concerning the rules by which government is to be conducted. This depends upon the existence of a "community"—an underlying unity of beliefs and interests. In the absence of moral as well as political consensus, "of common interests and of common standards of life and happiness," there is no community.[19] Opinion therefore is a crucial factor in constitutional regimes.

But Wilson allows for and stresses change. The underlying consensus of a people will be modified from age to age in accordance with changes in the conditions and attitudes of the people. For instance, Americans agree on the broad principles of the Declaration of Independence—on the right of the citizens to judge their government and alter it to suit their wants. But the specific meaning of the inalienable rights to life, liberty and the pursuit of happiness will be determined, and determined somewhat differently, by each generation:

It [The Declaration] expressly leaves to each generation of men the determination of what they will do with their lives, what they will prefer as the form and object of their liberty, in what they will seek their happiness.[20]

The meaning of liberty and of happiness cannot be fixed and specified once and for all. Altered conditions of life will inevitably require and produce change in the import of the Declaration and of the Constitution as well. It would seem that neither the ideas of the Declaration nor those of the Constitution can contribute very much to the definition of the ends and values of American life—the "object" of our liberty and the character of our happiness. Each generation will do that for itself. How, then, are the indispensible "common standards of life and happiness" to be provided for? The argument of *Constitutional Government* seems to presuppose that, once a people has become prepared for popular government, a common way of life will inevitably prevail among them. Each generation will maintain a consensus, with only a rather general, if not vague, sort of guidance from the standards that presided over the founding of the country.

In the last two chapters of *The State*, Wilson addresses himself more systematically than anywhere else to the functions and purposes of government. He rejects what he regards as the extreme views on the subject. The extremists of the "laissez faire" school are hostile to government as such; they would confine its role to that of a mere policeman in the interest of an unqualified individualism. Their errors derive from the assumption that the state is at best a necessary evil, whereas it is really the indispensible organ of social

[19] *Constitutional Government*, p. 26.
[20] *Constitutional Government*, p. 4.

cooperation; the "only potent and universal instrument" of society.[21] The other extreme is represented by the political life of the ancient city-states of Greece and Rome and by the modern Socialists. Wilson finds something to admire in the Socialists' emphasis upon partnership and harmony among men and in the "splendid public spirit" and "public virtue" generated by the ancient polities which regarded the individual as living for the service of his community. But these viewpoints would exalt social solidarity and the power of the state at the expense of "privacy of the individual life" and "personal independence."[22] It is the distinctively modern view that the individual lives for his own sake.

In his effort to define the ends of government, Wilson seeks the middle ground—a mean that would involve rejection of what is harmful and adoption of what is valid in the extreme views. Government is the primary organ of society:

What, then, are the objects of society? What *is* society? It is an organic association of individuals for mutual aid. Mutual aid to what? To self-development. The hope of society lies in an infinite individual variety, in the freest possible play of individual forces. . . .[23]

Society is an association in which men cooperate in providing the things necessary for the individual self-development and self-direction of each man; it is a fraternal *partnership* in the promotion of *individuality*. To serve this end of society it becomes the overriding purpose of government to ensure that all citizens have a fair chance to work for their self-fulfilment. Government exists to promote the "equalization of the conditions of personal development."[24] Wilson is at great pains to distinguish state regulation designed to provide the conditions of individuality or to "equalize conditions" and state "interference" in the affairs of individuals. The latter consists of the effort to dictate how people shall live and for what ends they shall live. The government must act to remove obstacles and provide opportunities; it must not seek to shape the personal goals and private morals of individuals—a function belonging to the family.

But the activities or specific objects of government will vary as the social prerequisites of equal opportunity vary. The modern state cannot leave the organization of industrial and commercial life to the free play of unregulated self-interest: "Certainly modern individualism has much about it that is hateful, too hateful to last."[25] Among things hateful in the prevailing economic system

[21] *The State*, p. 660.
[22] *The State*, p. 657.
[23] *The State*, p. 660.
[24] *The State*, p. 667.
[25] *The State*, p. 659.

of Wilson's day were the ruthless exploitation of factory workers, including women and children, and the unscrupulous methods of business competition by which monopolistic power is attained. The author of *The State* condemns such practices for their immoral selfishness, but even more for the gross inequalities they promote. As a result of vicious individualism, a few men gain exclusive control of vast commercial and industrial enterprises, thus controlling the conditions for the happiness of great multitudes. Although it is contrary to the ends of society to permit the rich to gain despotic power over the poor, Wilson does not allow the socialist solution to these evils. The solution is to purify the competitive system, not to get rid of it. Somehow, the maximal autonomy of individuals must be reconciled with cooperation for communal ends.

These themes reappear in and prevade Wilson's speeches as candidate for governor of New Jersey, as governor, and as candidate for the presidency of the United States in the campaign of 1912. A number of his major campaign speeches are compiled in a volume called *The New Freedom*. The programs of the Wilsonian "New Freedom" arise from a diagnosis of the ills and evils that have infected American democracy. Relentlessly, powerful economic forces have been transforming the character of American society. In the new age into which we have emerged, the independent action of individuals is gradually replaced by the action of great impersonal organizations and corporations. Our "individuality is swallowed up" in vast complex associations that we do not control and whose operations we cannot clearly understand.[26] Increasingly, our lives are determined, not by direct and personal relations among neighbors or among workers and employers, but by remote and impersonal relations among strangers.

Associated with these conditions is a growing concentration of economic power in the hands of those who rule the great monopolies, trusts, and banking institutions of the country. Through interlocking corporate directorships and financial manipulations, a small number of men manage to dominate the major industries, railroads, banks, and commercial enterprises. Many of these monopolists, having become such by unfair methods of competition, continue to use these devices to secure themselves from competition. Banks under their control will deny credit to new enterprises, and if a new enterprise does get underway, it can be undersold and driven out of its market by price-fixing agreements. Individual enterprise and initiative is stifled. The conditions of labor are often unhealthy and inhumane. Men, women, and children work for long hours, at low wages, in unsanitary places.

The capstone of this system of wrongs, and the means by which it is

[26] *The New Freedom,* p. 20.

maintained, is the corrupt alliance between Big Business and the political machines. Thus:

The government, which was designed for the people, has got into the hands of bosses and their employers, the special interests. An invisible empire has been set up above the forms of democracy.[27]

By means of secret deals between "the special interests" and "the bosses," monopoly works its will in the legislature, obtaining high tariff schedules and other privileges that preserve its domination of both economic and political life. While denouncing such arrangements, and proposing the means for their abolition, Wilson is always careful to avoid the kind of appeal that would arouse class antagonisms or "any prejudice against wealth."[28] The emphasis is always upon defects in the economic *system* which permits *a few* unscrupulous men to exploit the many. When declaiming such men Wilson almost never misses the opportunity to attribute good motives and public spirit to the great majority of the business community. The New Freedom is emphatically not a call to the lower calasses to unite against an oppressive upper class. It is a call to all citizens, including misguided members of Big Business, to unite in recognition of their "greater community of interest."[29]

Wilson's program seeks to return the government to the people and to break up the vast interlocking combinations of economic power. The former objective is to be fostered by such democratizing measures as the direct primary for the nomination of congressmen and state officials, and the popular election of United States senators. These were measures long advocated by the Progressive Movement, but Wilson's advocacy of them bears the stamp of his own political thinking. In his view, these reforms are not designed to place the power of decision-making directly in the hands of the people, or to modify representative democracy in the direction of populistic democracy. They are designed to substitute for the private and secret political processes of the bosses the public and open political processes of common counsel, and to ensure that representatives will be responsive to the common interest rather than to private interests.

The proposed economic policy of the New Freedom involved major reductions in the tariff, elimination of trusts and other restrictions upon competition, legislation to outlaw business practices that foster monopoly, an end to the monopoly of credit by centralized banking directorates, and improvement in the conditions of labor. A substantial portion of this program became law

[27] *The New Freedom*, p. 36.
[28] *The New Freedom*, pp. 50–51.
[29] Woodrow Wilson, *The Public Papers of Woodrow Wilson*, ed. Ray Stannard Baker and William E. Dodd, 6 vols. (New York, 1925–1927), II, 352. Referred to hereafter as *The Public Papers of Woodrow Wilson*.

in the first administration of President Wilson through the Underwood Tariff Act, the Clayton Anti-Trust Act, the Federal Trade Commission Act, the Federal Reserve Act, the Child Labor Act, an act making credits available to farmers on special terms, and the Adamson Act providing a maximum eight-hour day for railroad workers.

Wilson saw tariff reform, banking and currency reform, and anti-trust legislation as interrelated and mutually supportive measures. The reduction of tariff rates was calculated to withdraw from the giant business establishments their artificial protection from competition and to require American business to become more efficient, imaginative, and productive under the spur of competition. Opportunities would thus be opened up for new enterprises and for small business. The Federal Reserve System was to insure that credit would be available to new and small enterprises, not merely to the great and powerful. And it would serve to prevent financial crises, while providing the kind of elastic currency that an expanding economy requires. The Clayton Act legislated against certain practices that tend to promote monopoly, including mergers and interlocking directorates. The Federal Trade Commission was to define and prevent unfair methods of competition, such as price-fixing and collusive boycotts.

President Wilson's sponsorship of these measurse was vigorous and effective. Shortly after taking office he moved decisively to organize congressional support, to overcome opposition, and to arouse public opinion. On April 8, 1913, he addressed a special session of Congress which he had called to consider the tariff. This was the first time since the administration of John Adams that a president had personally appeared before the Congress. Wilson's efforts on behalf of tariff reform were quickly followed by his struggle to establish a Federal Reserve System that would be largely under government control. Over the strenuous opposition of powerful bankers, he was able to insist that members of the Federal Reserve Board must be appointed by the president, not by the banking community. Wilson's activist conduct of the presidency is also exemplified by his intervention in labor negotiations resulting from a threatened railroad strike in the spring of 1916 and his subsequent successful advocacy of legislation for the eight-hour day on the railroads. The president urged this policy "in the interest of health, efficiency, contentment, and a general increase of economic vigor."[30] But, perhaps most exemplary of all are Wilson's systematic and vivid appeals to the public on behalf of his domestic programs. In accordance with what he had previously written on the role of the president, Wilson used his office and his rhetoric to dramatize the legislative programs of the New Freedom—relating them to the larger purposes and values of American life.

[30] *The Public Papers of Woodrow Wilson*, IV, 269.

The measures constituting the Wilsonian economic policy are means to an end. What is the end? By what vision of the social good is the New Freedom inspired and justified? Wilson's domestic policy is sometimes interpreted as little more than an effort, by the decentralization of American business, to restore the old competitive and materialistic individualism. And it is sometimes interpreted as a giant step toward the enlarged concept of "social justice" that came to fruition in the New Deal of Franklin Roosevelt. Both views can find some support in Wilson's justifications of the New Freedom.

He certainly sought an emancipation of small business from the restraints imposed by private economic power, a restoration of the freedom to compete. The New Freedom was to bring "the liberating light of individual initiative, of individual liberty, of individual freedom, the light of untrammeled enterprise."[31] Economic liberty would promote prosperity. But, beyond this, it was the aim of the New Freedom to bring about a renewal of personal independence in many vital areas of life and, consequently, a massive release of autonomous human energies. Social justice can be seen as instrumental to this end. Wilsonian pronouncements upon justice often seem to identify it with measures curtailing the ability of the strong to prevent the weak from "entering the race," from using their own talents and energies for self-chosen ends. Just as frequent, however, is an identification of justice with humane considerations such as safe and sanitary conditions of labor, moderate working hours, and compensation for industrial injuries. Even these considerations could conceivably be viewed as subservient to individual liberty, for a man compelled to work in miserable circumstances may be incapacitated for autonomous endeavor; he does not have "a fair chance to live and to serve himself."[32]

Yet the justice of the New Freedom is not simply a means of attaining the greatest amount of freedom of choice for the greatest number. It is also represented as a demand for mutual sympathy, a demand for generous and compassionate collaboration among citizens. One of Wilson's most persistent themes is our urgent need to turn away from the pursuit of special interests and join together in the service of the general welfare of the whole nation. In 1914, looking back upon the crisis through which the country had passed, he defined it in this way:

There was ominous antagonism between classes. Capital and labor were in sharp conflict without prospect of accomodation between them. Interests harshly clashed which should have cooperated.[33]

The overriding aim of the New Freedom was the promotion of social harmony by the righting of wrongs that stand in the way of cooperation. Once

[31] *The New Freedom*, p. 165.
[32] *The New Freedom*, pp. 130–31.
[33] *The Public Papers of Woodrow Wilson*, III, 211.

the injustices are removed men will see and act upon that fundamental communion of needs and aspirations in the light of which all differences are secondary and resolvable. This theme of united effort for an all-embracing common good is at least as pronounced in Wilsonian thought as is the theme of liberated individuality and the freedom to serve one's own good. How are these commitments to be reconciled? Wilson the scholar teaches us that only men bound together by common values or standards of happiness can form a republican polity, *and* that republican polity is devoted to the development of a spirited personal independence. His policies as candidate and president aim at the promotion of a communion of citizens *and* the emancipation of each individual to make of his life what he will. Why would such individuals join in such a communion?

The New Freedom is not merely a movement for the removal of economic restraints. It is also a movement for the moral regeneration of economic life. When the injustices that divide us into conflicting classes and groups have been abolished, men will be free to pursue their own interests in a spirit that takes account of the well-being of the whole. They will pursue their own good, but they will be able to "link those pursuits in at every turn with the interest of the community as a whole."[34] Each citizen will be in a position to recognize that his true welfare depends on that of the community, and he will be constantly reminded of that dependence by the democratic statesman. Further, Wilson attributed to man inherent capacities for the transcendence of merely self-interested concerns; natural sympathies and inclinations toward cooperative association that are strengthened by the habits of mutual responsibility generated in self-governing societies. Wise political programs and inspiring political rhetoric will liberate these higher human faculties; they will "release the generous energies of our people."[35] The emancipation of the individual to serve himself is also an emancipation of enlightened self-interest and disinterested social concern.

Thus, in the Wilsonian Good Society a multitude of highly diverse, independent persons are joined together in devotion to profoundly shared interests and purposes. At the heart of Wilsonian thought is an image of the perfect fusion of private liberty and public duty, a union of utmost individuality with a high degree of public solidarity.

Are Wilson's views of government and politics characterizeable as "progressive" and "liberal" views? In some circles there is the tendency to identify him as a conservative who came only lately and partially to embrace more liberal attitudes about the role of government in the advancement of

[34]Woodrow Wilson, *A Crossroads of Freedom,* ed. John Wells Davidson (New Haven, 1956), p. 74.
[35]*The New Freedom,* p. 64.

social justice. Clearly, Wilson did not understand by "social justice" a movement toward substantial equality in men's incomes, possessions or material gratifications. He understood it as an equalizing of the preconditions for individual self-direction and growth; the removal of inequitable and crippling obstacles to the pursuit of happiness. In general terms, he regarded the activities of government as confined to the performance of these functions. But these can be interpreted in such a way that they become rather broad functions. They are defined in abstract terms that allow for differing interpretations and for varying applications with varying circumstances. Men may disagree about what are the indispensible preconditions for personal "self-development" that need to be equalized. Equality of opportunity as a purpose of government is a highly flexible and adjustable concept. Its meaning can change and its requirements expand as social forces and opinions change. Thus it can come to require of government specific undertakings previously held to be unnecessary or forbidden.

In *The State* Wilson wrote:

In politics nothing radically novel may safely be attempted. No result of value can ever be reached in politics except through slow and gradual development, the careful adaptations and nice modifications of growth.[36]

His campaign speeches appear to constitute a sharp break with this earlier view; they stress the urgent need for new measures to meet the problems of a decisively new age. In some speeches the voters are told that, so serious are the dangers and discontents of the new age, that a radical political and economic reconstruction will be necessary if outright revolution is to be prevented.[37] Yet Wilson did not regard his policies as radical innovations; he regarded them as necessary means for the conservation of basic American institutions and values. The measures of the New Freedom were always introduced to Congress with the assurance that they did not constitute any sweeping change or wholesale uprooting of old American practices. This expresses his own understanding of the relation between Wilson the conservative and Wilson the reformer: "If I did not believe that to be progressive was to preserve the essentials of our institutions, I for one could not be a progressive."[38] Among the essentials to be preserved are representative democracy, individual liberty, the rule of law, and the federal system. Wilson placed a high value on respect for law and on the constitutional powers of the states and corresponding limits on the federal government. Yet as president he supported novel federal legislation limiting the hours of labor, and, in spite of earlier constitu-

[36] *The State*, p. 667.
[37] See *The New Freedom*, pp. 31–32.
[38] *The New Freedom*, p. 40.

tional misgivings, a federal child labor law. This need not be interpretated as self-contradiction or a mere change of viewpoint. From the very beginning Wilson's understanding of revered constitutional and other traditional imperatives was sufficiently flexible or pragmatic to allow for practical modifications with changing times.

Wilson's "conservatism" does not really involve a reverence for what is old and for the ideas of Founding Fathers. It is not any kind of traditionalism. It is, rather, a certain way of recognizing the importance of continuity in human affairs, and the dangers that arise when settled habits and expectations are suddenly uprooted. The preservation of continuity might be thought to require substantial innovation, particularly if the only alternative envisioned is revolution.

III

The innovations for which Woodrow Wilson is most widely known concern his vision of a new order in international relations and the role of the United States in the promotion of a peaceful world. The president's view of this country's role in world affairs, epitomized in his "Fourteen Points" and the struggle for a League of Nations, was deeply rooted in his interpretation of the American experience and the American purpose. Wilsonian "internationalism" is inseparable from a certain conception of the American nation. "Americans," said Wilson, "must have a consciousness different from the consciousness of every other nation in the world."[39] He saw the United States as a special country, unique in two respects—in its origins and in its historic experience. The new continent, to which men came from great distances deliberately and for a purpose, afforded an opportunity for a new beginning in human affairs. They came here to be free of autocratic rule, of privileged classes, and of all the artificial distinctions that divide men and stand in the way of universal friendship. The founders of the country intended it to be an example and an encouragement to all nations and peoples. America was "founded for the benefit of humanity."[40] As a result of these early ideals we have opened our doors to all the peoples of the world and have become a nation composed of all the peoples of the world.

America, for Wilson, is unique, but what is unique about it is its concern with and embodiment of general human interests. The consciousness of other nations has been, like that of a family, inward-looking and parochial. The United States is distinguished because it represents, not one small and separate segment of the human race, but mankind. America is the universal nation.

[39] *The Public Papers of Woodrow Wilson*, III, 321.
[40] *The Public Papers of Woodrow Wilson*, III, 318.

Wilson did not regard this as a mere historical fact or an accident of history that we are free to interpret as we please and in accordance with the interest of the moment. He regarded it as a providential fact, imposing upon us a duty or mission. The American mission is, "to unite mankind" by breaking down barriers and promoting that equality which is the foundation of human solidarity or brotherhood.[41] It follows from this that, in its dealings with others, the United States is not at liberty to act simply with a view to the advantage of those living within its borders. We are not at liberty to be guided simply by our national interest, or, more precisely, we are not to regard our national interest as something distinct from and possibly opposed to the interests of other peoples. This is the meaning of Wilson's oft-quoted statement that "it is a very perilous thing to determine the foreign policy of a nation in the terms of material interest."[42] The "material interest" is an advantage that one gains at the expense of others. The real national interest of the United States may be served without cost to any one else, for it consists of the advancement of certain democratic values that are identical with the common good of all humanity.

When the European war began the president insisted that the United States maintain a rigorous neutrality in order to be in a position to act as impartial mediator and proponent of a just peace. But German submarines were sinking ships that carried American passengers. At the risk of war, Wilson demanded that Germany accord full respect to the right of American citizens under international law to travel with safety in belligerent zones. In justification of the refusal to allow any compromise of American rights to freedom of the seas the president offered two arguments. Compromise would entail an abridgment of American sovereignty; "the honor and self-respect of the Nation is involved." *And* compromise would mean an abdication of our moral position "as spokesman even amidst the turmoil of war for the law and the right."[43] In Wilsonian thinking these two considerations were inseparable. Maintenance of national honor is the precondition for America's capacity to serve its transnational cause as the world's impartial representative of law and right. And the service of that cause is the meaning of our national honor.

As the danger of American involvement in the war increased, the president began to devote himself to more exact articulation of the ideas underlying American foreign policy. And in the two years following our entry into the war he devoted increased attention to public statements defining the principles and purposes for which we fought. Among the most important of these statements are the "Peace Without Victory" speech (January 22, 1917), the Second

---

[41] *The Public Papers of Woodrow Wilson*, III, 319. See also III, 67.
[42] *The Public Papers of Woodrow Wilson*, III, 67.
[43] *The Public Papers of Woodrow Wilson*, IV, 123.

Inaugural Address (March 5, 1917), the address to Congress asking for a Declaration of War (April 2, 1917), the address on the Fourteen Points (January 8, 1918), and two speeches (July 4, and September 27, 1918) in which nine more points were explicitly added to the original fourteen. At first, these definitions and specifications of purpose were designed to promote such agreement among belligerents as would, hopefully, shorten the war. But, more important than this, they reflect the Wilsonian conviction that the clear and public articulation of basic principles must contribute to a durable peace, and that a durable peace is not possible without such articulation.

The following are the major imperatives embodied in the Fourteen Points. There must be an end to all secret diplomacy: "open covenants of peace, openly arrived at . . . diplomacy shall proceed always frankly and in the public view." All nations must enjoy freedom of the seas. Economic barriers to free trade among nations should be removed or substantially reduced. National armaments should be drastically curtailed. And a League of Nations shall be established "affording mutual guarantees of political independence and territorial integrity to great and small states alike."[44]

Among the additional imperatives later formulated by Wilson are these: Any autocratic governmental power capable of disturbing the peace must be abolished or reduced to harmlessness. All questions of territory and of economic or political relationship must be settled in a manner acceptable to the people concerned: the principle of self-determination. The settlement of international issues shall be on the basis of impartial justice, not the special interests of particular nations. "It must be a justice that plays no favorites and knows no standard but the equal rights of the several peoples concerned." And there shall be no special political alliances or economic combinations within the League of Nations. The primary allegiance of each member must be to the "common family of the League of Nations."[45]

The president understood that implementation of these principles would involve and require a radical transformation of world politics. For the prevention of major war the old international system, with its military alliances and balances of power, would have to be thoroughly uprooted. Wilson did not regard this transformation as a mere alternative that statesmen are free to choose or to reject. He regarded it, rather, as a conclusion imposed upon us by stubborn political realities and historical events—a mandate of History. This imperious mandate was thought to be embodied in an emerging world

---

[44] *The Public Papers of Woodrow Wilson*, V, 159–61. Point I concerns secret diplomacy; Point II concerns freedom of the seas; Point III deals with economic barriers and Point IV with armaments. The concept of a League of Nations is advanced in Point XIV.

[45] *The Public Papers of Woodrow Wilson*, V, 257.

public opinion generated inevitably by the war and by perception of the causes that had led to it. Aroused by the grievances and pointless sufferings of the war, this great world opinion becomes steadily more conscious, coherent, and demanding. Progressively, "the common will of mankind has been substituted for the particular purposes of individual states."[46] A powerful moral force is at work in the world, and behind this moral force and the opportunity it provides for political reconstruction, Wilson sees the hand of Divine Providence.[47]

A new world order is possible, and it is urgently required for the preservation of both democracy and civilization. The prerequisites for the effective waging of modern war, Wilson holds, are incompatible with the prerequisites of democratic government and liberty. And future wars are likely to be of such magnitude as to imperil civilization itself. But Wilson had yet another reason for insisting upon the urgency of political reconstruction. In the two years following the Bolshevik Revolution in Russia the president became increasingly concerned about the threat posed by communism for Western democratic civilization. Wilson came to regard the Communist organization of society as a despotism at least as vicious as that of the Prussian autocracy. But Communist revolution is a reaction against the wrongs of the old international system—its conflicts, exploitations, repressions, and wars. As long as these evils remain, Bolshevism will continue to be a "poison . . . running through the veins of the world."[48] The Wilsonian reorganization of international relations was envisioned as a liberal-democratic alternative to traditional injustice and violence on the one hand and revolutionary injustice and violence on the other. With these considerations in view, we can return to the exploration of that plan for reorganization and its philosophy or premises.

The president summarized the objectives of his twenty-three points in one sentence: "What we seek is the reign of law based upon the consent of the governed and sustained by the organized opinion of mankind."[49] This formulation (and the political arrangements it is intended to summarize) embodies two essential principles: the relations among states must be governed by law, or by legal considerations, and they must be governed by democratic standards. These two principles are related to each other and to the Wilsonian diagnosis of the causes of war.

Wilsonian statements present us with three interpretations of the causes of war in the modern world. According to one of these, modern wars are the

[46] *The Public Papers of Woodrow Wilson*, V, 254.
[47] *The Public Papers of Woodrow Wilson*, V, 551–52.
[48] *The Public Papers of Woodrow Wilson*, VI, 108.
[49] *The Public Papers of Woodrow Wilson*, V, 234.

result of competetive strivings for economic advantage. Economic causes, such as "commercial and industrial rivalry," are held to be primary, and political ones secondary.[50] More often, however, the causes are traced to political ambitions, to the lusts for power of politically irresponsible rulers, to "the existence of autocratic governments backed by organized force which is controlled wholly by their will, not by the will of their people."[51] The third interpretation finds the roots of international violence ultimately in injustice: "war comes from the seeds of wrong."[52] As examples of such war-producing wrongs, one might consider: the government of a people by a foreign power to which they do not consent, competition among strong powers for the political domination or commercial exploitation of weaker ones, and economic discrimination—the denial or restriction of a nation's access to vital markets and raw materials.

The third explanation for war underlies the other two and it can assimilate them. If violent conflict among nations is the result of inequities, political or economic, then it can be prevented by the removal of inequities. And, for Wilson, the eradication of inequities requires, if it is not synonomous with, the democratization of intercourse among states. The equality of all nations in their rights and moral claims must be acknowledged by all. "The guarantees exchanged must neither recognize nor imply a difference between big nations and small, between those that are powerful and those that are weak."[53] If states will deal with each other as equals, regardless of the differences between great and small, then exploitation, one of the major sources of grievance and tension, will be eradicated. If all peoples and nationalities are guaranteed the right of self-determination or autonomy, if no people is ever compelled to live under an alien regime, then another major source of conflict has been removed. The principles of freedom of the seas and free trade follow from these doctrines of national equality and self-determination, and they serve a similar function in the maintenance of peace. The strong shall not be in a position to deny to the weak the necessities of life or the opportunity for prosperity. And, when no one can become strong or weak as a result of such discrimination, then men are relieved of another age-old cause of hostilities. Thus, in Wilsonian teaching, the alleviation of the world's moral ills and the solution of its practical problems require one and the same remedy—the establishment of justice. This and only this is a real resolution of international conflict. And justice is understood largely as a duty to recognize an equality of rights.

Wilson saw that such democratized international relations would be possi-

[50] *The Public Papers of Woodrow Wilson*, V, 637–38.
[51] *The Public Papers of Woodrow Wilson*, V, 11.
[52] *The Public Papers of Woodrow Wilson*, V, 598.
[53] *The Public Papers of Woodrow Wilson*, IV, 411.

ble only among democratic nations. Or, at least, the self-governing countries would have to predominate in the world and constitute the League of Nations. "No autocratic government could be trusted to keep faith within it [the League] or observe its covenants."[54] Arbitrary or oligarchic governments are the nurseries of selfish ambitions from which proceed exploitation and aggression. And within such governments the plots of aggrandizement can be developed in secrecy. Wilson held that a democratic polity is incompatible with an aggressive and militaristic foreign policy. Democracies do not tend to produce power-seeking leaders who are accustomed to use their fellow men as mere instruments of their ambition. Moreover, in a self-governing community where public opinion is active, far reaching decisions cannot be made and worked out under the cover of secrecy. Political leaders laying a plan for conquest or war could not long succeed in keeping their actions from public disclosure. Wilson presupposes that the people, having discovered the existence of such a plan, will inevitably oppose it. Democratic peoples will emphatically prefer peace and justice to such national glory or economic advantage as may come from an imperialistic policy. Wilson's reasons for holding this conviction derive from his understanding of the way of life fostered by democracy. "Only free peoples can . . . prefer the interests of mankind to any narrow interest of their own."[55] But why are free peoples *likely* to do so? Wilson has not provided a direct answer to this question, but it is the premise of his whole democratic teaching that a regime of equality liberates the individual from what is parochial and fosters his identification with the things that all men have in common.

It is also a major premise of Wilsonian doctrine that nations can and do act in their foreign relations on the principles and propensities that govern their domestic polity. Thus a democratic nation will wish to conduct a diplomacy of "open covenants openly arrived at," and democratized peoples will reject illiberal covenants and accept liberal ones when they find out about them. And, since free societies seek to resolve domestic controversies by the application of rules of law, they will be willing and able to do likewise in their international disputes.

This is not to say that Wilson envisioned a world wholly free of any need for resort to force or threats of force. The first draft of the League of Nations Covenant, prepared by the president, provides for a total economic blockade, and, if necessary, military action against an offending state. The president never thought that a just peace could be maintained simply by appeals to reason, morality, or compassion. It must be maintained by "a community of

[54] *The Public Papers of Woodrow Wilson*, V, 12.
[55] *The Public Papers of Woodrow Wilson*, V, 12.

power."[56] The decisive consideration is reflected in the word "community." Wilson regarded the traditional balancing of power among nations as an uncertain and grossly defective preventative for war and aggression. The uncertainties and defects lay in the reliance placed upon the self-interested employment of countervailing power by individual states for particular national objectives. For unilateral action based upon self-interested national purpose, the League would substitute concerted action of all self-governing states based upon their common interst in the security of a just peace. A potential aggressor would be deterred by the certainty that an overwhelming preponderance of coercive power would be brought against him.

The successful functioning of this system of collective security would be dependent upon two conditions. First, the self-governing states must be willing at all times to act on the principle that "the peace of the world" takes precedence over any national concerns, ends, or values of their own, however genuine. For instance, the United States would be morally obliged to contribute its human and material resources to action against an "aggressor," whether or not his particular acts threaten American security or American purposes. Secondly, the members of the League must be willing to be governed by rigorously impartial rules as the sole or overriding standard by which international disputes are to be settled. Consider a hypothetical conflict between nation "A" and nation "B" that vitally affects several other states. In its approach to settlement of the conflict, the United States may not be guided by considerations of who are its friends and who are its antagonists, and what would be the consequences of one solution or the other for the vital interests of its friends. It must play no favorites; it must decide on the basis of general rules to be applied in the same way to any and all states.

This is how the judge decides, or ought to decide, controversies between individuals in a court of law. But a court is the agent of a civil society; its major rules have been either enacted or sanctioned by the legislative representative and will be enforced by the executive representative of that society. The citizens are in fundamental agreement on the rules and the enforcement. The Wilsonian world community is composed of separate civil societies which make their own laws and which retain the power to act independently. How are all these independent communities to be induced to act as if they were members of a single world civil society?

Some Wilsonian answers to this question have already been suggested. The free countries will be bound together by their commitment to democratic institutions and ideas. This common democratic commitment is expected to promote agreement on crucial issues, such as the definition of "aggression"

[56] *The Public Papers of Woodrow Wilson,* IV, 410.

and other unjustifiable acts among states. Free trade will unite the nations by mutually beneficial economic intercourse. And most significant of all, there is the emerging common will and concerted judgment of an aroused mankind demanding the subordination of self-centered nationalism. To Wilson this united world opinion was a palpable reality, and one destined to predominate over all other political realities. Of course, the fulfilment of that destiny would require the exertions of statesmanship, that imaginative statesmanship which can sense, articulate, and give rational form to the just passsions of the people. For the real connecting thread of popular opinion is not reason, it is a humane passion that requires its representative and its spokesman.[57] The primary function, the ultimate function, of a world organization would be to provide a forum wherein this great passionate opinion could be channeled, focused, and made effective. The League of Nations was to be a tribunal where the conflicts of the nations and the doings of the powerful would be brought "under the scrutiny of mankind."[58]

The president was mistaken in his assessment of the power or the reality of a united world public. The nations did not unite. It was not the case that "the common will of mankind has been substituted for the particular purposes of individual states." And today the world is still divided into different and opposing regimes embodying different ways of life and opposing moral commitments. And these differences are taken quite seriously. The diverse peoples of the world continue to suggest, through behavior, that they regard their diversity as a vital fact, at least as important as their common humanity.

Woodrow Wilson's most pervasive concept was an idea of the unity of Mankind. But he did not conceive of a unification of men achieved at the expense of their variety or autonomy. The world as he wished it to be was a world of independent nations and peoples in full possession of their rights and powers of *self-determination.* But may not the autonomous strivings and self-directed development of various groups of men lead to conflicting aspirations, postures, and demands? Wilson did not regard the rights and claims of self-determination as a possible source of international tensions any more than he regarded the promotion of personal autonomy or individuality as a possible source of national tensions. His writings on every political subject reflect the conviction that, with regard to all fundamental questions, there is an ultimate or underlying agreement among men. All men desire and need peace, freedom, and justice. The basic interests as well as the basic values of individuals and peoples are in ultimate harmony. Human and political conflicts are not natural or inevitable; they are the result of wrongs and injustices that temporar-

[57] *The Public Papers of Woodrow Wilson,* V, 602–03.
[58] *The Public Papers of Woodrow Wilson,* VI, 73.

ily obscure our underlying agreement. The wrongs and injustices can be eradicated, and when they are eradicated then the full self-determination of men and communities is highly compatible with their amicable union on all vital matters. These notions of human nature and society were, for Wilson, first principles. He did not subject them to any systematic questioning or philosophic inquiry. To do so he would have had to engage in some of that theoretical reflection which, long ago, he had rejected as a possible source of political wisdom.

Woodrow Wilson is sometimes praised and sometimes criticized for his "idealism." It is often asserted that the president was ahead of his time and that, if the human race is to survive, it must rise to his moral perspective. Equally as often it is asserted that he vastly and dangerously over-estimated the capacity of ideals and ethical principles to prevail in human affairs. To the questions raised by these and other conflicting assessments it is difficult to give a simple answer. Wilson's early writings on governmental matters reflect ample awareness of the inevitable role that power and personal ambitions must play in political life. He recognized that ideals and principles cannot gain ascendency without the support of power, ambition, and practical institutional arrangements. But his whole career was devoted to the promotion of arrangements to bring about that ascendency. He taught that progress in any society is always a matter of gradual development and growth. Even in the midst of the battle for the League he warned hopeful men not to expect "immediate emancipation," but, rather, "slow disentanglement from the many things that have bound us in the past."[59] But he did expect emancipation; he did, finally, envision a world in which justice rules and organizes human endeavor. In that world the same rules of civility would obtain among nations as obtain among individuals, fellow citizens, and friends.

These Wilsonian views and expectations are of more than academic interest to us, if only because of their influence upon both American foreign policy and the perspectives from which American foreign policy is criticized. Wilson taught that, in its posture toward the rest of the world, America must stand for something more than its own security and prosperity. And he taught that democracy cannot be safe in an anti-democratic world. These things came to mean that America must always act in the service and with the consent of a world majority, and that democratic countries are committed to the use of democratic means in their foreign relations. Wilson's understanding of the kind of world that would be safe for democracy, and the way to achieve it, is profoundly related to his conception of the nature of self-governing communities. He saw the democratic community as the home and nursery of certain

[59] *The Public Papers of Woodrow Wilson,* V, 478–79.

moral virtues—qualities of mind and character which provide a solid foundation for international justice and cooperation.

Wilson regarded these virtues as necessary concomitants and products of democracy, but he was by no means contented with the degree of their attainment and perfection in twentieth century America. In his last years he returned to an old theme: the antagonism of capital and labor and the evils of our economic life. Too many employers continue to exploit their workers and too many men manipulate each other as mere means to the end of profit. Such exploitation and manipulation is a cause of the mass unrest and discontent that erupted in the Russian Revolution and threatens the democratic world. The great task now confronting us is to make "the world safe against irrational revolution" by correcting "the too great selfishness of the capitalist system."[60]

In May of 1919 the president proposed that Congress explore ways and means to encourage "the genuine democratization of industry," involving the participation of workers in decisions that affect their welfare.[61] This reform would be accomplished largely by voluntary efforts of business and labor, with government playing a limited role. Presumably, private property was to retain its rights and its importance and private enterprise its vital function in the advancement of prosperity. The end was not to equalize incomes and powers, but to promote fraternal cooperation in the economic sphere. Wilson did not see any contradiction between such efforts to promote fraternal cooperation in the conduct of industry and the maintenance of property rights in a free enterprise system.

Woodrow Wilson never desired the abandonment of capitalism but, rather, its moral purification by application of the ethical resources he saw inherent in democracy. Wilson can be said to be an advocate of democratic capitalism, with the capitalist element purged of low selfishness by the democratic element and devoted to the service of human happiness. This democratic capitalism would be more than a match for its revolutionary adversary.

In the eyes of Woodrow Wilson, egocentric individualism was the major defect, and the only major defect, of American life. It was his conviction that this blemish on the honor of the Republic could be removed; this evil could be overcome within the basic framework of American life. He assumed that a society wholly committed to personal liberty and individuality can rid itself of egocentric individualism. Behind this Wilsonian assumption about what is attainable in America lies an ultimate vision of the political good—a noble democracy where self-interest no longer prevails over benevolence as the foundation of human conduct.

---

[60] *The Public Papers of Woodrow Wilson*, VI, 538.
[61] *The Public Papers of Woodrow Wilson*, V, 486–88.

SELECTED SUGGESTED READINGS

Congressional Government. Cleveland: Meridian Books, 1956.

Constitutional Government in the United States. New York: Columbia University Press, 1961.

A Day of Dedication: The Essential Writings and Speeches of Woodrow Wilson. Edited by Albert Fried. New York: The Macmillan Company, 1965. See pages 281–339.

The New Freedom. Englewood Cliffs: Prentice-Hall, Inc., 1961.

An Old Master and Other Political Essays. New York: Charles Scribner's Sons, 1893. See Chapter II, The Study of Politics, and Chapter IV, Character of Democracy in the United States.

★ FRANKLIN DELANO ROOSEVELT *Morton J. Frisch*

I

There is no doubt that Franklin D. Roosevelt, considered as a thinker and a statesman, rates lower than Abraham Lincoln. While one must admit that he proceeded with practical wisdom and moderation, one cannot compare him to Lincoln in depth of understanding. The successful handling of the situation of the Great Depression, that is, the preservation of liberal democratic institutions in a period of crisis, was one which involved an unusual degree of practical wisdom and moderation. Those qualities Roosevelt had, but that is not to say that he possessed theoretical wisdom. Roosevelt was emphatically a politician, a master politician. That the American people were able to withstand the shock of an unparalleled depression and that their concern for their well-being did not deteriorate into despair was, in large measure, due to the sobriety and restrained character of his statesmanship. And that sobriety and restraint were as much a part of the action of the New Deal as were the major pieces of New Deal legislation.

Roosevelt's New Deal has been described by some as "the prologue to Communism in America"[1] and, in order to substantiate that view, his critics have emphasized that he was fomenting class war by talking about the great industrial and financial interests as moneychangers and economic royalists. As a matter of fact, Roosevelt leveled the charge of "money-changers" against big industry and finance in his First Inaugural Address, and complained about "economic royalists" in his second presidential campaign, giving the impression of a conspiracy on their part. His rhetoric clearly exaggerated the existing state of the danger, at least from them, but his intention was to expose the threat to capitalism by exaggerating it. It seems to be clear that Roosevelt recognized and generally exercised moderation. That he wanted at the same time to appeal to popular prejudice is not at all surprising considering the resistance of powerful moneyed interests to his programs and policies. The way in which he did this indicates, however, that he sometimes departed from a course of moderation, but there is no suggestion here that Roosevelt ever intended to undermine the tradition. Roosevelt's First Inaugural Address is one of the great presidential inaugural speeches in American history, clearly

---

[1] See Robert E. Sherwood, *Roosevelt and Hopkins* (New York, 1948), p. 73.

ranking with those of Thomas Jefferson and Abraham Lincoln. If that speech is indicative of anything at all, it shows how deeply he was steeped in the American political tradition and in the rhetoric of that tradition. We find ourselves prepared for this fact by the realization that the New Deal does not emerge through the rejection or annihilation of the tradition, but through its reshaping or reinterpretation.

Roosevelt had a number of serious political setbacks in his presidential career—the Supreme Court's invalidation of critical New Deal legislation in 1935 and 1936, the defeat of his court-packing plan in 1937, and his failure to purge recalcitrant Democratic congressmen in the 1938 party primaries. But the supreme test of the practicality of his politics was that none of these setbacks proved disastrous, for he was able to get the welfare and regulatory legislation he needed, change the complexion of the Supreme Court for the better (the Roosevelt Court was distinguished), and prevent the Congress from blocking his interventionist foreign policy prior to the Japanese attack on Peark Harbor. We do not know how Roosevelt himself would have characterized it, but we do know that his approach to the problems of the 1930s was intensely Hamiltonian. Roosevelt never forgot that government requires competence, energy, force, foresight, and something approaching wisdom. There was an emphasis in the New Deal on the positive function of government, a function which had been insufficiently acknowledged by the earlier liberalism. But it must emphasized that, while the thrust of the New Deal points more clearly to Hamilton than to any other statesman, the New Deal is more than a mere restatement of Hamiltonianism. The objective of the New Deal is the welfare state and the coming-into-being of the welfare state requires the emergence of a higher plane of thought regarding the American ends than that which informed the Progressive Movement. That higher plane restores the vigorous view of active government which the Founding Fathers themselves had and restores the proper relation between the purposes of the Preamble and the provisions of the body of the Constitution. Surely the New Deal pointed in the direction of the restoration of the highest aims of the Constitution. If it can be said that the New Deal *changed* the Constitution, or went beyond it, our argument is that it did so in the direction toward which the Constitution itself pointed.

The purpose of this chapter is to try to understand the character of the Roosevelt Revolution, that is, to try to understand the character of the changes wrought by the New Deal, and the extent to which those changes altered the course of the American political tradition. But the transformation of the traditional American Democracy into a welfare state, with its regulated or controlled economy, seems more revolutionary than it really is. It is our belief that one of the great lessons of the past thirty years (and this is something which

Roosevelt clearly understood) is the extent to which America's traditional democratic order has proven compatible with far more welfare and far more regulation than anyone had hitherto thought possible. Roosevelt rejected the paternalistic welfare state when he rejected socialism. So, instead of saying that the traditional American Democracy became undermined in the period of the New Deal, it would be more accurate to say that the meaning of the American political tradition underwent a profound reinterpretation at that time. Roosevelt surely reinterpreted the tradition very profoundly, for there is no doubt that the welfare state is incompatible with certain features of the traditional American Democracy. But Roosevelt, the statesman who introduced the welfare principle, did not consider it to be a radical change; that is, it was not a change which went to the *root* of the system. It preserves it. The New Deal fulfilled a function which was essentially restorative or conservative rather than constitutive.

II

By 1933, the Great Depression had produced an economic crisis unparalleled in American history, and the National Recovery Act of that year was part of a comprehensive effort made by the New Deal Administration to remedy the depressed state of the nation's economy. The Recovery Act grappled with that depression as it directly affected labor and industry, and there was a reliance placed upon the commerce clause as sufficient in itself to support the Act. But a unanimous Supreme Court's invalidation of the NRA in May 1935 in *Schechter Poultry Corporation* v. *United States* brought the whole structure of New Deal regulatory legislation into jeopardy. The NRA was declared unconstitutional ostensibly because it delegated legislative power to the president, but a more specific act of Congress could have remedied that. Far more crucial was the Court's determination that the trade and labor practices of the Schechter Poultry Corporation might not be regulated by the national government under its power over interstate commerce. The importance of this determination issued from the fact that it threatened all economic regulatory legislation based on the commerce clause of the Constitution. Therefore the real question behind the Court's decision that Congress could not delegate legislative power to the president was whether Congress ever had the legislative power under the commerce clause to regulate the business of the Schechters in the first place.

The crucial political issue of the 1930s was the extent of the economic regulatory powers of the national government allowable under the commerce clause. The problems of the depression were economic, and the commerce clause was the constitutional power most directly concerned with economic or financial matters. Hence legislation directed at controlling or regulating many aspects of the national economic system was primarily predicated upon that clause. In his famous "horse and buggy" press conference, the president discussed the Court's narrow construction of the commerce clause as the most significant aspect of the Schechter decision.[2] He wanted a more comprehensive meaning to be attributed to the commerce clause, and he wanted the constitutional enumeration of the fundamental powers of government to be interpreted with enough flexibility to accomodate the new regulatory activities of the national government.

Foremost among the criticisms of President Roosevelt and the New Deal was the charge that their understanding of the Constitution had departed significantly from the essentially democratic character of the American political tradition in the direction of centralization. And the Supreme Court justices whose great concern was the centralizing tendencies of the New Deal Administration contended that a comprehensive commerce power would obliterate the distinction between what is local and what is national, and result in a decisively centralized nation. Justices Willis Van Devanter, James McReynolds and George Sutherland obviously wanted to destroy the New Deal, as they tried to use the Constitution as an instrument to deprive the country of economic legislation under the supposed necessity of maintaining the states in their powers over local concerns. After the Schechter decision was announced, even Justice Brandeis, who had little in common with the Van Devanter-McReynolds-Sutherland group, told one of the president's closest advisors, Tom Corcoran: "This is the end of this business of centralization, and I want you to go back and tell the President that we're not going to centralize everything. It's come to an end. As for your young men, you call them together and tell them to get out of Washington—tell them to go back to the states. That is where they must do their work."[3] Brandeis wanted a political system which would be as free as possible from centralized direction, and hence would not sap the vitality of the local communities. Bigness, as he saw it, was a curse. The argument for federalism is that it prevents centralization and therefore mitigates some of the evil effects of bigness.

The Court's understanding of the Constitution, as stated by Chief Justice Charles Evans Hughes in the Schechter case, was that increased activities by the national government, penetrating deep into the local communities, violates the traditional federal division of local and national functions, and that that violation prepares the way for a dangerous centralization. The decisive premise of this argument is that there is a province of freedom with which no govern-

---

[2]Franklin D. Roosevelt, Press Conference #209, May 31, 1935, *Press Conferences of Franklin D. Roosevelt* (Hyde Park, New York, 1956), V, 322–23.
[3]Quoted in Arthur M. Schlesinger, Jr., *The Politics of Upheaval* (Boston, 1960), p. 280.

ment, not even a democratic government, is entitled to meddle. One way of controlling the government and hence guaranteeing that freedom is to maintain a system in which, according to that understanding, the powers of government are distributed between various levels of government. However important economic stability is, it was freedom that finally assumed an overriding importance in the Hughes Court's treatment of New Deal regulatory legislation, at least prior to the court-packing plan, and freedom is held to depend upon a federal division of powers. It is hardly unreasonable to suppose that the Hughes Court was radically democratic and reactionary at the same time, for it seemed to think that the Constitution means whatever freedom means. But the fact that the Constitution which delineates the American system of government is in general democratic does not mean that every aspect of that Constitution establishes some element of freedom.

The critical question, as Roosevelt saw it, was whether or not the national government could be entrusted under the Constitution with the task of dealing with national economic problems and economic crises. He had to defend a very large increase in the regulatory powers of the national government as being constitutional and his understanding of the Constitution gave the national government the necessary power (unless specifically prohibited in the Constitution) to alleviate national economic emergencies. There was no reason to suppose that the national government was intended to be confined to mere delegations of power, especially in light of the necessary and proper clause. But Roosevelt knew that the problem of determining the extent of the national commerce power, important as it was, was not the fundamental problem. A power is a *means* by which certain *ends* are accomplished. The powers delegated to the government or to certain branches of the government are powers to do certain things or perform certain tasks and are therefore related to certain ends or purposes of government. Those ends which can be inferred from the particular powers of government are specified in the Preamble to the Constitution. Roosevelt conceived of a national government as having powers fully adequate to accomplish the ends or purposes which the Preamble sets forth, but not transcending those ends. The Hughes Court, however, misread the broad language of the commerce clause in the Schechter case and, reviewing the argumentation of that Court's opinion, we are moved to conclude that FDR had a better understanding of the scheme of the Constitution. The commerce clause permits a flexibility which the Hughes Court simply refused to recognize.

The Great Depression has demonstrated certain inescapable realities. Surely one of these realities was that the general welfare or common good requires a limitation on freedom, a limitation which can be imposed only by government. The Hughes Court tried to make the Constitution an instrument to deprive the United States of economic legislation (of a regulatory type) in the interest of preserving freedom. This allows us to say that the Hughes Court's preoccupation with freedom caused it to lose sight of some of the great objects of government, such as that of providing for the general welfare. It is probably not an overstatement to assert that its overriding concern with freedom (that is, that the economy should be allowed to act on its own without substantial government regulation or control) was the crucial failing of the Hughes Court.

It has always been thought, since the most obvious action of FDR's New Deal was the reform of democratic institutions, that he was an innovator. But he did not actually institute any reform that resulted in a major change in the American Constitution. From the rash of Supreme Court decisions in 1935–1936 invalidating crucial New Deal measures to the court-packing crisis in 1937, Roosevelt was absorbed with the danger to the American Constitution rather than with its change. He wanted to make certain that the Constitution remained in harmony with the fundamental requirements of the nature of the regime. His understanding of that danger emphasized the Hughes Court's strained or narrow construction of the commerce clause.[4] That Court handed down a series of decisions, the cumulative effect of which amounted to a corruption of the Constitution, for a majority of that Court attempted to sever the practical connection between the commerce power and the needs of the country which the commerce power was originally intended to serve. The question of the relationship between the government and the economy therefore was central to that great political confrontation between the Hughes Court and the president.

The Hughes Court was faced with New Deal statutes of a most controversial character, representing as they did a marked departure from the traditional conceptions of the partition of power between the states and the nation, and accordingly many members of that Court resisted the trend of these statutes. One can go further and say that the Supreme Court went out of its mind in 1935 because the moment had occurred for a prudential change in practice that previous constitutional tradition had frowned upon. The Hughes Court's error was not its refusal, prior to the re-election of President Roosevelt in 1936, to budge to popular demand. Popular demand was not that unified (especially with regard to such statutes as the NRA). And, of course, it is possible to have popular demand go in the wrong direction. The Constitution, moreover, ought not to mean whatever popular opinion wants it to mean, merely to sanction popular demand. The Hughes Court's error was its refusal to face up

---

[4]See *Railroad Retirement Board* v. *Alton R. R.* 295 U.S. 330 (1935) and *Carter* v. *Carter Coal Co.*, 298 U.S. 238 (1936).

to the hard and unpleasant realities of the times, and the simple falsity of its representation of the constitutional document.

The crucial controversy of the New Deal period prior to 1937 was whether the Constitution prohibited the national government from dealing with the problems of a nationwide integrated economy (outside the field of public utilities) no matter how great the public need. The big question for the Hughes Court during that period was deciding which things, under the various clauses of the Constitution, should be done by which level of government. That Court challenged the NRA, which was avowedly based on the commerce clause, with the argument that the enterprise of the Schechters was too remote from interstate commerce and too insignificant in its effect on that commerce. It argued that the national commerce power had to cease to operate before it touched the Schechters because, if the trade and labor practices of persons who process and sell for local consumption were removed from state power, the states would lose some of the autonomy reserved to them by the Constitution. Any effort to increase the regulatory activities of the national government to the point of its participation in purely local functions would mean increased governmental centralization.

The constitutional revolution of 1937, if it can be called a revolution at all, was constituted by the expansion of the limits of the commerce power so as to make the power to regulate commerce the power to regulate the national economy. The prime duty of the Supreme Court is to interpret the law and therefore it is supposed to say what the law is. But that duty to say what the law is, is not always simple. It may very well lead to some far-reaching interpretations. For example, the Court can enlarge the meaning of the commerce clause, through the necessary and proper clause, and thereby enlarge the powers of the national government. The Hughes Court believed that a commerce power intended to exercise the function of economic regulation would introduce a radical and impermissible change in the system. That Court seemed to assume that democracy requires that the regulatory activities of the national government be suppressed in the interest of freedom, and it carried the point no further than that.

III

FDR managed political life in America more effectively than any other twentieth century leader, for more than anyone else he came to grips with the problem of the class struggle, arguing that economic freedom is an essential part of political freedom. Surely Roosevelt's statesmanship cannot be seen apart from the class struggle because statesmanship involves dealing with concrete circumstances, and the circumstances here involved the class struggle more than anything else. The masses were disaffected by great dislocations in the economy, and he used the rhetoric of the class struggle in order to persuade the *demos* that his was a sympathetic ear. Indeed, the rhetoric of the class struggle was one of the facts of political life that had to be accepted or approved or stolen in order to be moderated. That is, appreciable moderation might well involve riding the crest of the rhetoric of that which was being moderated. And under the circumstances of the Great Depression, moreover, Roosevelt had every right, and even an obligation, to start from the premise that the common good was equivalent to the immediate interests of the many as many, and more precisely, to the economic interests of the many. His battle against the "economic royalists," or in plainer language, the rich, took the form of a limitation on their freedoms, a limitation he conceived to be in the common interest or common good. But the notion of the common good implicit in his statesmanship was of a higher order than that implicit in the doctrine of the class struggle, for he rejected the radical egalitarianism of the Marxian doctrine.[5]

Roosevelt had a humane man's dislike of poverty, probably a belief that poverty makes men worse in a certain way, and a democrat's prejudice against inequality. If we take what he regarded as the best political scheme (that is, the welfare state), the end or purpose of government is the greatest good of the greatest number.[6] The greatest good of the greatest number may very well appear to be the good of everyone, but it is actually the good of the large majority, perhaps even the good of the common people as distinguished from the good of the wealthy. Achieving this may even require severe limitations on the freedom of the wealthy. The problem of political freedom therefore becomes one of finding that point of coincidence between freedom and restraint on which the greatest good of the greatest number or the political common good rests. Roosevelt's New Deal did not wish to place property at the mercy of the propertyless nor make freedom the preserve of the propertied. The New Deal attempted to achieve the right mean, not by avoiding restraints over the processes of the economy on the one hand and the freedoms of the individual on the other, but by integrating restraints and freedoms into a regime which could provide for the greatest good of the greatest number.

On the occasion of the Supreme Court's invalidation of the NRA, an editorial in the *New Republic* stated: "Either the nation must put up with the confusions and miseries of an essentially unregulated capitalism, or it must

---

[5]Franklin D. Roosevelt, *The Public Papers and Addresses of Franklin D. Roosevelt,* compiled by S. I. Rosenman 13 vols. (New York, 1938–1950), IV, 17. Hereafter cited as *Public Papers and Addresses.*

[6]*Public Papers and Addresses,* II, 186; III, 288; IX, 596.

prepare to supersede capitalism with socialism. There is no longer a feasible middle course."[7] The fact is that the New Deal involved a considerable interference with private property. It operated on the assumption that government is entitled to interfere with property and, to some extent, to redistribute property. Roosevelt was in favor of private property, but he was not opposed to government interference with property which he conceived to be in the public interest or common good. Inheritance taxes and corporation taxes tend to interfere with the property right in itself, without actually destroying property. In other words, the emphasis was on private property, but not necessarily on private property wholly at the disposal of the individual or individual corporation. Roosevelt understood that an essentially unregulated capitalism leads to concentrated economic power, the nakedness and violence of the class struggle and ultimately to socialism. As he stated to the Congress in 1938: "Capital is essential; reasonable earnings on capital are essential; but misuse of the powers of capital or selfish suspension of the employment of capital must be ended, or the capitalistic system will destroy itself through its own abuses."[8] And this is precisely why Marxism teaches that capitalism, simply speaking, leads inevitably to socialism by its own logic. What has evolved in America is a semi-free or controlled capitalism, that is, an economic system which the government *regulates*, but does not *operate*. But the radical advocates of free private enterprise have never understood that government regulation is not socialism. And if properly guided, it prevents socialism.

Roosevelt rejected the notion of the inevitability of class divisions and the tendency of labor and capital to conflict. The programs of the New Deal, we are not surprised to learn, found their basis in the Madisionian system. Roosevelt described that system as one "founded on the principle that many men from many states with many economic views and many economic interests might, through the medium of a national government, build for national harmony, national unity and independent well-being. . . .[The Madisonian system] means that government is intended to be the means by which all of these interests and policies are brought into equilibrium and harmony within a single Republic."[9] The function of government, as Roosevelt understood it, consists of reconciling the different claims of the different groups and interests in the society, but that reconciliation is not be confused with securing a consensus, for a considerable portion of the moneyed classes did not concede to the New Deal. Therefore also, and of overriding importance, it is the function of government to determine the common benefit or interest in which

[7]"Social Control vs. the Constitution," *New Republic* (June 12, 1925), p. 118.
[8]*Public Papers and Addresses*, VII, 9–10.
[9]Franklin D. Roosevelt, *Public Papers of [Governor] Franklin D. Roosevelt, 1932* (Albany, New York, 1939), p. 664.

the rival claims of the different interests can be resolved.[10] The particular resolution the New Deal achieved, which aimed at redistributing benefits between the various groups and interests in the society, had a powerful moderating effect on that portion of the society most susceptible to the attractions of a class orientation. The New Deal, accordingly, consciously nourished the expansion of the middle class which constituted a stabilizing and moderating force in American life, for it tended to blur all distinctions of class without blurring all distinctions between interests.

Conservative critics of the New Deal claim that Roosevelt moved too fast during the depression. The charge behind that charge is that to do *anything* is to move too fast. Yet for the government to leave old laws and modes of economic relations standing—to refuse to introduce new laws and new modes —in the midst of radical changes in material conditions is *itself* governmental redistribution of property, for the old modes were set by government in the light of *old* conditions. Not to change the modes in harmony with changing conditions is just as much governmental activity as is the harmonious changing of modes, and is in some ways more preservative of the status quo. Roosevelt, of course, did more than preserve the proportions. But our point here is simply this—that there is no such thing as government "leaving the economy alone" for the economy does not stand still—it moves. Roosevelt's conservative critics have helped to promote the false notion that the public concern for the economic interests of the many is the preserve of Marxism. This would seem to imply that whenever a difficult problem presents itself, the best solution would be the avoidance of any solution, or to let time take care of the problem. But Roosevelt could not afford to wait. He was dealing with unprecedented economic circumstances that had brought into question the basic Madisonian assumption that modern liberal democracy could arrest and even overcome the wastes and destructions of the class struggle.

IV

Roosevelt's New Deal constituted a profound modification of the traditional American Democracy, a modification arrived at through a break with the earlier liberalism. We can see most clearly what that break effected by the New Deal means when examining the establishment of the welfare state. The question naturally arises as to whether we should understand the changes effected by the New Deal (that is, the coming-into-being of the welfare state) as a regime-change or as a continuation of the existing regime. If there is any lesson to be learned from studying Roosevelt's statesmanship, it is that of

[10] *Public Papers and Addresses,* III, 436; V, 148.

seeing how the American Democracy could be improved *without* being fundamentally changed. The great task for Roosevelt was that of recreating democratic political institutions which was tantamount to the introduction of a new quality into the regime. But the introduction of that new quality was done in such a way as to preserve the essential nature of the regime, that is, its democratic nature. We may go so far as to regard the establishment of the welfare state as the most important event in American history in the twentieth century, at least on the domestic side. The establishment of the welfare state constitutes the most profound modification of the earlier liberalism which has occurred, but it is not the end of liberalism.

It is of some importance for an understanding of the welfare state to realize that it is a relatively recent phenomenon in American politics. Therefore the welfare state presupposes somewhere and somehow a change in the earlier practice and all changes of any importance constitute a break with the earlier practice. It seems that the accepted interpretations of the New Deal do not pay sufficient attention to the distinctive character of its innovations and, furthermore, the accepted interpretations are based on what amounts to a depreciation of the welfare state as a departure from the earlier liberalism. Owing to the collapse of the earlier liberalism, it became necessary to reexamine liberalism with a view to the question of whether the traditional understanding of the relationship between the government and the economy was adequate. The central errors of the earlier liberalism, Roosevelt maintained, were its unrestricted individualism, its policy of encouraging smallness and discouraging economic concentration (that is, its anti-trust approach of breaking down and destroying concentrated economic power), and its narrow and inflexible view of the functions of government. The Great Depression had thrust upon the government the responsibility for the general performance of the economy. FDR's New Deal rejected the notion that an economic system such as that of the United States would regulate itself automatically by the uncontrolled competition of private enterprise, and therefore it imposed regulations and controls on the economy as a whole. But this was accomplished only with very great difficulty as it involved a struggle against the established pattern of earlier liberal beliefs and attitudes.

The hostility of the earlier liberalism to the regulatory and welfare measures of the New Deal, as we have suggested, rested on a narrow understanding of the functions of government. We must never forget that an important part of the earlier liberalism was the simple consideration that all the important things in life are done by society, setting society apart form government, and that the function of government is primarily to secure the *conditions* of happiness. The earlier liberalism held especially that government has the function of guaranteeing life, liberty and the pursuit of happiness, but *not* the enjoyment or possession of happiness. The view that the happiness and well-being of the greatest number should be provided for by government is, in modern terms, a welfare-state view, and it emerged in this country in the period of the Great Depression.

Roosevelt was undoubtedly correct when he said that "heretofore, Government had merely been called upon to produce the *conditions* within which people could live happily, labor peacefully, and rest secure. Now it was called upon to [raise the standard of living for everyone; to bring luxury within the reach of the humblest; . . . and to release everyone from the drudgery of heavy manual toil]."[11] He pointed out that "it is a relatively *new thing* in American life to consider what the relationship of Government is to its starving people and its unemployed citizens, and to take steps to fulfill its governmental duties to them. A generation ago people had scarcely given thought to the terms 'social security,' 'minimum wages,' or 'maximum hours'."[12] The president most assuredly shared the earlier liberal view as far as it went, but he gave it a *new dimension* when he insisted that "all reasonable people must recognize that government was not instituted to serve as a cold public instrument to be called into use after irreparable damage had been done. If we limit government to functions of punishing the criminal after the crimes have been committed, of gathering up the wreckage of society after the devastation of an economic collapse, or of fighting a war that reason might have prevented, then government fails to satisfy those urgent human purposes, which, in essence, gave it its beginning and provide its present justification."[13] The president's statement draws a distinction between preventive and remedial measures, and argues for government's acting to forestall, through constructive economic and social measures, rather than always merely acting to repair the damage.

The earlier liberalism and the New Dealers shared the view that the concentration of economic power constitutes a threat to democracy, but the earlier liberalism had similar fears about the concentration of governmental power. Accordingly, the earlier liberalism sought to decentralize concentrations of economic power, while the New Dealers were more inclined, with some exceptions, to use regulatory legislation to control such concentrations. The New Dealers, in contradistinction to the earlier liberalism, envisioned a cooperation, not a conflict, between governmental power and private economic power, that is, between politics and private property, but with the political as the controlling element.

The earlier liberalism could be characterized as follows. The more fundamental issue of political reconstruction is almost entirely subordinated to the

---

[11] *Public Papers and Addresses*, I, 747. The italics are mine.
[12] *Public Papers and Addresses*, IX, 440. The italics are mine.
[13] *Public Papers and Addresses*, IV, 442.

restoration of the old competitive system (that is, improving private competition or freedom of competition) that would require only a limited government. That liberalism called for the destruction of monopolies and trusts, not their regulation. There was the ill-defined recognition that some regulation was necessary and proper, but no principle was stated. In the New Deal, on the other hand, there was a principle stated that the government must undertake responsibility for the maintenance and health of the economy as a whole to the point of rearranging that economy, if necessary, and redistributing its benefits. This moves away from an emphasis on the *conditions* of happiness toward the enjoyment or possession of happiness understood as material happiness or well-being. The welfare state is a society in which material happiness or well-being is no longer merely privately pursued. The question arises therefore as to whether one should understand this shift in emphasis as a qualitative shift in American politics as opposed, say, to a mere acceleration of political actions. This question, in turn, raises the further question whether, if qualitative, the change in action was based upon a conscious change in political understanding.

Basil Rauch, a New Deal historian, asks whether the great series of New Deal measures, which included the National Labor Relations Act, the Social Security Act and the Fair Labor Standards Act, represent a "new departure" in American political thought and practice. His answer is that the sheer quantity of governmental reformist activity initiated by the New Deal produced a "qualitative change" in American government—what is called positive government or the welfare state. Something new enters the tradition, Rauch admits, but it must be understood as derivative from the sheer quantity of reformist activity.[14] The quantitative change, from a certain moment on, becomes a qualitative change and therefore the New Deal can be reduced to a series of legislative acts initiated by the Roosevelt Administration. This interpretation of the New Deal leads to the consequence that there was no change, strictly speaking, that there was only a *fast* deal and not a *new* deal, and that all the fuss raised by the opposition was merely a reaction to the speed with which the series of New Deal legislative acts unfolded.

In Rauch, one sees reflections of the notion that the New Deal did unthinkingly what it was driven to do, and that the driving force was the boiling up of events and not the grasp of the significance of those events by FDR nor the direction given them by New Deal legislation. For to say that the qualitative change that had come about did so by the sheer force of the multiplicity of *ad hoc* responses to immediate problems is simply to say that the New Deal did not know what it was doing. The problem can be formulated as follows: did FDR lead or follow, and, if he led, did he really know where he was going?

---

[14]Basil Rauch, *The History of the New Deal* (New York, 1963), pp. ix, x.

Everyone agrees that Roosevelt was not a theoretical man, but a politician. What we do say, however, is that Rauch reflects the prevalent view that practice makes theory and we, on the other hand, believe that in the case of the New Deal in particular, as well as political events in general, it is the other way around. FDR did not know the deepest roots of, nor could he foresee, the fullest consequences of his political actions. But he did act, and he did know, *in principle*, the character of the changes his actions were bringing about. Hence we may conclude that that principle was the directing force of the several legislative acts which made up the New Deal, no matter how clumsy some of those acts might have been. It is no small evidence of this that FDR gave a name to the whole before any of its parts were cast, for he introduced the term "New Deal" in his acceptance speech for the presidential nomination in July 1932. "I have . . . described the spirit of my program as a 'new deal,' which is plain English for a changed *concept* of the duty and responsibility of Government toward economic life."[15]

We must repeat: the aim of the New Deal was the welfare state. To understand the welfare state means to understand it in its relation to the Lockean-Jeffersonian tradition. By viewing the welfare state in the light of the Lockean-Jeffersonian tradition, one can fairly state what Roosevelt's principles were. The Declaration of Independence defines the function of government in terms of a certain understanding of the relation between happiness and the conditions of happiness. According to that understanding, life, liberty and the pursuit of happiness constitute the conditions of happiness, and it is the function of government to guarantee those conditions, but not happiness itself. FDR, on the other hand, believed the function of government to be that of achieving the greater happiness of the greater number. He seemed to consider happiness as well-being and he defined his own understanding of the change in terms of the movement from political to economic rights. It is *this* fundamental change in emphasis which gives the New Deal its distinctive character as a political movement, for, from then on, government furnished not only the conditions of happiness, but, to a considerable extent, the enjoyment or possession of material happiness which might properly be called well-being. Well-being or welfare is a kind of in-between concept, in-between the conditions of happiness and happiness itself. It seems clear therefore that Roosevelt, with a consideration of political principle in mind, tried to develop a thoughtful view of what the country ought to do in order to meet the crisis at hand. He was able, moreover, to articulate what was happening more successfully than any other man of that period.

It suffices here to emphasize that there was a sudden breakthrough in

---

[15] *Public Papers and Addresses,* I, 782. The italics are mine.

American political thought in the 1930s which was accomplished by FDR and the New Deal. As a result of the climactic experience of the Great Depression, and the manner in which that Depression was understood, the earlier liberalism became seriously threatened. What is of immense importance in understanding the politics of the New Deal period is that the controvery between FDR and the earlier liberalism was not merely constituted by the latter's reaction to the speed with which the series of New Deal legislative acts unfolded. It derived ultimately from different understandings of the intents and purposes of democratic society. The contribution which the New Deal made to the American political tradition consisted in its correcting the earlier liberal view to the extent of correcting its narrow understanding of the functions of government (or of the relationship between the government and the economy), and only in this light can we see the case for FDR and the New Deal in its full dimensions. Fundamental to the welfare-state position was Roosevelt's contention that "government has the final responsibility for the *well-being* of its citizenship," that is, for securing the material happiness or well-being of its citizens,[16] while the earlier liberalism, setting society apart from government, continued to believe in government as being necessary only under certain conditions.

The specific New Deal thesis was that government has the responsibility to provide not merely for the *conditions* of happiness (that's the Lockeanism implicit in the American Founding), but for something approaching happiness itself or what we may call well-being or welfare. The difference between the welfare-state and the Lockean-Jeffersonian liberalism would then seem to be rooted in the fundamental difference between happiness or well-being and the pursuit of happiness as the end or aim of the state. The essential failure of the earlier liberalism consisted in a one-sided and over-simplified concentration on individualism and all that this implies for politics and government. The correction of that view involves a realization that the function of government is more than a mere matter of guaranteeing life, liberty and the pursuit of happiness, as has been so often supposed in our traditional political thinking. Surely Woodrow Wilson's New Freedom began to question the authority of the earlier liberalism. FDR transcended some of the limitations of liberal democracy and even enlarged its horizons by teaching us that a democratic society requires for its preservation the guaranteeing of equality of opportunity through governmental provision for welfare or well-being. But FDR did not seem to realize that, in constantly seeking to strengthen economic equality, the human personality could in fact become submerged in the interest of a better regulated economic life with its emphasis on health, welfare and freedom from

---

[16] *Public Papers and Addresses*, VII, 14. The italics are mine.

want. FDR may not have foreseen it, but the humane passion for welfarism could result in what Tocqueville referred to as a soft despotism. This is perhaps the greatest difficulty underlying the New Deal.

V

The great achievement of Roosevelt's statesmanship consists in his preserving the continuity of the American political tradition and, accordingly, that statesmanship was able to distinguish between preserving rigidly its practices and flexibly its principles. The "Nine Old Men," as the Hughes Court came to be called, saw only preserving rigidly these practices and not flexibly these principles. Within a living tradition, such as the American political tradition, the innovations introduced are not necessarily the opposite of the tradition. They may very well represent its strengthening, and one cannot understand *our* political tradition in its depth unless one understands it is the light of that strengthening. A typical mistake of the conservative is his concealing the fact that the continuous and changing tradition which he reveres so much would never have come about through conservatism, or without discontinuities, revolution and upheaval at the very beginning of the tradition. With this thought in mind, Roosevelt pointed out at the beginning of his second presidential campaign that preservation is never simple preservation without any changes. To preserve is to reform. Therefore reform becomes preservation for the far-sighted conservative.[17]

Shortly after the court-packing plan was announced in early 1937, Felix Frankfurter wrote to the president that there was no easy way out of the difficulty with the Supreme Court, that all possible courses of action had their advantages and disadvantages, and that any major tampering with the body politic would involve some shock to the body politic.[18] But Roosevelt was willing to take that risk. The Hughes Court had argued that the emergency of the depression did not make a difference. Roosevelt argued that the emergency did make a difference, but he went further than that. He wanted the court to understand the various currents and trends prevailing in the country, not so much to simply reflect the changing wants and wishes of the populace, as to direct it toward the preservation of the principles and institutions of government intended to protect the interests of the society as a whole.

What may help us to understand the New Deal is the fact that periods of crisis have always been periods when the American mind achieved its greatest insights into the nature of politics and political society. The period of the New

[17] *Public Papers and Addresses*, V, 389.
[18] Max Freedman, annotator, *Roosevelt and Frankfurter—Their Correspondence, 1928–1945* (Boston, 1967), p. 381.

Deal represents the innermost character of American politics, for in a crisis, what is essentially political is revealed in the extreme. The inevitable consequence, when profound economic and political issues are debated and resolved, is the level of political controversy so characteristic of the New Deal generation. We have tried to suggest our reasons for believing that FDR's New Deal was not a mere extension of the earlier liberalism. The consciousness of the critics of FDR, both from the left and the right, has been so dominated by the notion that he was a "pragmatic" politician that they have failed to recognize the distinctive contribution of his statesmanship. Roosevelt's statesmanship added a new dimension to American political thought, for in the tension between progressivism and socialism, he and, through him, the country, rose above those alternatives.

SELECTED SUGGESTED READINGS

The Public Papers and Addresses of Franklin D. Roosevelt. Compiled by S. I. Rosenman. 13 vols. New York: Random House, 1938; The Macmillan Company, 1941; Harper and Row, 1950.

See the following selections from *Public Papers and Addresses:*

"Commonwealth Club Address," September 23, 1932, *Public Papers and Addresses,* I, 742–56.

"Press Conference #209," May 31, 1935, *Public Papers and Addresses,* IV, 200–22.

"Address to the Young Democratic Clubs," August 24, 1935, *Public Papers and Addresses,* IV, 336–44.

"The Continuing Struggle for Liberalism," Introduction to 1937 Volume, *Public Papers and Addresses,* VI, xlvii–lxxii.

"Fireside Chat on Reorganization of Judiciary," March 9, 1937, *Public Papers and Addresses,* VI, 122–32.

"Address on Constitution Day," September 17, 1937, *Public Papers and Addresses,* VI, 359–67.

"Fireside Chat on Party Primaries," June 24, 1938, *Public Papers and Addresses,* VII, 391–400.

"Address on Election of Liberals," November 4, 1938, *Public Papers and Addresses,* VII, 584–93.

"Address at Jackson Day Dinner," January 8, 1940, *Public Papers and Addresses,* IX, 25–35.

"Address at University of Pennsylvania," September 20, 1940, *Public Papers and Addresses,* IX, 435–42.

★ FELIX FRANKFURTER   *Richard G. Stevens*

Felix Frankfurter had four careers, any one of which would have been enough to fill another man's life. Born in Vienna in 1882, he came with his family to New York at the age of 12 not knowing a word of English. He attended City College in New York and then the Harvard Law School where he was splendidly successful and from which he was graduated in 1906. By that time his facility with the English language was great. The precision, the driving force, and the colorful beauty of his English, both written and spoken, continued to develop throughout his life.[1]

His first and his longest career was that of a reformer—longest because it lasted throughout his life. While he often praised the ordinary, small-town attorney with a general practice of law,[2] he never desired such a practice for himself. He really wanted to be a lawyer without clients.[3] He wanted, that is, to immerse himself in the law itself, both because he had a zeal for justice (and law is in the service of justice),[4] and because he had a keen desire for learning. After his graduation from the Harvard Law School in 1906 he quickly abandoned private practice in favor of a poorer-paying but more satisfying post in the office of the United States Attorney for the Southern District of New York, Henry L. Stimson.[5] He followed Stimson first into a short interlude of private practice and then into the War Department and, being asked in 1913 to teach law at the Harvard Law School, joined that faculty in 1914.

His second career was that of an academic. It did not so much follow upon as change the manner of the first. He went back to the Law School as much to reform it and, through it, the law and public life, as to escape the " 'intellectual hand-to-mouth living' "[6] he had found in serving the government. With occasional interruptions, such as his service back in the War Department (1917 to 1919), a year at Oxford (1933–34) and service on a variety of commissions, he was at the Law School from 1914 until his appointment to the United States Supreme Court in 1939.

[1]See H. B. Phillips, ed. *Felix Frankfurter Reminisces,* (New York, 1960), p. viii.
[2]See, for example, Felix Frankfurter, *Of Law and Life and Other Things that Matter,* ed. Philip B. Kurland (Cambridge, 1965), pp. 161 ff.
[3]Phillips, ed. *Felix Frankfurter Reminsces,* pp. 34, 47.
[4]Frankfurter dissenting in *Elkins* v. *United States,* 364 U.S. 207 (1960) at pp. 233 and 235.
[5]Phillips, ed. *Felix Frankfurter Reminsces,* pp. 38–40.
[6]Phillips, ed. *Felix Frankfurter Reminisces,* pp. 80–84. The quotation is from p. 84.

Frankfurter's third career—and "career" is not too strong a word for it —was as a confidant of Franklin D. Roosevelt. They had not met while both were students at Harvard, but they did meet shortly after Frankfurter's graduation from the Law School, and they came to know each other well in 1913 while the one was in the War Department and the other in the Navy Department.[7] Just as the second career had not put a stop to the first, so the third was an addition to and an extension of the first two. The association of the two men became ever closer after Roosevelt's election as governor of New York in 1928, and continued so throughout his governorship and presidency. Frankfurter's advice on all matters of state was so bountifully given and was so well received by Roosevelt that their association excited great envy, fear and suspicion.

In January 1939, President Roosevelt appointed Felix Frankfurter an associate justice of the United States Supreme Court. This was his fourth, and his crowning career. He served on the Court for more than twenty-three years until a stroke forced him to retire in 1962. While on the Court, his correspondence with Roosevelt continued unabated until the latter's death in 1945. His affection for Roosevelt was part and parcel of his affection for the United States. While it would be a mean and petty disservice to the memory of both men to suggest that Frankfurter "used" Roosevelt, it would be true to say that he saw Roosevelt as the vehicle of much good that might be done to the country—that is, the vehicle of reform. And, while on the Court, he kept up a prodigious output of papers and addresses, ranging from the anecdotal to the scholarly, such that it can truly be said he remained an academic just as he remained a confidant, despite his elevation to the Court, and, all three of these activities, scholar, confidant and judge, went to the service of reform.

But if reform was the warp, surely restraint became the woof of the fabric of his judicial career, for, while any calling has its attendant restraints, he clearly saw and firmly asserted that the judicial place imposes a very special set of proprieties on its holder. Whether his understanding of judicial restraint subverted his judicial capacity, as was the case with Holmes,[8] or purified it, is the determining question in understanding and appreciating his judicial statesmanship. Whatever he may have thought about how Franklin Roosevelt ought to deal with the Russians, or with the depression, or with the war, it is what he thought about justice and about the United States Constitution and about the place of the Supreme Court under that Constitution that formed his highest acts as a statesman, his judicial decisions and the opinions supporting them.

Anthony Lewis rightly corrected the *Economist* for referring to Frank-

[7]Max Freedman, ed., *Roosevelt and Frankfurter: Their Correspondence, 1928–1945* (Boston, 1967), pp. 10–11.
[8]See p. 177.

furter as a "Democrat"[9] but, while Frankfurter was never a party man, surely he was a New Dealer. He believed that it was both expedient and in accord with the Constitution for the national government to take vigorous action forming and regulating the economy of the nation. The country turned to that task early in the New Deal, of course, and the crucial cases wherein the Supreme Court showed its agreement with the president and the Congress in the view that it was lawful and prudent for the nation to do so came down before Frankfurter joined the Court.[10] But there were nonetheless a great many opportunities for Frankfurter to shape the law on that question. His very first opinion was the opinion for the Court in *Hale* v. *Bimco Trading Co.,*[11] a case testing a Florida tax on imported cement, and his last opinion was a dissent in *National Labor Relations Board* v. *Walton Mfg. Co.,*[12] a case raising questions as to the proper mode of review by the courts of NLRB orders. Thus, his judicial career begins and ends with questions engendered by the Commerce Clause.

To say that a judge has opportunities to "shape the law" inevitably and immediately raises the question as to what it is that shapes the understanding of the judge. What is the pattern to which he looks when he "shapes" the law? Now, every Supreme Court justice has always contended that the Constitution was his pattern. But the Constitution is brief, and comprehensive and "intended to endure for ages to come, and consequently to be adapted to the various *crises* of human affairs"[13] and so requires interpretation. So, what passes for an answer must itself be treated as a problem. Confronted with that problem directly, Frankfurter told us in the Barnette case:

In the past, this Court has from time to time set its views of policy against that embodied in legislation by finding laws in conflict with what was called the "spirit of the Constitution." Such undefined destructive power was not conferred on this Court by the Constitution. Before a duly enacted law can be judicially nullified, it must be forbidden by some explicit restriction upon political authority in the Constitution. Equally inadmissible is the claim to strike down legislation because to us as individuals it seems opposed to the "plan and purpose" of the Constitution. That is too tempting a basis for finding in one's personal views the purposes of the Founders.[14]

Tempting it surely is, but can one safely deny plan and purpose or spirit to the Constitution in order to be led not into temptation? What could Frank-

---

[9]*Economist,* CCXXXIII (December 6, 1969), 4. Letters.

[10]See *NLRB* v. *Jones and Laughlin Steel Corp.,* 301 U.S. 1 (1937) and *Steward Machine Co.* v. *Davis,* 301 U.S. 548 (1937).

[11]*Hale* v. *Bimco Trading Co.,* 306 U.S. 375, Decided February 27, 1939.

[12]*National Labor Relations Board* v. *Walton Mfg. Co.,* 369 U.S. 404, Decided April 9, 1962.

[13]Mr. Chief Justice Marshall, for the Court, in *McCulloch* v. *Maryland,* 4 Wheaton 316 (1819) at p. 415.

[14]Dissenting in *West Virginia State Board of Education* v. *Barnette,* 319 U.S. 624 (1943) at p. 666. Cf. Felix Frankfurter, *Mr. Justice Holmes and the Supreme Court* (Cambridge, 1961), pp. 42–43, 95.

furter mean when he says "the letter killeth"[15] unless he means that the spirit giveth life? It would make no sense to suggest that Frankfurter, dealing with the Constitution in the one case and with a statute in the other, meant to say that constitutions are to be construed narrowly and statutes, subject to amendment, correction and supplementation from hour to hour by the very legislative power which enacted them, should be construed generously. Perhaps he meant in *both* cases to set the legislative power free to work its will, for, in the Barnette case, it was *restraint* of that power which he said was not to be found in the "spirit" or "plan and purpose" of the Constitution. But his formulation is none the less problematic. Hamilton, in showing that judicial review was to be expected in the scheme established by the Constitution, had argued that limitations, even very narrow and precise limitations, such for instance as the one that the legislature shall pass no *ex post facto* laws, "can be preserved in practice no other way than through the medium of courts of justice, whose duty it must be to declare all acts contrary to the manifest tenor of the Constitution void."[16]

Frankfurter's formulation is seen to be even more problematic when it is noticed that he does not hesitate to rely on his *own* view of the "spirit" or "plan" of the Constitution. In *San Diego Union* v. *Garmon,* raising the question as to whether a congressional establishment of certain regulations of labor relations had pre-empted action by the states, he said that "due regard for the presuppositions of our embracing federal system, including the principle of diffusion of power not as a matter of doctrinaire localism but as a promoter of democracy, has required us not to find withdrawal from the States of power to regulate where the activity regulated was a merely peripheral concern" of the congressional act.[17] *What* federal system? *Why* promote democracy? Are either of these things called for by the Constitution? Maybe so, but *if* so, only by its "spirit" or "plan." Can it have escaped Frankfurter's notice that the Constitution *never once* uses the word "federal"? Neither does it use the word "democracy."[18] Surely the first three words of the Preamble *imply* something that deserves to be called "democracy," but there is room for honest argument. Surely the first sentence of the first article, in vesting only those legislative powers therein granted in the Congress, *implies* that there are *other* legislative powers and so leads to the *possible* conclusion that something like a "division" of powers between the "federal" government and the states was intended. But the "division" of powers—one for the nation, one for the states; two for the

[15]Dissenting in *United States* ex rel. *Knauff* v. *Shaughnessy,* 338 U.S. 537 (1950) at pp. 548 and 550.
[16]*Federalist,* ed. E. M. Earle (New York, 1937), No. 78, p. 505.
[17]*San Diego Union* v. *Garmon,* 359 U.S. 236 (1959) at p. 243.
[18]This is as true of the amendments as it is of the Constitution proper.

nation, two for the states—which the textbooks all describe[19] as the essence of "federalism" is simply nowhere to be found in the Constitution. The bland assurances of the Tenth Amendment notwithstanding, there is not one word in the Constitution which, analogous to the terms of Article I Section 8, says "The States shall have Power to . . . etc." It will not do to say that, oh well, everybody now *agrees* that it is a "federal" and "democratic" Constitution, for it is precisely against such a universally accepted concession that the passage quoted from the Barnette case is directed.[20] One could by another route show that Frankfurter's assertion in the Barnette case is self-defeating, for how *else* could one know that Supreme Court justices ought not to make their judgments in the light of the "spirit" of the Constitution except by understanding how, according to the "spirit" of the Constitution, Supreme Court justices ought to perform their duties, for the Constitution surely does not say how.

The bottom question then is not whether he did or did not defy his own stricture regarding the spirit of the Constitution, for he did, but rather what his understanding of that spirit was. The passage previously quoted from his opinion for the Court in *San Diego Union* v. *Garmon*[21] indicates that his view of the tenor and plan of the Constitution can be summarized by the words "federalism" and "democracy," and, as it happens that indication is supported by a study of all his published writings, both on and off the Court. Of course, both of those words, especially the former, are enormously problematic. He surely does not mean that we have a "federal" system in the *proper* sense of the word.[22] He does not even seem to mean that there is a "division of powers" in the sense that the Constitution clearly gives one thing to the nation and another to the states. He seems to mean that there is a realm of things in which the states may constitutionally act, and that realm is cut into by the constitutional grant of legislative powers to Congress. To say that is not in any way surprising. But he *also* seems to say that it is Congress that decides what the division of things between itself and the state legislatures is. That is a strange division in which one of the two beneficiaries keeps rewriting the distribution of benefits.

[19]Rightly or wrongly. Wrongly, we think.

[20]The implications of the first sentence of the first article could as easily lead one to the distinction which Locke makes between the legislative power in the complete sense, which is identical to the "supream power" residing in the whole people and that legislative power which is vested *by* the supreme power in an actual legislative institution and which is "limited". If the implications led to that, then they would suggest nothing at all of a "division" of powers between a national legislature and state legislatures. See John Locke, *Treatises*, II, Chap. xi.

[21]*San Diego Union* v. *Garmon*, note 17. And see Felix Frankfurter, *The Commerce Clause under Marshall, Taney* and *Waite*, (1937) (Chicago, 1964), p. 12; and *The Public and its Government* (New Haven, 1930), pp. 49 and 73–74.

[22]*Federalist*, No. 9, pp. 51–52. See also Martin Diamond, "The *Federalist's* View of Federalism," G.C.S. Benson *et al, Essays in Federalsim* (Claremont, 1961), and "What the Framers Meant by Federalism," *A Nation of States*, ed. Robert A. Goldwin (Chicago, 1963).

Suffice it to say that due regard for our federalism, in its practical operation, favors survival of the reserved authority of a State over matters that are the intimate concern of the State unless Congress has clearly swept the boards of all State authority, or the States' claim is in unmistakable conflict with what Congress has ordered.[23]

Small comfort to the advocates of states' rights to hear that matters of "intimate concern" to the state and, so, "reserved" to the state (the language, be it remembered, of the Tenth Amendment) may be swept from the boards by Congress.

The process of adjusting the interacting areas of national and state authority over commerce has been reflected in hundreds of cases from the very beginning of our history. Precisely the same kind of issues has plagued the two great English-speaking federations the constitutions of which similarly distribute legislative power over business between central and subordinate governments.[24] These are difficulties inherent in such a federal constitutional system.

The interpenetrations of modern society have not wiped out state lines. It is not for us to make inroads on our federal system either by indifference to its maintenance or excessive regard for the unifying forces of modern technology. Scholastic reasoning may prove that no activity is isolated within the boundaries of a single State, but that cannot justify absorption of legislative power by the United States over every activity. On the other hand, the old admonition never becomes stale that this Court is concerned with the bounds of legal power and not with the bounds of wisdom in its exercise by Congress. When the conduct of an enterprise affects commerce among the States is a matter of practical judgment, not to be determined by abstract notions. The exercise of this practical judgment the Constitution entrusts primarily and very largely to the Congress, subject to the latter's control by the electorate.[25]

But if a country in which there is a strong tradition of local self-government but in which the limits of local competence may periodically be expanded and contracted according to the practical judgment of the central legislature may be called a "federal" government, then *England* has a federal government—nay, *all* governments are "federal," even the governments of the individual states themselves. In such a usage the adjective goes automatically with the noun and so adds nothing descriptive to the noun. To say that we have a "federal" system of government is to say nothing at all about it. Note well that Frankfurter abandons almost entirely in his words and perhaps quite entirely in his meaning any judicial check on the legislature such as that which had been retained by the nineteenth century resolution of this problem. The

---

[23]Frankfurter dissenting in *Rice* v. *Santa Fe Elevator Corp.*, 331 U.S. 218 (1947) at p. 241.

[24]Here Frankfurter cites several sources. Among them he cites Section 91 (He ought to have cited Sections 91 and 92) of the British North American Act of 1867. The very "division" of powers which, as we said above, is *lacking* in the United States Constitution is made in explicit terms in the "constitution" of Canada.

[25]Frankfurter for the Court in *Polish National Alliance* v. *National Labor Relations Board,* 322 U.S. 643 (1944) at pp. 649–50. Cf. his opinion for the Court in *International Association of Machinists* v. *Gonzales,* 356 U.S. 617 (1958) at p. 619 and his opinion for the Court in *Palmer* v. *Massachusetts,* 308 U.S. 79 (1939) at p. 84.

question as to whether the mere grant of power over commerce which the Constitution made to the Congress abolished all power over that matter by the states, whether or not Congress got around to exercising that power, was raised in *Gibbons* v. *Ogden*[26] but was not settled there. After much reflection and hesitation the Court did settle the question, after a fashion, in *Cooley* v. *The Board of Wardens of the Port of Philadelphia.*[27] The answer there was to the effect of "sometimes, sometimes not," but the Court reserved to *its* judgment the question as to when and when not. Frankfurter says that is not a fit question for judicial judgment. It is a matter for practical judgment, that is, legislative judgment.

If, then, the word "federal" in the phrase "our embracing federal system" does not explain our system to us, some other word, perhaps the word "our," if properly understood, would explain it. The "short of it" to use one of Frankfurter's own favorite expressions, is that Frankfurter believed that the Constitution intended both national and state legislatures to have free sway except where constrained by explicit prohibitions and those prohibitions were to be construed very, very narrowly. Of course, if the actions of a state legislature and those of the nation are inharmonious, then the former must give way. Thus, the "division" between the national legislature and the state legislatures is determined by how much the national legislature is willing to leave to the states. Now that might be a good system and it might be "our" system, as well, but a most important question arises. If Frankfurter believed, as he clearly seems to, that the system would become ever more national over time, at the expense of the states—and, so, at the expense of anything that might be called "federalism"—one would have to ask whether he believed, on the one hand, that the Constitution itself provides, by its very terms or by its very "spirit," for such a gradual nationalization by granting *nothing* to the states, by putting only a few precise limits on the United States, and by granting the most ample and elastic powers to the United States, which powers are progressively to be fulfilled as the exigencies of the day demand and the capacities of Congress allow or whether, on the other hand, he believed that the Constitution *itself* changed over time: whether or not, that is to say, the Constitution by some process other than "by some solemn and authoritative act" of the people[28] is now one thing and now quite another.

It seems that Frankfurter thought the Constitution itself changed. In one case, be referred to the law as "living," but that was only in a footnote.[29] He did, in *Wolf* v. *Colorado*, speak of the due process clause (to which this chapter

---

[26] *Gibbons* v. *Ogden*, 9 Wheaton 1 (1824).
[27] *Cooley* v. *The Board of Wardens of the Court of Philadelphia*, 12 Howard 299 (1851).
[28] *Federalist*, No. 78, p. 509.
[29] Frankfurter concurring in *Bernhardt* v. *Polygraphic Co.*, 350 U.S. 198 (1956) at p. 209.

will later turn) as a "living principle."[30] This much is only a hint, but examination of his writings off the Court discloses his meaning. In *The Commerce Clause Under Marshall Taney and Waite*, published in 1937, he said that the "robust English psychology of common sense whereby law is evolved case by case rather than by deduction from general principles, finds illusory application when the technique of adjudication of the common law is carried over to the statesmanship of constitutional decision."[31] That would seem to show a clear distinction between common law adjudication and constitutional adjudication, but if it is carefully examined and read in full context, one sees that, however "illusory," there *is* still "application," for the common law method *is* "carried over." Judicial statesmanship, as Frankfurter understands it, amounts to carrying off such a carrying over. The constitutional judge differs from the common law judge, apparently, more in his subtelty than in anything else.

In 1930, Frankfurter argued that there had been, a hundred years before, "strong legal and political resistances to the intervention of federal authority into matters outside of its narrowly conceived scope, though in the promotion of local improvement through public roads the strict legal theory early yielded to pressure of need."[32] It is not, be it noted, simply one of two arguable positions respecting the Constitution, but the "strict" legal theory of it that resisted national activity. That theory did not yield to superior argument about the true meaning of the Constitution but to "pressure of need." The constitutional breeches were too tight. By 1830, barely forty years after the founding, the country had grown out of its Constitution. Something had to give.

How is one to account for the survival of the Constitution for a nation of less than four million scattered along the Atlantic seabord, in our present empire stretched across the whole continent, and beyond, in the Asiatic waters of the Pacific? The seeming puzzle is accentuated by the fact that the Constitution is not a dead document. It is, perhaps, the liveliest of our political traditions. It is in a true sense the organ of our political life. The continuing serviceability of the Constitution during cycles of bewildering changes in the society which it governs must mean either that its forms have been adapted to wholly new uses, or that many political results are attained through accomodations outside the constitutional structure, or that the Constitution within its own ample and flexible resources permits adequate response to changing social and economic needs.[33]

Thus far, one could still see a possibility that the Constitution might come through this argument unscathed, but the very next paragraph dashes one's hopes.

In truth, all these three factors have combined to make the Constitution workable. In no single respect has the expectation of the framers of the Constitution been more

[30]Opinion of the Court, *Wolf* v. *Colorado*, 338 U.S. 25 (1949) at p. 27.
[31]Frankfurter, *The Commerce Clause*, note 21; *Wolf* v. *Colorado*, at pp. 25–26.
[32]Frankfurter *The Public and Its Government*, p. 14.
[33]Frankfurter, *The Public and Its Government*, pp. 61–62.

completely frustrated by history than through the popular election of Presidents. Yet the forms of the Constitution have been retained and through them, in conjunction with the machinery devised by our political parties, are registered those very democratic forces against which the constitutional mechanism was directed.[34]

Elsewhere might be a good place to dispute Frankfurter's view that, by 1930, the democratization of the election of the president had defied the intention of the Framers. It is a favorite theme of twentieth century sophisticates that the Constitution was anti-democratic, but that its strictures had been outgrown and outsmarted.[35] What is of importance for the immediate argument is not the question of whether Frankfurter's view that the Constitution was intended to be undemocratic is correct or not, but rather his view that the Constitution had been turned topsvy-turvy and was yet the "same" Constitution. A change in the most fundamental principles, without that "solemn and authoritative act" by the people, of which Alexander Hamilton spoke, appears here not as a defiance of the Constitution but as an evolution or growth or progress in it. The great Supreme Court justices are to Frankfurter "those to whom the Constitution is not primarily a text for interpretation but the means of ordering the life of a progressive people."[36] He even uses the very expression "living Constitution."[37]

If the Thames is "liquid history," the Constitution of the United States is most significantly not a document but a stream of history. And the Supreme Court has directed the stream.[38]

Frankfurter has been accused of being an "Anglophile." Perhaps that is unfair, but surely he is such an admirer of the common-law mode of adjudication as to raise the question whether or not he really misses the fundamental difference between the English and the American constitutions. "Publius" clearly indicated a belief that constitutionalism is a peculiarly American thing.[39] England simply does not *have* a constitution in the sense in which the United States has one. Indeed, England *has* a constitution. *Every* country has one. But to speak of "constitutional government" in one breath and admit in

[34]Frankfurter, *The Public and Its Government*, pp. 61-62.
[35]S.E. Morison, and H.S. Commager, *The Growth of the American Republic*, 4th ed. (New York, 1960). See the first couple of pages of Chapter 13 of the Fourth Edition. J. Allen Smith, *The Spirit of American Government* (New York, 1919), pp. vi–vii and 30–31; R. Hofstadter, *The American Political Tradition* (New York, 1954), pp. 12–13. But see pp. 51 ff. of this text and Martin Diamond, "Conservatives, Liberals and the Constitution," *Left, Right and Center*, ed. Robert A. Goldwin (Chicago, 1965).
[36]Frankfurter, *The Public and Its Government*, p. 76.
[37]Frankfurter, *The Commerce Clause*, p. 9. As far as I know he *never* used that phrase in a Supreme Court opinion.
[38]Frankfurter, *The Commerce Clause*, p. 2 and cf. Felix Frankfurter *Of Law and Men*, ed. Philip Elman (New York, 1959), p. 149 and F. Frankfurter and J. Landis, *The Business of the Supreme Court* (New York, 1928), p. 310.
[39]*Federalist*, No. 53, p. 348.

the next that every country has a constitution, because every country is somehow constituted this way or that is to agree that *every* government is "constitutional government" and therefore to talk into meaninglessness what was
meant to be a distinction. England may jolly well have a "living constitution"
if it likes, but that is because when one speaks of the English constitution one
is not speaking of a solemn and authoritative charter of powers and limitations,
but rather one is speaking of a state of affairs. Dicey saw that clearly.[40] One
need not be an Anglophobe to insist that, despite the many worthy and
wondrous things in England, the English simply do not look at their constitution in the way in which the Americans look at theirs which enables the
Americans to speak of "constitutionalism." Americans may wonder whether
or not this or that congressional action is in accord with the Constitution.
Macaulay's schoolboy knows that Parliament *cannot* act out of accord with the
"English constitution," for what the one enacts the other becomes. The alleged anti-democratic character of the United States Constitution pales in
significance as a repudiation of the principles of the American Revolution
alongside the thunderous destruction of the uttermost principles of the Revolution contained in the doctrine that the American Constitution, like the English, is a "living Constitution." While, unlike the English, it *pretends* to be a
solemn limitation on those who hold for the time being the reins of government, it can in fact, just like the English, be *changed* by those who hold the
reins.

One cannot get out of this problem by having recourse to that favorite
current shibboleth which is to shout "absolutist" at the head of anyone who
calls in question the doctrine of the "living Constitution." One is not claiming
absolute knowledge of the absolute truth about what is absolutely good for man
if he insists that, when a given bunch of men said a given thing on a given day
after three months of patient and lively argument and after commitment of the
fruit of their deliberation to a committee of style so that what they said would
be well said, they said *something* and not any old thing and that they really
meant what they said. The interpreters who insist on a living Constitution
easily suppose that "they," the Framers of the Constitution, could not possibly
understand our problems. It may be that more patience and more open-
minded study of what the Framers wrought would show that they quite
understood the root of our problems. "Understanding" is a two-way street.
Before we can assert that they didn't understand us, we must try very hard
to understand them.

Such an understanding of the true "spirit" or "plan and purpose" of the

---

[40]See A.V. Dicey, *An Introduction to the Study of the Law of the Constitution* (1885) (London,
1961), pp. 127, 129, 137 and *passim*. And see J. Bryce, *The American Commonwealth*, Vol. I, the
chapter entitled "The Courts and the Constitution."

Constitution as might be had after an open-minded study of it, by which we mean a study which is not swept off its intellectual feet by ready acceptance of current doctrine, might lead to a grasp of the fundamental motivation of the authors of the Constitution. Even a bare glimpse of that motivation by a beginning student suggests that to fly to the doctrine of the "living constitution" in order better to preserve those liberties which are thought to be ill-preserved by the Constitution, is, to borrow another of Frankfurter's phrases, "to burn the house to roast the pig."[41] To appreciate this, one can turn from Frankfurter for a moment to Justice Thurgood Marshall. If it is true, as some black men say today, that the Constitution was a "white racist" document and if it is then true that it *called for* segregation in 1896 but, as Thurgood Marshall said before the Senate Judiciary Committee inquiring into his nomination to the Court, the Constitution *now* does *not* call for segregation, but for integration, because it is a "living Constitution"[42] then there is nothing whatsoever in the Constitution to prevent it from changing back. That is not much of a Constitution. It would be a "living" thing, all right, just as a cancer is a living thing. It is only a small step to go from a poker-faced assertion of constitutional rights in the name of a living Constitution to a situation in which any and all claims of rights in the name of the Constitution may be rejected, and not necessarily cynically, by the rejoinder that such a right might have been a "constitutional" right yesterday, when the case was commenced, but is not today, when it has come for decision.

But to return from the general question of a "living Constitution" to Frankfurter's version of it, we are struck by another troubling question. If judges have a hand in this stage-play of limited government, then a dark shadow is cast over all the fine talk we have heard about judicial restraint. And, that judges *have* a hand in it is clear.

Marshall's use of the commerce clause greatly furthered the idea that though we are a federation of states we are also a nation and gave momentum to the doctrine that state authority must be subject to such limitations as the Court finds it necessary to apply for the protection of the national community. It was an audacious doctrine which, one may be sure, would hardly have been publicly avowed in support of the adoption of the Constitution.[43]

It surely appears from this that the kind of "federal" government we have is not only very, very national, as we have shown, and is not only a radical change from the Constitution that was ratified, but that the change is largely due to the inventiveness, not to say usurpations, of the "great Chief Justice,"

---

[41]See his dissent in *International Salt Co.* v. *United States*, 332 U.S. 392 (1947) at p. 403.
[42]United States Congress, Senate, Committee on the Judiciary, 90th Congress, 1st Session, Hearings, *Nomination of Thurgood Marshall* (Washington, 1967), p. 49.
[43]Frankfurter, *The Commerce Clause*, pp. 18–19.

John Marshall. Has that change progressed? Could the course of change be reversed? What, if anything, should judges do to facilitate the change? In the name of what do they decide whether to lead or to follow? Which way is forward? What Frankfurter thought about the nature of the judicial process can better be appreciated by turning now to the due process clause.

Chief Justice Marshall had in *Barron* v. *Baltimore* in 1833 ruled that the first eight amendments to the Constitution were meant to be restrictions only on the actions of the United States and not upon the actions of the states. Therefore, if Maryland were forbidden to take private property for public use without paying just compensation, it was not because of that clause in the Fifth Amendment which says, "nor shall private property be taken for public use, without just compensation." Marshall compellingly shows that implicit in the whole list of amendments known as the "bill of rights" is a directedness toward the actions of only the United States such that the very clause in question ought to be understood as reading "nor shall private property be taken *by the United States* for public use, without just compensation."[44] It would be silly to say as some have said that Marshall there ruled that it was permissible for states to violate the Constitution. What he ruled was simply that the Constitution puts different restraints on the nation and on the states such that action which would be unconstitutional if taken by the one would not be if taken by the other. That this is *obviously* the case in general may be seen by noting that Article I Section 10 forbids the states to make laws impairing the obligation of contracts whereas Article I Section 9 puts no such restraint on the United States.[45] It would be equally foolish to argue that the Constitution authorizes unjust actions by the states. The whole understanding behind the Constitution may be such as to include the view that it is unjust for *any* government to take private property for public use without just compensation. All that one can make of this matter from Marshall's opinion is that, comprehensive as the Constituion is, it does not attempt to cure *every* evil that might arise. Whether this is because it simply fails to reach some evils, or because it regards some cures as worse than the diseases, or because it regards some cures as visionary and doctrinaire, cannot be fully pursued here.

It might be argued that the Constitution intends to guard against such evils as that borne by Barron by establishing, on the one hand, the guarantee of republican government to each state in Article IV and, on the other hand, the few limitations imposed on the states by Article I, Section 10. If one answers to this that it would be foolish to suppose the Founders would impose

---

[44] *Barron* v. *Baltimore*, 7 Peters 243 (1833). We are not here quoting the case but characterizing it.

[45] See Thomas Schrock, "The Liberal Court, the Conservative Court, and Constitutional Jurisprudence," *Left, Right and Center*, ed. Goldwin, pp. 87–120.

only those few limits on the states while imposing "all those" limits on the United States, one must remember that the premiss of such a rejoinder is an anachronism. The Founders *didn't* impose "all those" limits on the United States. They imposed only the limits found in Article I, Section 9, plus a few more spread here and there in the constitutional document.[46] One must not forget that amendments, even the most revered ones, are amendments to a *Constitution* and that *they* cannot be understood unless *it* is, and that *it* cannot be understood unless one wholly forgets *all* the amendments for a time. If one thinks it strange to suppose that the Founders should simply form the national government well and name the right form which is to be guaranteed for the state governments and then place separate and very, very brief lists of prohibitions against the one and the other, it must not be forgotten that such a scheme is strikingly in accord with the argument of John Locke's chapter entitled "Of the Extent of the Legislative Power."[47] What is more persuasive is that such a Constitution, burdened with only a very brief list of explicit prohibitions, is *precisely* what Hamilton argues for in *Federalist*, No. 84.

If the Constitution is so looked at and if one remembers the apprehension felt about the new national government founded by it, Marshall's ruling can be seen to be perfectly consistent with the view that a "bill of rights" putting a whole set of additional explicit limits *on the United States only*, was the price the Founders had to pay to get acceptance of the new Constitution. Thus, Marshall's ruling in the Barron case makes sense.

But the few limits on the states did not prove to be enough. The states, as the Founders themselves well understood would be the case, proved to be far greater sources of injustice than the United States. Slavery, which the Constitution had been ashamed to name, but which, in its caution, it failed to suppress, of course led the train of injustices, but it *was* a train. Several states, in their official capacities, had denied to United States citizens the consideration and respect which, as such, they deserved; invidiously discriminatory legislation was passed; and individuals, black as well as white, were subjected to unjust trials and to the tyranny of unchecked police oppressions.

Slavery, twentieth century revisionist history to the contrary notwithstanding, led to the Civil War and, the Union, stronger in the aftermath of the war than it had been before, imposed a series of additional limitations on the states, just as the "bill of rights" had imposed a list of additional limitations on the United States. The Thirteenth Amendment abolished slavery. The Fifteenth Amendment, in a word, gave the franchise to black men. The second,

---

[46]See Article I, Section 3; Article III, Section 3.
[47]Locke, *Treatises*, II, Chapter xi.

third and fourth sections of the Fourteenth Amendment constituted, so to speak, the treaty of peace between the victorious Union and the rebellious states. The first section of the Fourteenth Amendment defined citizenship and then stated:

No state shall make or enforce any law which shall abridge the privileges or immunities of citizens of the United States; nor shall any state deprive any person of life, liberty, or property, without due process of law; nor deny to any person within its jurisdiction the equal protection of the laws.[48]

What do these limitations mean? In 1873, Justice Samuel Miller for the Court narrowly confined the application of the privileges and immunities clause of the Fourteenth Amendment, and perhaps rightly so. The due process and equal protection clauses have sometimes appeared to overlap, but they have surely had lives of their own such that one can justifiably speak of one without paying much heed to the other. In *Hurtado* v. *California*,[49] in 1884, Justice Stanley Matthews for the Court rejected the contention that the due process clause, *ex vi termini,* applied to the states the constraints which the first eight amendments applied to the United States. In principle, that view was reaffirmed in 1908 and again in 1937.[50] Interestingly enough, while claims made on behalf of those accused in criminal cases in the name of the due process clause were often rebuffed by the Court, claims made by taxpayers and others that state legislation, in substance, deprived them of property without due process of law, were often sustained.[51] Frankfurter was among those who believed the Court wrong to interfere with state legislation on due process grounds. Perhaps he never reconciled himself to the due process clauses in the Fifth and Fourteenth amendments, but *surely* his earliest recorded thoughts on them showed that he regarded them as investing an unwarrantable discretion in judges. In 1912, he had some hope that judges might be able to handle such tasks if "the stream of the Zeitgeist" was "allowed to flood the sympathies and the intelligence of our judges."[52] But, by 1924, he had firmly decided that that was too much to hope for. Perhaps Theodore Roosevelt had put the fear of God in the Supreme Court for a time, but "the 'fear of God' is too capricious, too intermittent . . . . The due process clauses ought to go."[53] They ought to go because they enable judges, under the guise of reliance on the Constitution,

---

[48]Constitution, Amendments, XIV, Section 1.

[49]*Hurtado* v. *California*, 110 U.S. 516 (1884).

[50]*Twining* v. *New Jersey*, 211 U.S. 78 (1908) and *Palko* v. *Connecticut*, 302 U.S. 319 (1937).

[51]See *Lochner* v. *New York*, 198 U.S. 45 (1905); *Coppage* v. *Kansas*, 208 U.S. 412 (1908). Compare the state court case of *People* v. *Marx*, New York Court of Appeals, 99 N.Y. 377 (1885) where the connection between "substantive due process" and criminal justice shows itself.

[52]Felix Frankfurter, *Law and Politics*, ed. E.F. Prichard, Jr. and Archibald MacLeish (New York, 1962), p. 7.

[53]Frankfurter, *Law and Politics*, pp. 15–16.

to stand in the way of needed reform being sought by the legislature. Of all that has been written on Frankfurter, there does not come to mind a criticism which uncovers the ultimate self-contradiction between the view that judges ought to be restrained and the view that the due process clauses ought to go. We shall have to come back to that.

In 1932, Frankfurter saw in the Scottsboro boys case some hope that the due process clause might be put properly to some good use by the Court.[54] If ever he became reconciled to the clause, it was then. Perhaps his greatest contribution to an understanding of the clause was his concurring opinion in *Adamson* v. *California* in 1947. He there defended at length the traditional view of the clause that one could not, out of the very language of the due process clause of the Fourteenth amendment, conclude that the states were thereby forbidden to do all the things which the first eight amendments forbade the United States to do. The late Professor Edward Corwin, in 1953, called the Adamson case the "high-water mark of dissent" against the traditional view.[55] Four justices—Hugo Black and William O. Douglas in one opinion and Frank Murphy and Wiley Rutledge in another—contended that the Court had been wrong all along. Mr. Justice Black's opinion declared that the traditional view —the view that the due process clause called for "essential fairness," to be determined by the Supreme Court on an examination of all the circumstances of the case and not by measuring the process against the list of processes catalogued in the first eight amendments—threw judges back upon their own notions of justice, that is, upon a discredited doctrine of natural law.

Despite the fact that several clauses of the First, Fourth, Fifth and Sixth amendments are now said to have been "absorbed" by the due process clause, the traditional view has, in principle, still not been overthrown. This according to no less an authority than Mr. Justice Douglas who, to say the least, would have it otherwise.[56] Thus, it is with more than merely historical curiosity that one attempts to understand Frankfurter's defense of the traditional view. Black's dissent in the Adamson case had charged that the traditional view, with all its talk about "civilized decency" and "fundamental principles of liberty and justice," wrongly vested in the Court "boundless power" under " 'natural law' " to "roam at will in the limitless area of their own beliefs."[57]

The whole temper of Mr. Justice Black's opinion is that of a complete

---

[54]Frankfurter, *Law and Politics*, p. 189. See *Powell* v. *Alabama*, 287 U.S. 45 (1932).
[55]*Adamson* v. *California*, 332 U.S. 46 (1947). See E.S. Corwin, *The Constitution of the United States of America, Revised and Annotated* (Washington, 1953) p. 1115.
[56]Mr. Justice Douglas concurring in *Gideon* v. *Wainwright*, 372 U.S. 335 (1963) at p. 346.
[57]Mr. Justice Black dissenting in *Adamson* v. *California*, 332 U.S. 46 (1947) at pp. 69–70, 75, 77–80, 90–91 and see his concurring opinion in *Federal Power Commission* v. *Natural Gas Pipeline Co.*, 315 U.S. 575 (1942) at p. 601, note 4.

dismissal of natural law. And, in the context of that dismissal, it seems strange for him to say:

I think [the *Twining*] decision and the "natural law" theory of the Constitution upon which it relies degrade the constitutional safeguards of the Bill of Rights and simultaneously appropriate for this Court a broad power which we are not authorized by the Constitution to exercise.[58]

Change for the worse is reason for one's deploring degradation, but if there is no natural or intrinsic standard of what is better and what worse, what right and what wrong, what lawful and what arbitrary, then mere change could not call forth the moral indignation which pervades Black's opinion. If there is nothing which is naturally worthy of being guarded, then one could not speak in a laudatory manner of "constitutional safeguards," nor complain of their "degradation." He could only speak of constitutional "clauses" or "provisions," and remark on their change or passing. And, why be upset by the Court's appropriating for itself broad power not authorized by the Constitution? If nothing is naturally lawful, then it is not unlawful for the Court to run counter to the Constitution. That is, if nothing is by nature right and just, then being constitutional is no more right and just than being, say, "creative." Mr. Justice Black would have no call to criticize his breathren for appropriating power as long as they got away with it. A mere transfer of power from the dead words of the Constitution to the lively fiat of the judiciary ought not to disturb anyone unless it disturbs the public and one should only be disturbed *then* if he believes, as Hobbes did, that civil peace if *naturally* preferable to civil war. If *nothing* is naturally preferable, then what others call "civil war" the sophisticated would simply regard as an interesting social science datum—a laboratory experiment in democratic action—if, indeed, one thing is by its nature more interesting than another.

Frankfurter accepted the term "subjective" as an appropriate label for the things Black's dissent proscribed, but he contended that "natural law" had a "much longer and much better founded meaning and justification" than such "subjective" things.[59] One is not compelled, he argued, to resort to "private notions" or else lapse into "mechanical jurisprudence."[60] But, if not to the

---

[58] *Adamson* v. *California*, 332 U.S. 46 at p. 70.

[59] *Adamson* v. *California*, 332 U.S. 46 at p. 65.

[60] See *Adamson* v. *California*, 332 U.S. 46 at pp. 60–62 and compare his dissent in *United States* v. *Bethlehem Steel Corp.*, 315 U.S. 289 (1942) at p. 326; dissent in *Elkins* v. *United States*, 364 U.S. 207 (1960) at p. 235; dissent in *West Virginia State Board of Education* v. *Barnette*, 319 U.S. 629 (1943) at p. 647; for the Court in *Kirschbaum* v. *Walling*, 316 U.S. 517 (1942) at p. 522; for the Court in *Addison* v. *Holly Hill Co.*, 322 U.S. 607 (1944) at p. 618; for the Court in *Osborn* v. *Ozlin*, 310 U.S. 53 (1940) at p. 66; concurring in *United States* v. *Spelar*, 338 U.S. 217 (1949) at p. 224; for the Court in *Universal Camera Corp* v. *National Labor Relations Board*, 340 U.S. 474 (1951) at p. 489; for the Court in *Carpenter's Union* v. *National Labor Relations Board*, 357 U.S. 93 (1958) at p. 100; concurring in *Sweezy* v. *New Hampshire*, 354 U.S. 234 (1957) at p. 267; concurring in *Pennekamp* v. *Florida*, 328 U.S. 331 (1946) at p. 367. And see *Of Law and Men*, ed. Elman, p. 42.

black letters of the Constitution or into one's own viscera, where does one look?

A variety of terms has been employed by Frankfurter and by commentators upon him to characterize the source of that judgment which is neither "mechanical" nor "subjective," but the terms most commonly employed are "history" and the "conscience of the community" or the "conscience of mankind."[61] But there are some strange contrasts between what Frankfurter found to be contrary to due process and what he found to be in accord with it. In one case, despite a personal revulsion, he believed it was permissible for a state to send a man to the electric chair a second time after a first trip, with all its attendant terror, had failed to kill him.[62] In other cases, he has insisted that "our historic heritage" forbids the execution of the insane.[63] But if what is forbidden is not what revolts this or that judge, but rather what has always revolted everybody, or at least all Englishmen, or at the very least all Englishmen in America, can it truly be said that "we" have been or are now more revolted by the execution of the insane than by a second attempt to execute where a first attempt failed?

The reliance on history is surely problematic, for, if one goes far enough back in English history one runs into such things as the sentence given to one Charles Batemen:

That he should return to the place from whence he came, from thence to be drawn to the place of execution, there to be hanged by the neck, and whilst alive be cut down, and his bowels to be taken out and burnt; his head to be severed from his body, and his body divided into four parts, and that his head and quarters be disposed at the pleasure of the king.[64]

If Georgia or Alaska should choose to draw, disembowel and quarter fully sane and manifestly guilty doers of great wrongs, would the due process clause bar them from doing as they chose?

The Court has to "thread" its way, term after term, through particular cases to determine due process,[65] for the "standards of justice" imposed by due process are "not authoritatively formulated anywhere as though they were prescriptions in a pharmacopoeia."[66] Perhaps this imposes a great burden on the judges who must thread the way, but there "is no escape" from an appeal

---

[61]Frankfurter concurring in *Louisiana* ex rel *Francis* v. *Resweber,* 329 U.S. 459 (1947) at p. 471. Cf. *Bartkus* v. *Illinois,* 359 U.S. 121 at p. 128.

[62]*Louisiana* ex rel *Francis* v. *Resweber.*

[63]Dissenting in *Solesbee* v. *Balkcom,* 339 U.S. 9 (1950) at p. 16.

[64]*The Trial of Charles Bateman for High Treason* XI *State Trials* 467 (1 James II, 1685) at p. 474. This is not a unique sentence. It illustrates the times. Frankfurter knew the Bateman case. He cites it in *Solesbee* v. *Balkcom,* 339 U.S. 9 at p. 18.

[65]Frankfurter concurring in the result in *Kingsley Pictures* v. *Regents,* 360 U.S. 684 (1959) at p. 696.

[66]Separate opinion of Frankfurter in *Malinski* v. *New York,* 324 U.S. 401 (1945) at p. 417.

to due process.[67] And, while due process is not a technical formula, not an authoritative prescription, neither is it personal whim,[68] but "respect enforced by law for that feeling of just treatment which has been evolved through centuries of Anglo-American constitutional history and civilization."[69]

History is a dark subject. It is, in a way, everything that ever happened. But that cannot be what is meant, for almost everything imaginable *has* happened and, on the other hand, all that has happened is not open to us. Maybe "history" is what has been written about what has happened but that, too, is unsatisfactory for the record is nearly as bulky and just as enigmatic as the series of events it imperfectly records. Perhaps "history" is the "stream" of history—the direction in which the events ineluctably move—but then that is not history but something which it is said is seen within it. But it must be something more like the latter than like the former two, for much of what has happened is irrelevant.

In order to know what are significant data, limits must be assigned to what we will consider. Drawing limits, however, means having regard for what is wanted and what is wanted is due process, and we are back at the beginning. Why, for example, *Anglo-American* history? Frankfurter does not hesitate to cite an Indian case[70] when he picks his way along the "slippery slope of due process."[71] But, obviously, Anglo-Indian law inextricably marries what is Anglo to what is Indian. Will not what is Indian then make its way through what is Anglo-Indian and, then through the Anglo-American to affect what is American? In the "gradual process of exclusion and inclusion" should the Indian be let in or kept out? Whichever way, why?

We are back to the "living Constitution." It appears that it is not the conscience of "mankind" but of only a part, if an ill-defined part, of mankind which guides judges in their search for due process. And, it is not that part at any particular time in history, but as it shows itself in the stream of history—in what is immanent in the coming-into-being of things. Will what is immanent not show itself in innovations? Suppose a truly creative future session of the Alaska legislature should decide to restore drawing and quartering as a punishment. Is there no rock in the stream of history to which we might make fast the judicial ark?

An exhaustive treatise on the problematic character of history is thank-

[67] Judgment of the Court in an opinion by Frankfurter joined by Murphy and Rutledge, JJ., in *Watts* v. *Indiana*, 338 U.S. 49 (1949) at p. 50.

[68] "The vague contours of the Due Process Clause do not leave judges at large. We may not draw on our merely personal and private notions. . . ." Opinion of the Court by Frankfurter in *Rochin* v. *California*, 342 U.S. 165 (1952) at p. 171.

[69] Frankfurter concurring in *Joint Anti-Fascist Refugee Committee* v. *McGrath*, 341 U.S. 123 (1951) at p. 162.

[70] Frankfurter, *Of Law and Men*, p. 16.

[71] Frankfurter, *Of Law and Men*, p. 15.

fully not requisite here. An indication of the difficulties posed by one part of history—precedent—will serve as an example sufficient for the present purpose. In one instance, Frankfurter spoke of the "whole philosophy of our law" as being "based on precedent."[72] Even when constitutional questions are involved, the Court "should not be unmindful . . . of the principle of *stare decisis* by whose circumspect observance the wisdom of this Court as an institution transcending the moment can alone" be effective.[73] Special explanation is called for "when an important shift in constitutional doctrine is announced after a reconstruction in the membership of the Court. Such shifts of opinion . . . must be duly mindful of the necessary demands of continuity in a civilized society."[74]

We recognize that *stare decisis* embodies an important social policy. It represents an element of continuity in law, and is rooted in the psychological need to satisfy reasonable expectations.[75]

Continuity is, in itself, a good thing and change, while inconvenient, is necessary. Whenever changes are necessary, they are to be made with the least inconvenience to continuity which is possible, that is, continuity is to be preserved whenever possible. But that change is allowed *at all* demonstrates that continuity is not the ultimate measure.

It would disregard [*stare decisis*] for a judge stubbornly to persist in his views . . . after the contrary had become part of the tissue of the law. Until then, full respect for *stare decisis* does not require a judge to forego his own convictions promptly after his brethren have rejected them.[76]

How long does it take for a view to become "part of the tissue of the law"?

As one swallow does not make a summer . . . one ruling hardly establishes a practice. . . .[77]

How many swallows make a summer? Apparently four swallows make a summer, for in an opinion rendered one week after this statement, we are told that four uniform decisions make law that should not be overruled.[78] But the comfort derived from such mathematical neatness is short-lived, for, in disposing of a case which revolved around the legal status of women, Frankfurter dismissed Sir William Blackstone's views on the subject as "self-deluding romanticism" and overturned six centuries of precedent.[79]

Neither history in the simple sense of the store of past experience nor

---

[72]Dissenting in *Milanovich* v. *United States*, 365 U.S. 551 (1961) at p. 562.
[73]*Green* v. *United States*, 355 U.S. 184 (1957), Frankfurter dissenting, at p. 215.
[74]Frankfurter concurring in *Graves* v. *New York ex rel O'Keefe*, 306 U.S. 466 (1939) at p. 487.
[75]Frankfurter for the Court in *Helvering* v. *Hallock*, 309 U.S. 106 (1940) at p. 119.
[76]Frankfurter dissenting in *Radovich* v. *National Football League*, 352 U.S. 445 (1957) at p. 455.
[77]Frankfurter dissenting in *Commissioner* v. *Wodehouse*, 337 U.S. 369 (1949) at p. 415.
[78]*United States* v. *I.C.C.*, 337 U.S. 426 (1949), Frankfurter dissenting, at p. 446.
[79]Frankfurter for the Court in *United States* v. *Dege*, 364 U.S. 51 (1960) at p. 54.

history in the more sophisticated sense of "evolution" or "process" can possibly be taken as the standard for due process, for history in the simple sense argues that what is old is good and, in that sense, it is embarrassed by such things as Batemen's sentence, whereas history in the "evolutionary" sense is incapable of distinguishing between a violation of and a development of due process. History cannot be left to its aimless meanderings. It must be guided. That this is true, and that judges participate in its guidance—i.e., make law— is acknowledged by Frankfurter, but he says that "judicial law-making power ultimately rests for its authority" on "reason," that we might know "whither we are going."[80]

"Reason," however has no independent potency in Frankfurter's opinions. Every time he refers to it, it fades back into the "conscience of the community." Justice turns out to be indistinguishable from "prevailing standards of justice."[81] He cheered heartily Holmes' statement that "law is not a brooding omnipresence in the sky"[82] without ever seeming to notice that the "conscience of the community" is quite as much the will o' the wisp as the thing which Holmes' remark laughs to scorn. For, if what is due process is what the "conscience of the community" cries out to be the "prevailing standards of justice," would that not be more likely to show itself in what the legislature enacted than in what the judges, isolated as they are from the community at large, draw from the atmosphere?

The striking thing is that Frankfurter acknowledges that fact and fashions his view of judicial duty accordingly. "In the day-to-day working of our democracy it is vital that the power of the non-democratic organ of our Government be exercised with rigorous self-restraint."[83] This is because "holding democracy in judicial tutelage is not the most promising way to foster disciplined responsibility in a people."[84] This doctrine of "restraint" and "humility" has been much praised and contrasted with judicial willfulness. But we are again back at the beginning. Is there no alternative to the plain choice between judicial tyranny on the one hand and, on the other, an abandonment of the Constitution as a limitation on government? It is no consolation to the minority to know that its rights cannot be trampled on by the majority except when the majority feels so inclined.

[80]See his concurring opinion in *Hannah* v. *Larche,* 363 U.S. 420 (1960) at p. 493; his dissent in *Larson* v. *Domestic and Foreign Commerce Corp.,* 337 U.S. 682 (1949) at pp. 705–06; his dissent in *Mitchell* v. *Trawler Racer Inc.,* 362 U.S. 539 (1960) at pp. 550–51. Cf. his opinion in *New York* v. *United States,* 326 U.S. 572 (1946) at p. 575.

[81]Frankfurter dissenting in part in *United States* v. *Commodities Trading Corporation,* 339 U.S. 121 (1950) at p. 134.

[82]See Frankfurter for the Court in *Guaranty Trust Co.* v. *York,* 326 U.S. 99 (1945) at p. 101 and compare Holmes dissenting in *Southern Pacific Co.* v. *Jensen,* 244 U.S. 205 (1917) at p. 222.

[83]*American Federation of Labor* v. *American Sash and Door Co.,* 335 U.S. 538 (1949) at p. 555.

[84]Frankfurter, *Of Law and Men,* p. 18; compare pp. 41 and 193.

It can never be emphasized too much that one's own opinions about the wisdom or evil of a law should be excluded when one is doing one's duty on the bench. The only opinion of our own even looking in that direction that is material is an opinion whether legislators could in reason have enacted such a law.[85]

As Walter Berns has shown, this means that the "Court will excercise its powers only when the legislators are idiots." Not even *then*, really.[86] For, as Clyde Summers has pointed out, Frankfurter's "dominant conception of the Court's role in a democracy is both pervasive and rigid," and is based on the premise that ours is a "government of unfettered majority rule" in which "rigid judicial abstinence is required."[87]

Frankfurter said in 1924 that the "due process clauses ought to go,"[88] and we raised here the question of whether he had ever become reconciled to the clauses. We believe he never truly reconciled himself to them, for, though he said that the Court could not "escape from an appeal to due process," his way of responding to that appeal is no more than a sophisticated escape from it. We have said that it was self-contradictory to speak of "judicial self-restraint" and to demand that the due process clauses go.[89] The self-contradiction lies in this: Frankfurter's view of the "role of the judge" is said to be drawn from the Constitution, but a truly restrained judge is not one who reads out of the Constitution those duties by which he does not wish to be bound. The Constitution, which nowhere speaks of democracy, in two distinct places binds governments in the United States to due process of law, but Frankfurter told us that "a democracy need not rely on the courts to save it from its own unwisdom."[90] That is why, when faced with due process cases, he has thrown the issue back into the hands of the democracy by allowing "the stream of the Zeitgeist . . . to flood [his] sympathies and intelligence."[91]

Let us here affirm that it is our belief that the Constitution founds an emphatically national government only laced here and there with an occasional federal principle and so, Frankfurter was right that the national legislature has an enormous say in what will be left to the states, and that the national legislature is bound by only a few distinct restraints. But it is the *Constitution* which, all along, has allowed for such a national and an increasingly national government. We need no recourse to a "living" Constitution which is no Constitution at all in the American sense. Let us also here affirm that it is a

---

[85]*West Virginia State Board of Education* v. *Barnette,* 319 U.S. 624 (1943) at p. 647.

[86]Walter Berns, *Freedom, Virtue and the First Amendment* (Chicago, 1965), p. 180.

[87]Clyde Summers, "Frankfurter, Labor Law and the Judge's Function," *Yale Law Journal,* LXVII (December 1957), 281.

[88]See footnote 53.

[89]See p. 251.

[90]*American Federation of Labor* v. *American Sash and Door Co.,* 335 U.S. 538 (1949) at p. 556.

[91]See note 52.

democratic government which is founded. But it is one in which the majority, whether Frankfurter liked it or not, emphatically chose to impose upon itself "auxiliary precautions"[92] precisely because in its soberest moments it knew itself to be capable of "unwisdom" in its worse moments and would need now and then to be restrained by courts even though those courts were its own creation. Finally, let us here affirm that, while the first eight amendments forbid the United States several courses of action, the due process clause of the Fourteenth Amendment only imposes the more general restraint on the individual states that they not take life liberty or property—that is, that they not kill, imprison or fine—except by a process which, on full examination, is essentially fair. This might very well mean, for example, that a particular thing is explicitly forbidden to the United States and yet quite permissible for a state.

To what does a judge turn to find what is essentially fair? Well, to begin with, let us say that if it is to some brooding omnipresence or other, its name might well be the "conscience of the community" understood *precisely* as that sober sense of a healthy people that they *ought* to do right and that they sometimes do not do so. But let us emphatically insist that it cannot be found in the "stream" of what that people has chosen to do.

Why does it make sense for a people to vest in its courts power to bind its own hands which power, to be employed, must be informed by studied judgment which, in its turn, seems on the surface to be quite unchecked? A clue can be found in the fact that a great deal *more* leeway is left to the judges in the realm of criminal justice than, say, in the realm of economic legislation. This is because criminal justice is precisely the place where the sovereign people, in their sober and conscience-stricken moments, know themselves to be weakest and most foolish and so most in need of the services of the wise and disinterested.

Frankfurter is not wrong because he, contrary to his protests about the "spirit" or "plan and purpose" of the Constitution, relies on such a spirit. That is inescapable. He is wrong because he does not quite rightly grasp that "plan" in our view. When he says that judges can do their duty only if they properly understand the "role of a judge" in a "democratic society," he fails to see that this is a democratic society which means to be the first truly successful democracy in history and that its hopes are based in no insignificant way on the restraints which it imposes upon itself by reliance on "auxiliary precautions." If one responds to this by insisting that Frankfurter is concerned with the role of the *judge* and that this, including the definition of that "judicial power" which is vested in the Courts, can only be understood by understanding what, in the nature of things, judges have done and can do, we come closer to

---

[92] *Federalist*, No. 51, p. 337.

proper understanding. One more problem remains, however.

Unlike Holmes, whom Berns has described as not at all interested in government and human affairs,[93] Frankfurter was, from his first to his last breath, passionately concerned with everything that went on in politics and finance. His life-long career as a reformer was motivated by his abiding belief that a vigorously active government could do great good for a people. But, ultimately, Frankfurter's problem goes back to Holmes. The passage of Holmes, which Frankfurter loved to quote, reads in its entirety this way:

> The common law is not a brooding omnipresence in the sky but the articulate voice of some sovereign or quasi-sovereign that can be identified; although some decisions with which I have disagreed seem to me to have forgotten the fact.[94]

Frankfurter often conveniently forgot the word "common" when he quoted Holmes, but we believe that Frankfurter was, in this, being perfectly true to the intention of Holmes. We believe Holmes would have applied the substance of his statement here to all law, including constitutional law. But both Holmes and Frankfurter seem to have forgotten that the *old* view of judges—that judges were narrowly confined to following what legislatures had done—was coupled with another old view that *both* the judges *and* the legislatures were bound by some such "brooding omnipresence" as Holmes scornfully dismisses. The view, that is, that it was the proper business of judges to "find" and not to "make" law was *not* coupled with the view that the legislature *did* make law out of whole cloth. If a judge "restrains" himself to "finding" the law and yet reduces "the law" to that which has been enacted by a "sovereign" that can be and is "identified" as the legislature, then one destroys altogether the fundamental principle of due process, stated when the due process clause of the Fifth Amendment was first explicated; that the "article is a restraint on the legislative as well as on the executive and judicial powers of the government, and cannot be so construed as to leave Congress free to make any process 'due process of law,' by its mere will."[95]

Frankfurter wrote more words than most men. He even wrote more words than most Supreme Court justices. He was, for more than half a century, a considerable influence on American life. Like Holmes, whom he greatly admired, he has often been regarded as a "philosopher." But there is a difference between an intellectual and a philosopher. Frankfurter's problem was the problem of the twentieth century. He was too much a vehicle of the "Zeitgeist." Invested with judicial power by a Constitution which its founders believed to be aimed at justice, he construed that Constitution as though it was

[93]See p. 190.
[94]Dissenting in *Southern Pacific Co.* v. *Jensen,* 244 U.S. 205 (1917) at p. 222.
[95]Mr. Justice Curtis for the Court in *Murray's Lessee* v. *Hoboken Land and Improvement Co.,* 18 Howard 272 (1856) at p. 276.

an altogether neutral document. He confounded impartiality with neutrality and construed the Constitution as though the Framers, also, had confounded the two. Instead of impartial justice coming forth without fear or favor, a kind of wilfullness insinuates itself which does not favor justice or fear consequences. Perhaps it was more or less harmless for Frankfurter to think what he thought. His character had been formed by an earlier view and so he could preach one way according to his thoughts, and yet practice another way, according to old-fashioned standards of justice and decency. But what about those whose understanding is formed in the image of the law he helped to make? What about those whose view of justice is fashioned by the mountain of words Frankfurter wrote into *United States Reports* and into the literature of the twentieth century; those of us who come after and who may have a lesser intellect than Frankfurter, our teacher? What will restrain us if we believe, as we have been taught to believe, that, finally nothing is just but as we declare it so? Can a country that abandons itself to such a doctrine survive, or will it not abandon the Constitution and all the glorious hopes it embodies? Can a nation, so conceived and so dedicated, long endure?

SELECTED SUGGESTED READINGS

The Commerce Clause under Marshall, Taney and Waite. Chicago: Quadrangle Books, 1964.

Law and Politics. Edited by E. F. Prichard, Jr. and Archibald MacLeish. New York: Capricorn Books, 1962. See the articles entitled "The Zeitgeist and the Judiciary," "The Red Terror of Judicial Reform," "The Supreme Court of the United States," and "The Young Men Go to Washington."

Of Law and Men. Edited by Philip Elman. New York: Harcourt, Brace, 1956. See the articles entitled "John Marshall and the Judicial Function," "The Judicial Process and the Supreme Court," and "The Reading of Statutes."

Roosevelt and Frankfurter: Their Correspondence, 1928–1945. Annotated by Max Freedman. New York: Atlantic, Little, Brown, 1967. See especially the sections covering the years 1936–1937 at pages 303–417.

See also the following United States Supreme Court decisions:
United States v. *Bethlehem Steel Corp.,* 315 U.S. 289 (1942).
West Virginia State Board of Education v. *Barnette,* 319 U.S. 624 (1943).
Adamson v. *California,* 332 U.S. 46 (1947).
San Diego Union v. *Garmon,* 359 U.S. 236 (1959).
Baker v. *Carr,* 369 U.S. 186 (1962).

THE CONTRIBUTORS

MORTON J. FRISCH is Professor of Political Science at Northern Illinois University. He is co-editor and co-author of *The Thirties: A Reconsideration in the Light of the American Political Tradition* (1968), and has published articles in the *Journal of Politics*, the *Review of Politics*, *Ethics* and the *Cambridge Journal*.

RICHARD G. STEVENS is Associate Professor of Political Science at the University of Waterloo. He has published articles in the *Political Science Quarterly*, *Social Research* and the *William and Mary Law Review*.

HARVEY C. MANSFIELD, JR. is Associate Professor of Government at Harvard University. He is the author of *Statesmanship and Party Government: A Study of Burke and Boling-broke* (1965), and has published articles in the *Political Science Quarterly*, the *American Political Science Review* and *Nomos*.

MARTIN DIAMOND is the Burnet C. Wohlford Professor of American Political Institutions at Claremont Men's College. He is co-author of *Essays on Federalism* (1961); joint author of *The Democratic Republic* (1966, 1970); co-editor of *The Thirties: A Reconsideration in the Light of the American Political Tradition* (1968); and has published articles in the *American Political Science Review* and *The Public Interest*.

ROBERT K. FAULKNER is Associate Professor of Political Science at Boston College. He is the author of *The Jurisprudence of John Marshall* (1968) and has published an article in the *Journal of American History*.

RALPH LERNER is Associate Professor of the Social Sciences at the University of Chicago. He is co-editor of *Medieval Political Philosophy: A Sourcebook* (1963), and has published articles in the *American Political Science Review* and the *Supreme Court Review*.

HARRY V. JAFFA is Professor of Political Philosophy at Claremont Men's College and Claremont Graduate School. He is the author of *Thomism and Aristotelianism* (1952); *Crisis of the House Divided, An Interpretation of the Issues in the Lincoln-Douglas Debates* (1959); *Equality and Liberty, Theory and Practice in American Politics* (1965); co-author of *Shakespeare's Politics* (1964); co-editor of *In the Name of the People* (1959); and has published articles in the *American Political Science Review*, the *Journal of Politics* and *Comparative Studies in Society and History*.

HERBERT J. STORING IS Professor of Political Science at the University of Chicago. He is co-author of *The State and the Farmer* (1962); editor and co-author of *Essays on the Scientific Study of Politics* (1962); editor of *What Country Have I? Political Writings by Black Americans* (1970); and has published articles in the *Political Quarterly* and the *Public Administration Review.*

WALTER BERNS is Professor of Political Science at the University of Toronto. He is the author of *Freedom, Virtue and the First Amendment* (1957), and has published articles in the *American Political Science Review,* the *Journal of Politics,* the *Western Political Quarterly,* the *Yale Law Journal* and *Law and Contemporary Problems.*

HARRY M. CLOR is Associate Professor of Political Science and Director of the Public Affairs Conference Center at Kenyon College. He is the author of *Obscenity and Public Morality, Censorship in a Liberal Society* (1969), and has published articles in *Midway* and the *Denver Quarterly.*